Strategic Ignorance

STRATEGIC IGNORANCE

**Why the Bush Administration Is Recklessly
Destroying a Century of Environmental Progress**

CARL POPE
and
PAUL RAUBER

SIERRA CLUB BOOKS

SAN FRANCISCO

The Sierra Club, founded in 1892 by John Muir, has devoted itself to the study and protection of the earth's scenic and ecological resources—mountains, wetlands, woodlands, wild shores and rivers, deserts and plains. The publishing program of the Sierra Club offers books to the public as a nonprofit educational service in the hope that they may enlarge the public's under-standing of the Club's basic concerns. The point of view expressed in each book, however, does not necessarily represent that of the Club. The Sierra Club has some sixty chapters through-out the United States and in Canada. For information about how you may participate in its programs to preserve wilderness and the quality of life, please address inquiries to Sierra Club, 85 Second Street, San Francisco, California 94105, or visit our website at www.sierraclub.org.

Published by Sierra Club Books
85 Second Street, San Francisco, CA 94105
www.sierraclub.org/books

Produced and distributed by
University of California Press
Berkeley and Los Angeles, California
University of California Press, Ltd.
London, England
www.ucpress.edu

SIERRA CLUB, SIERRA CLUB BOOKS, and the Sierra Club design logos
are registered trademarks of the Sierra Club.

Library of Congress Cataloging-in-Publication data is available
from Sierra Club Books.

ISBN 1-57805-109-6

Book and jacket design by Blue Design

We gratefully acknowledge permission to reprint the following cartoons: Page 90 (2003), page 106 (2001), page 180 (2003), page 199 (2003) by Oliphant; page 58 (2001) and page 148 (2003) by Auth; all © Universal Press Syndicate. Reprinted with permission. All rights reserved. Page 75 © The New Yorker Collection 2003, Lee Lorenz, from cartoonbank.com. All rights reserved.

Appendix, *The Bush Record on the Environment,* © 2004 by the National Resources Defense Council; used with permission.

Printed in the United States of America on New Leaf Ecobook 50 acid-free paper, which con-tains a minimum of 50 percent post-consumer waste, processed chlorine free. Of the balance, 25 percent is Forest Stewardship Council certified to contain no old-growth trees and to be pulped totally chlorine free.

08 07 06 05 04

10 9 8 7 6 5 4 3 2 1

This book is dedicated to the volunteers and staff of the Sierra Club.
Teddy Roosevelt would have been proud of them:
they are citizens of the republic " in the arena."

Contents

Preface

Paul Rauber and I wrapped up the final chapter of *Strategic Ignorance* last Thanksgiving weekend. Given the Bush administration's penchant for announcing stunning new environmental retreats on Friday afternoons of holiday weekends, we knew this was a risky approach. Sure enough, when I picked up Saturday's paper I nearly dropped it: America's future, it seemed, was now being scripted as a disaster movie. Bush's Nuclear Regulatory Commission had decided that, rather than requiring nuclear reactors to shield the cables connecting the control room and the reactor from fire, the utilities need only designate certain technicians to play Harrison Ford. Should a fire disable the control cables, these technicians would run—through the fire, if necessary—and try to shut down the reactor by hand before it suffered critical damage. The National Research Council followed up with its own disaster plan: to hand out potassium iodide pills to everyone living in the vicinity of a nuclear power plant.

Like many of Bush's initiatives, this Hollywood version of disaster management would be laughable if it were not so terrifying. This new NRC rule covers more than 100 operating nuclear power plants—many of them badly managed, antiquated, and falling apart. All are near American communities and families. And a fire disabling the reactor control cables is not an implausible, worst-case scenario; just such a fire disabled the Brown's Ferry nuclear plant in Tennessee back in 1975. Fire extinguishers and redundant safety systems are required in office buildings and parachutes. Is it too much to ask for them in nuclear power plants as well?

Only three days later, on December 2, 2003, the administration announced that it was postponing the cleanup of mercury emissions from power plants for yet another decade. The vehicle was a poison trading system, whereby the dirtiest plants could pay for improvements elsewhere while they continued to deposit neurotoxins into the atmosphere. As we send this book off to press, the dismantling of our environmental standards seems to be accelerating.

Why would the Bush administration, so eloquent about protecting America from the threat of terrorism, do such things? Attempting to explain why, as this book does, was not easy. It was made more difficult by the sheer volume of examples, which have the odd effect of making the story less believable rather than more so. Most Americans are understandably reluctant to believe that their commander in chief would knowingly place them at greater risk. So readers seeking chapter and verse for our assertions will find them in the endnotes; those who want even more extensive back-up materials are directed to our Web site, www.StrategicIgnorance.org. There you will find more complete derivations of some of our data, additional examples that space in the book did not permit, further citations and references, as well as reading suggestions for a more in-depth understanding of the book's political and economic context.

We have, by necessity, had to limit the stories we tell; the full account of Bush's environmental recklessness and strategic ignorance will have to wait for the historians and the end of his administration. Readers looking for a more complete record of what the administration has done can turn to the chronological list in the appendix, graciously provided by our colleagues at the Natural Resources Defense Council. Production pressures force us to cut off the list at December 1, 2003, but the NRDC has continued its invaluable project at www.nrdc.org/bushrecord/.

Our aim here is more focused: to explain *why* Bush is doing what he is doing, and what it means. Those who feel that Bush is trying to drag us back are correct, but mistaken if they limit the extent of the retreat to 30 years, as some do. This administration's project is more audacious. We suggest that it is, in fact, a conscious attempt to return America to the status quo before Theodore Roosevelt challenged the robber barons and made conservation a national commitment.

This book has been a team effort, and we owe a great debt to the many friends and colleagues who helped us along the way. We would like to acknowledge, in particular, *Sierra* magazine, in whose pages some of this material originally appeared; Sierra Club Books editor Danny Moses, whose concept this project originally was; Sierra Club Books publisher Helen Sweetland, who gave us no choice but to meet our deadlines; and our editor, Diana Landau, who herded her cats with grace and aplomb. Thanks, too, to Sierra Club executive assistant Rod MacKenzie, copyeditor Julia Zafferano, and our interns/researchers/fact-checkers Mike Madison, Laurel Eddy, Josh Wein, and Lindsay Knisely. They did their best, but all errors of fact rest on our shoulders.

—Carl Pope

"Wouldn't it be nice if just once, on some issue, the Bush administration came up with a plan that didn't involve weakened environmental protection, financial breaks for wealthy individuals and corporations and reduced public oversight?"

— *New York Times* editorialist Paul Krugman

"[A] riot of individualistic materialism, under which complete freedom for the individual . . . turned out in practice to mean perfect freedom for the strong to wrong the weak."

— President Theodore Roosevelt, describing the social Darwinist economic philosophy of his day

"Ignorance is Strength."

— Slogan of Big Brother's Ministry of Truth in George Orwell's *1984*

Red in Tooth and Claw
A Compassionate Conservative
Joins the Ruthless Right

Most Americans know that George W. Bush is not an environmentalist. Unlike more than 70 percent of the American public, he cannot bring himself to use the "e" word to describe himself. (Even Vice President Dick Cheney thinks of himself as "a pretty good environmentalist, though the Sierra Club may not agree with that.") In truth most Americans do not trust Republican politicians on the environment, and they certainly do not trust oilmen. Bush is both. His polling numbers on protecting clean air, water, and wild places have remained consistently poor.

But few Americans realize that there is more to it than bad instincts on endangered species or a desire to help out his oil buddies. In fact, Bush has done his best, in only three years, to break our national compact on environmental progress and turn the clock back—not years or decades but a full century. That people have not been paying close attention is not surprising, given the shock of September 11, wars in Afghanistan and Iraq, and declining mass media coverage of domestic issues like the environment. People may be aware that Bush is easing air pollution rules for industry, that he is allowing excessive logging, and that he is too cozy with the oil and coal industries. But how many Americans are aware that the Bush administration has, just for a start:

- Approved a plan that would greatly increase the amount of toxic mercury in America's air, allowing more than four times as much as allowed by current law;

- Freed the nation's 51 dirtiest power plants from having to install readily available pollution controls, which could prevent 80,000 to 120,000 asthma attacks a year;

- Filled regulatory agencies with lobbyists and executives from the very industries they are now regulating, and suppressed scientific findings by those agencies that ran counter to the administration's aims;

- Shifted the economic burden of cleaning up toxic waste dumps from polluters to their victims;

- Cut by more than a third, for regulatory purposes, the value of a human life—the dollar value used to calculate how much it is worth to protect people from the impact of industrial processes; and

- Stripped environmental protections from one-tenth of our nation's surface area.

It is easy, in this cynical age, to chalk it all up to greed. Bush wants campaign contributions, and polluters write the checks. Americans easily connect these dots—campaign money from the oil industry means a government that sides with oil companies. When timber companies give the Bush campaign an unprecedented $1 million, our national forests are more likely to end up as two-by-fours than refuges for endangered species. When the vice president, the deputy interior secretary, and scores of other government officials have made bundles working and lobbying for oil, mining, and timber interests prior to their government service—and sometimes during it—few are shocked when official actions happen to profit the friends of political appointees and grease the officials' own future careers.

Yet greed alone cannot explain the depth and breadth of the current assault on the environment. Something of this magnitude can only be accomplished by people in the grip of an ideological fervor. This is what the American people do not know: the Bush administration is full of influential officials who believe—from the bottom of their hearts, not just their wallets—that weaker laws on clean air, less funding to clean up toxic waste dumps, and national parks and forests run for private profit are actually good for the country.

Americans, the Bush team believes, have become soft. They expect too much safety, and a free lunch besides. If people want to hike in the wilderness, they should be willing to pay for it. If people object to the pollution where they live, they can buy an air purifier, or move. And if some kids get cancer from old toxic waste dumps, that is the price of living in a rich, brawny, big-shouldered, free country.

Most Americans thought we had banished this robber-baron philosophy a long time ago. But Bush and his inner circle have broken with a century of American tradition and public faith about how we fit into the world. In their view, America went wrong when turn-of-the-century Republican President Theodore Roosevelt—whom some of them call "the patron saint of land grabs"—first committed the country to a national ethic of conserving and protecting our natural heritage. "The conservation of our natural resources and their proper use," TR once declared, "constitute the fundamental problem which underlies almost every other problem of our national life." Presidents as diverse as Franklin Roosevelt, Dwight Eisenhower, Lyndon Johnson, Richard Nixon, Jimmy Carter, and George H. W. Bush have embraced TR's legacy; the current president seeks to dismantle it.

If we want to rescue our nation's environmental legacy from an administration determined to squander it, just knowing that a threat exists is not enough. We hear about that nearly every Friday afternoon, when (usually too late to make the evening news) a bland White House announcement informs us that another piece of the environmental safety net has been shredded. More than this, we need to understand *why* Bush wants to undermine a history of progress most Americans are proud of—and why he believes he can get away with putting our health and heritage at risk. In order to put up an effective defense, we need a clear view of the attackers' strategy, which is what this book endeavors to give.

A Connecticut Texan in the White House

The Bush presidency did not start out looking like the Texas Chainsaw Massacre meets Bambi. As governor, Bush had developed a reputation as a conventional, likable, not-too-energetic Texas Republican. He was conservative because Texas was. As an oilman he was predictably hostile toward environmental standards, but he had gotten along pretty well with Democrats in the Texas legislature. He proved adept at developing good relationships with the Hispanic community, something his fellow Republicans envied. His father, George H. W. Bush, had not lived up to his promise to be "the environmental president" but had moderated some of Ronald Reagan's more egregious anti-environmental stands—and most people surmised that the apple had not fallen far from the tree.

There were differences, however, mostly having to do with George W.'s adopted home state. Texas has always been distrustful of government, and Governor Bush's approach to most problems was a vaguely compassionate attitude coupled with governmental passivity, reliance on private solutions, and total faith in the power of the market. Voluntary air pollution controls, privatized and pauperized state parks, and a hands-off approach to enforcement of clean water standards were how this attitude played out in the real world.

Texas's environmental policies are far from the current American mainstream. While other states were actively setting aside open space—often backed by voter-authorized financing—Texas under Bush did not add a single acre of new state parks, even though it ranked almost last in the nation in parkland per capita and was enjoying some of the largest budget surpluses in its history. Instead, Bush proposed to balance the state park system's budget by leasing some of its crown jewels to private developers for exclusive, high-priced resorts. During Bush's term, Texas also had one of the worst enforcement records for clean air and clean water of any state. Even the good old boys who fished for bass on Lake Sam Rayburn had to turn to the federal Environmental Protection Agency (EPA) to stop Bush from allowing a paper mill to dump its untreated effluent into the lake.

But for a Texan Republican, Bush could have been scarier. He was a far cry, at least, from House whip Tom DeLay, the former pest exterminator known, for his intimidation skills, as "the Hammer." Nor did Bush have the harsh, cutthroat quality of Senator Phil Gramm. So when he ran as a "compassionate conservative," most observers nodded approvingly. At worst, they assumed, the compassion was a shallow facade concealing a conventional, probusiness Republican.

Some, like *Washington Post* columnist E. J. Dionne, saw in Bush a new fusion between corporate conservatism and the traditionalist Republican strand of conservatism that emphasized community and virtue over profit and riches. Bush, Dionne initially rhapsodized, "like the traditionalists, understands that most people do not draw meaning from the marketplace alone, and that the marketplace is not the sole or most important source of virtue. . . . [T]he market's cool calculations should be tempered not so much by the state as by those havens in a heartless world—family, church and neighborhood."

Compassionate conservatism, however, quickly faded from view. As president, Bush continued to invoke family, church, and neighborhood at every opportunity, but his administration poisoned the family's air, trashed the Creation, and sold out neighborhoods to his corporate contributors. America had fallen for the old bait-and-switch—and is still learning the nature of the switch.

"Morning in America" Turns Dark

While George Bush was practicing his genial laissez-faire in Texas government, the Republican Party was changing in fundamental ways. A harsh, bitter virus had infected the American right and spread to the GOP.

When Reagan took office in 1980, American conservatism was a blend of three strands. Libertarians worshipped at Ayn Rand's altar of fierce individualism, scorning government as an infringement on their personal freedom. Traditionalists emphasized values and respect for established cultural patterns, faiths, and communities. (George H. W. Bush was an archetypal example.) These two strands came together in the 1950s and 1960s in "fusionism," the conservatism that took over the Republican Party, propelling first Barry Goldwater and then Reagan into national politics.

The third strand of conservatism paid the bills. The corporatist right believed that the purpose of government was to support business and those who controlled business. Like libertarians, its adherents were essentially antigovernment, but, like traditionalists, they were enamored of hierarchy and order.

For years both traditionalists and libertarians tried to separate themselves from the corporatist moneymen, claiming to reject the mindless worship of material success and corporate power. "Conservatism is something more than mere solicitude for tidy incomes," thundered Russell Kirk, one of Goldwater's traditionalist mentors, way back in 1954. "Economic self-interest is ridiculously inadequate to hold an economic system together, and even less adequate to preserve order." From the libertarian side, the Cato Institute's Jerry Taylor warned against conservatives shilling for "a society that chooses tangible wealth creation over preservation of ecosystems," and libertarian politicians like former representative John Kasich of Ohio labored to eliminate government subsidies that amounted to corporate welfare.

By the 1990s, this proud claim of independence had become a joke. The right-wing corporations whose bank accounts had long funded the right called in their chits, and corporatism simply took over conservatism. Behind the new think tanks that gave the radical right its intellectual veneer were huge contributions from right-wing corporate titans like ExxonMobil, General Motors, and foundations associated with the Scaife and Koch families. The campaign contributions that fueled Republican victories in the Newt Gingrich–led 1994 takeover of Congress were richly endowed by reactionary corporations like Chevron, RJR Nabisco, and Peabody Coal. (A proud few conservatives decried the trend; Edward Luttwak of the Center for Strategic and International Studies warned his fellows, "Any conservative who wishes to conserve will not be funded.")

Even with corporatism taking control, Goldwater and Reagan held fast to an optimistic, sunny vision of the world and the future, as in Reagan's 1984 promise of "morning in America." But following Bill Clinton's election in 1992, the sunshine turned to bile. President George H.W. Bush's defeat was as bitter a draught for the right as Al Gore's was for Democrats eight years later, with Ross Perot playing the spoiler role that Ralph Nader took on in the later election. The radical right felt itself cheated; its members did not believe that Clinton deserved to be president and never accepted his presidency. Out of power, fueled by revanchist rage, the darker strains of the conservative coalition gathered their forces. As cognitive linguist George Lakoff points out, the hard right came to embrace the morality of a strict father—one very, very disappointed with his children:

> The world is a dangerous and difficult place. . . . The government
> becomes the strict father. . . . The citizens are children of two kinds: the
> mature, disciplined, self-reliant ones who should not be meddled with
> and the whining, undisciplined, dependent ones who should never be
> coddled. . . . Without competition, people would not have to develop dis-
> cipline and so would not become moral beings.

Different elements of the radical right coalition came to this worldview by
different routes. For the Christian Coalition, it reflected the harsh, Old Testa-
ment fundamentalism heard from many of their pulpits. For foreign policy neo-
conservatives like Donald Rumsfeld and Paul Wolfowitz, it stemmed from a
belief that the world was a dark and dangerous place where institutions like
NATO and the United Nations could never substitute for American military
hegemony. For the Sagebrush Rebels of the Mountain West, paranoia was part
of their sense of history as a struggle—whether against hostile Indians, threatening wilderness, or the Sierra Club lady down the road. For the corporatists,
it was simply second nature.

The radicals' harshness was strategic as well. Gingrich demonstrated in
1994 how to use "wedge politics" to propel Republicans into a congressional
majority. That election went down as "the year of the angry white male," and
holding congressional power with Clinton still in the White House only made
them angrier. Finally, blowing on the embers of low-level scandals, Clinton's
enemies used the spark of Monica Lewinsky to ignite the conflagration that
ended in an impeachment vote.

Clinton's disgrace was only half the battle, however; next came taking
power. The angry men hardened by the impeachment battle coalesced around
the governor of Texas, recognizing in Bush a figure who was unthreatening to
most Americans but who quietly signaled to the radical right that he was a True
Believer. Moreover, he had demonstrated the talent that all successful Republican presidential candidates since 1900 had relied on: the ability to raise corporate money, lots of it.

History and opportunity thus combined to strip American conservatism
of the sunny optimism of Goldwater and Reagan, and led it to abandon even
George H. W. Bush's promise of a "kinder, gentler America." The harsh new
ethos that came to dominate the Bush administration was a modern variant of

social Darwinism, the ideology of the nineteenth-century robber barons. Back then, Darwin's concept of "survival of the fittest" was misapplied to the social and economic spheres, used to legitimize greed and make a virtue of cutthroat competition. Like anthrax spores, social Darwinism had lain dormant in the soil of American conservatism since Theodore Roosevelt routed it with his assaults on turn-of-the-century trusts and corporate robber barons. Now it burst into life again.

For social Darwinists, society as well as nature was divided into winners and losers, and the winners' triumph was accorded the inevitability of natural law. (A contemporary variant of "survival of the fittest" appeared on the bumpers of luxury cars in the 1990s: "He who dies with the most toys wins.") Lakoff sums up the notion: "Worldly success is an indicator of sufficient moral strength; lack of success suggests lack of sufficient discipline. Those who are not successful should not be coddled; they should be forced to acquire self-discipline."

Channeling their (largely mythic) frontier heritage, the neo–social Darwinists drew careless analogies of their opponents as wild animals. Representative John Mica from Florida compared welfare recipients to alligators who get "unnatural feeding" from well-meaning humans; his Wyoming colleague Barbara Cubin compared them to the wolves reintroduced in Yellowstone, who would not leave their pens until they were hungry. In his frustration with the Endangered Species Act, California Representative Sonny Bono even proposed an Armageddon solution: "Give them [endangered species] all a designated area and then blow it up."

Why did George W. Bush, the compassionate conservative, throw in his lot with this angry, bitter, and decidedly uncompassionate lot? Willie Sutton robbed banks because that was where the money was; Bush recruited the hard right because that was where the power was—and the burning zeal to return a Republican to the White House. In turn, the radicals saw in Bush's unthreatening persona the perfect vehicle for carrying out Gingrich's wedge politics. Together—and with the help of the U.S. Supreme Court—they squeaked into office and called it a mandate, which they used not only to reverse the gains of the Clinton era but also to turn back the clock to a time when business had its way and no questions were asked.

Ten Commandments for the Hard Right

In rolling back the social and environmental progress of the twentieth century, George W. Bush has been guided by a few simple, unwavering principles. Bush's backers might not state them quite so bluntly, but these rules match the cynical, winner-take-all ethos that guided the Republican Party in the Battle of Florida in 2000. They have been applied by his administration, with remarkable consistency and astounding effect, in taking us back to the social Darwinist notion of the struggle for existence as "red in tooth and claw." This time, however, the predators are ruthless corporations, not carnivores.

1. Reward the winners.

Winners are better than losers, not just luckier or more fortunate. They shouldn't be punished even if they cheated to win. Winning is everything: worrying about how you play the game is for losers.

Cheaters *do* prosper, it turns out. Enron and a multitude of other energy companies well wired into the White House took advantage of California's winter 2001 crisis to loot billions of dollars from the state treasury. Bush's Federal Energy Regulatory Commission did not see much amiss, refused to institute price caps to stop the looting, and to date has still refused to order the companies to return the extorted money. When farmers in the Klamath basin broke onto federal property and diverted river water being used under court order to sustain populations of endangered salmon, the secretary of the interior stood by and allowed them to do so. As seen in chapter 3, Bush assembled an administration that would see to it that winners continued to take all.

2. Get tough with America.

Playing safe is for sissies. Stop coddling the public. Only wimps and trial lawyers worry about parts per million.

Invoking the catchy, disparaging term "the nanny state," the tough guys of the Bush administration ridicule the notion that government should protect us from needless risk. John Graham, Bush's head of risk management, scoffs at the concept that industrial chemicals ought to be tested for safety before being released into the environment. America, he warned, is suffering from "a hypochondria raging among various consumer advocates and public interest groups." He dismisses the precautionary principle—the idea that new chemical substances ought to be proven safe before being released—as "a mythical concept, perhaps like a unicorn." Chapter 4 explores this tough-love approach to public policy and how it has been applied.

In keeping with this Beltway machismo, the Bush administration has played fast and loose with the health of people unlucky enough to live near power plants or toxic industrial sites. More than 16,000 old and dirty power plants, petroleum refineries, chemical factories, and industrial facilities were permanently exempted from having to install modern pollution control technologies. Under Bush's so-called Clear Skies proposal, many communities would be subjected to four times more toxic mercury from coal-fired power plants than they would if the Clean Air Act were simply enforced. Property contaminated with highly toxic PCBs (polychlorinated biphenyls) can now be sold without any obligation for the seller to clean it up. Caveat emptor: let the buyer beware.

The president allowed his brother, Governor Jeb Bush, to resume injecting untreated wastewater into Florida's drinking water aquifers. The administration allowed hazardous waste to be "recycled" into fertilizer, which could be used on playgrounds, golf courses, and parks—and then decided that such waste-based fertilizers could be used to grow food as well.

Are you ready to risk a world without polar bears or a New England without maple syrup? The hard right is. Faced with mounting evidence that global warming will massively disrupt the world's weather, devastate low-lying regions and countries, disrupt agriculture and water supplies, and destroy wildlife and ecosystems, the Bush White House still insists that global warming is not happening—or that, if it is happening, it may be a good thing, and anyway that trying to prevent it is either premature or too late. The message: what we really need to do is suck it up and get used to the idea of living on a hothouse planet. We look at the wishful thinking on climate change in chapter 10.

3. Say one thing, do another.

Never admit what you're up to. Rather, assert the opposite, repeatedly and despite all available evidence.

Why did Reagan's administration get such a terrible environmental reputation? Because, Bush decided, it had bad public relations: Reagan and his appointees did not sufficiently sugarcoat what they were doing. Interior Secretary James Watt baldly announced, "We will mine more, drill more, cut more timber." When asked if it might not be wise to save something for future generations, Watt replied, "I don't know how many future generations we can count on until the Lord returns." This made people worry.

Guided by political guru Karl Rove and pollster Frank Luntz, Bush's rhetoric is far more sophisticated. He regularly has his picture taken in natural settings and wraps his anti-environmental policies in benign names like "Clear Skies" and "Healthy Forests."

"The three words Americans are looking for in an environmental policy, they are: 'safer,' 'cleaner,' and 'healthier,'" Luntz advised Bush and Co. in a leaked memo. "[A]ny discussion of the environment has to be grounded in an effort to reassure a skeptical public that you care about the environment for its own sake—that your intentions are strictly honorable." So are they all, honorable men—even if Clear Skies results in increased pollution and if Healthy Forests chops down trees to save them from fire, as we see in chapter 5.

4. Take care of business.

Markets are smart, governments dumb. The magic of the marketplace will always outperform "command and control" regulations. Government is very good, however, for shoveling taxpayer money at businesses run by campaign contributors. And the most generous contributors are the outmoded, dirty, and dying industries and firms that can't compete without government assistance.

"I don't think you can litigate clean air and clean water. I don't think you can legislate clean air and clean water," Bush said on the campaign trail. His alternative is to ask business politely whether they would like to participate in a voluntary program. Immediately after Bush's inauguration, he invited American businesses to nominate the regulations they found burdensome and would like to eliminate. His zeal for deregulation has survived even the energy crises of New York and California as well as the October 2003 blackout of a large portion of the East. When dozens of states that had not yet deregulated fought to keep their secure, cheap, functional, *regulated* electrical grids, Bush pushed Congress to take away their freedom of choice.

The Bush administration's relationship to business was nicely summed up by Mike Smith, assistant secretary for fossil fuels at the Department of Energy, who told a friendly audience, "The biggest challenge is going to be how to best utilize tax dollars to the benefit of industry." Smith and his fellow officials (many of them plucked from the ranks of the same businesses they are now regulating) quickly rose to that challenge. Bush's energy policy, for example, contained $38 billion in subsidies and tax breaks to polluting, technologically backward industries which are also among Bush's most zealous campaign donors. These industrial dinosaurs, unable to compete in the market, limp along by buying government favors. Not only are they killing us—we are *paying* them to kill us. Chapter 6 tells why.

5. Privatize our heritage.

This land isn't your land—anymore. Public land and common resources are socialist notions; only individuals count. If people value wilderness and wildlands, they can buy or rent them.

One of Bush's first actions as president was seeking to eliminate the new national monuments declared by President Clinton. His most concerted public lands efforts have been to permit drilling for oil and gas in the Rockies, off the coasts, and in the Arctic National Wildlife Refuge. Under Bush, half of the critical habitat set aside for endangered species by previous administrations has been opened to development.

Not even the national parks are safe: Bush tried to turn over Yellowstone and Grand Teton national parks to the snowmobile industry for winter profits at the expense of park solitude and wildlife (not to mention the health of park personnel). Timber companies were allowed to invade Giant Sequoia National Monument and log one tree in every ten under the guise of "fire prevention." Sea turtle nesting grounds on Padre Island National Seashore were relinquished to oil companies for drilling. The coal industry was allowed to shear off entire mountaintops and dump them into public streams, creeks, and rivers.

Plans to restore wolves and grizzly bear populations on public lands in the West were abandoned. Up to 1,000 bison from the herds at Yellowstone National Park were permitted to be slaughtered each year so that 2,000 cows could continue to graze on public land without having to be vaccinated against brucellosis.

The "fee demonstration" program, a misguided Clinton-era pilot project to collect higher admission fees at national parks and forests, was made permanent. Meanwhile, government support for park acquisition was slashed. Bush did offer $100 million for improving wildlife habitat—but only to subsidize private landowners on land inaccessible to the general public. For a discussion of selling off our common heritage, see chapter 7.

6. Cultivate strategic ignorance.

Our science is "sound"; their science is "junk." Start from a desirable premise, and then find the facts to fit. When all else fails, blame "the bureaucracy."

"Facts are stupid things," said Bush's ideological mentor, Ronald Reagan. For Bush, facts are endlessly fungible—when one does not fit, it can be replaced by another. Scientific studies, no matter how well peer reviewed, can always be blamed on bureaucrats and disregarded, as Bush did with the EPA's comprehensive study of global warming.

Scores of reports—not to mention record heat waves, melting glaciers, and mosquito-borne diseases—have warned the administration that global warming is a serious threat requiring serious government action. They have all been ignored. Biologists conducted studies showing that fishing for tuna by encircling dolphins and entangling them in nets is not, in fact, "dolphin safe." Bush terminated the studies. When Interior's wildlife biologists sent Gale Norton a comprehensive, twelve-year study showing the catastrophic impacts of oil drilling in the Arctic, she called it "science fiction" and replaced it with a one-week report that said the opposite. Distinguished scientists have been bounced from scientific advisory panels overseeing vital federal health research, replaced by scientists with extreme views and/or close ties to the affected industries. Bush's politicized science is detailed in chapters 9 and 10.

7. Freeze out the public.

What citizens don't know won't hurt them. The less they know, the less they'll be able to interfere, and the easier it is to get the results we want.

Government of, for, and by the people does not always achieve the results desired by campaign contributors. Jane and John Q. Public tend to get sentimental over endangered furry critters or minority children suffering from asthma.

In the name of national security, the Bush administration cut off public access to crucial information. Web sites were stripped of potentially embarrassing information about the risks that nuclear power plants and chemical factories pose to surrounding neighborhoods. Attorney General John Ashcroft advised government agencies to seek every reason to reject Freedom of Information Act inquiries, making secrecy the norm in government agencies rather than the exception.

Millions of citizens responded to calls for public comment on preserving roadless wilderness; the vast majority was in favor of doing so. Then the administration rigged the rules to minimize the impact of such comments. It has sought to prevent citizens from objecting to plans for logging the national forests. It has also sought to restrict the number of projects that would be subject to the citizen-suit provisions of the National Environmental Policy Act (NEPA). Some Bush allies even propose that the ability to sue under NEPA be limited to those with a direct economic stake in the matter.

How much does Bush care about public opinion? Recent changes to the White House's e-mail system have made it much more difficult for citizens to voice their opinions. More hear-no-evil, speak-no-evil in chapter 11.

8. Clearcut the law, bulldoze the regulators.

Lawyers and judges get in the way of entrepreneurs. Environmental groups and ordinary citizens have too much power to block oil leases, timber sales, and sprawling developments. And regulations just hobble American industry.

Over the past century, America developed a body of laws and regulations requiring federal agencies to protect and respect the environment. Under Bush, government regulations have been rewritten to make it more difficult for judges to require public officials to comply.

Because so many courts had found the Forest Service guilty of so much illegal logging, national forest plans have been made essentially voluntary, and whole categories of timber sales were exempted from the law. When judges ruled that the navy was breaking environmental laws, the administration attempted to eliminate judicial review for anything to do with the oceans.

The administration's approach to troublesome courts is management by denial, foot-dragging, and bench-stacking. Seeking more favorable rulings, Bush sought to appoint judges far outside even mainstream conservative belief. And when called upon to defend environmental laws it does not like, the administration presents a halfhearted defense or none at all, essentially taking a dive and allowing its allies to win. More ideas on how to cripple environmental law are reported in chapter 12.

9. Make Uncle Sam the enemy.

If the federal government is solving real problems, people will support more federal government. But more government is never the answer, even when it appears to be getting the job done. So don't let it.

The hard right's goal for government, as articulated by influential Washington nabob Grover Norquist, is to "reduce it to the size where I can drag it in the bathroom and drown it in the bathtub." This is complicated by the fact that government does all kinds of things people want or desperately need. Programs that conserve soil, forests, water, and energy, or that clean up pollution, are especially loathsome to the hard right because they expand the sphere of public ownership, accountability, and commons management. New parks are wildly popular, so there must be no new parks.

The solution is to shrink the federal government—including those programs the public holds dear. So the Land and Water Conservation Fund is slashed to a fraction of its promised size, Superfund sites cease being cleaned up, veteran National Park Service staffers are let go when their positions are privatized, and funding to improve sewers and keep sewage off beaches is slashed. Chapter 13 examines how Bush makes government less popular by making it less effective.

10. Go it alone in the world.

Who needs allies? They have their own ideas, and sometimes those don't agree with ours.

One of Bush's first acts in the White House was to withdraw the United States from the Kyoto Protocol on Climate Change. He did so to signal to his supporters that he was not going to let the United States get pushed around by India and China—but the message he sent to the rest of the world was that America was going its own way. This message was reinforced at subsequent international conferences, increasing international anger. No wonder, then, that when Bush went looking for international support for war in Iraq, he found himself standing virtually alone. Chapter 14 examines America's self-isolation.

A Shrewd but Reckless Plan

These ten rules that govern the Bush administration's environmental policy sound harsh and even counterproductive. Obviously such strategies fly in the face of overwhelming public sentiment. Americans do not think cheating is a legitimate way of winning. They want air that is really clean and water that is really safe; they want security and protection for themselves from pollution and other risks they do not control. They like the fact that the national parks are there for everyone to enjoy. They do not want to live in a society controlled by corporations and the market. They expect government to respect both science and the law; they want both the information they need and the power to protect themselves. They do not think politicians should pay off their campaign donors—though, sadly, many have come to expect it.

Americans value the principle of the common good and do not think that ruthless competition is the path to a good life. They think they are part of something larger—a national community and even a global community. Along with those stunning photographs of Earth taken from space came an increasing realization that we are all in this together.

So how has the Bush administration pushed its harsh agenda so far and so successfully? By having a disciplined plan and by following its own rules, as the chapters of this book detail. *Strategic Ignorance* does not follow the conventional practice in environmental reporting of looking through the lens of the natural world, with chapters on air, water, wildlife, wilderness, and so on. Rather, it examines the Bush environmental record the way his administration approached the issue: as part of an ideological and political effort to undo a century of environmental progress.

Ignoring the nation's problems, of course, has not made them go away. Hiding data does not make the Superfund sites less toxic or bring back declining species. Slashing environmental budgets only compounds problems for the future, just as increasing the budget deficit leaves our debts to our children. Contrary to Big Brother's slogan in George Orwell's *1984,* ignorance is not strength. It is, in fact, this incurious administration's greatest weakness, which this book seeks to expose.

The Bush plan misjudges, too, how much Americans can be lied to before we see through the smoke. As Senator James Jeffords put it, "The president says one thing, but does another. . . . With a straight face he talks about protecting resources for our children—even as he abandons the federal protection of land and air and water as fast as he can. Does he think we don't notice?"

It is increasingly hard not to. Even if stories about beaches contaminated with sewage are not on page one, parents know that their kids cannot go in the water. Stories about Superfund may not be sexy enough for television news, but one out of four Americans lives within a bicycle ride of a contaminated site where cleanup has been blocked by budget manipulations. Talk radio does not cover how fire prevention funds are being diverted to help timber companies, but people are losing their homes to preventable blazes. When smog is not cleaned up, millions of asthmatic kids head for the emergency rooms. And there is nothing to ruin a weekend hike like suddenly coming upon the brutal ugliness of a fresh clearcut.

Americans started feeling the impact of the Bush administration's strategic ignorance on the environment mere weeks after he took office, and those impacts get more painful every day. This book explains why Bush made his choices and what we can do about it.

"All the great natural resources which are vital to the welfare of the whole people should be kept either in the hands or under the control of the whole people."

— **Theodore Roosevelt**

"When I got home at the end of 1890 . . . the nation was obsessed by a fury of development. The American Colossus was fiercely intent on appropriating and exploiting the riches of the richest of all continents."

— **Gifford Pinchot, on returning from his forestry studies in France**

"Our goal is to destroy, to eradicate the environmental movement. We want to be able to exploit the environment for private gain, absolutely."

— **Ron Arnold, founder of the "wise use" movement**

"I have never believed we had to choose between either a clean and safe environment or a growing economy. Protecting the health and safety of all Americans doesn't have to come at the expense of our economy's bottom line."

— **President Bill Clinton**

A Work in Progress
America's Compact on the Environment

Not since early humans made their way to Australia has there been a biological cornucopia like the one the Europeans found in North America, with its endless forests, teeming game, and rich fishing grounds. Settlers arriving in New England could smell the pine trees 150 miles off Cape Cod. Captain John Smith wrote of Chesapeake Bay, "We found . . . that abundance of fish lying so thicke with their heads above the water, as for want of nets we attempted to catch them with a frying pan, but we found it a bad instrument to catch fish with. Neither better fish more plenty or variety had any of us ever seene." In Massachusetts, lobsters were food for indentured servants and prisoners. To the west, bison herds stretched from horizon to horizon, and flocks of passenger pigeons obscured the sun.

We squandered most (but not all) of this natural wealth in two great waves of heedless destruction that swept over the continent like Ice Age glaciers. In the nineteenth century, driven by plow and harrow, axe and steam engine, buffalo gun and dredge, American settlers pushed west. In short order they laid waste to the pineries of the Great Lakes, the hardwood forests of Ohio and Kentucky, the riparian oak forests of California, the shad fishery of the Potomac, the oyster beds of the Chesapeake and San Francisco bays, the white pines of northern New England, and the great blue-stemmed grama prairie of Oklahoma. The roar of the native grizzly was heard no more in California, the green flash of the Carolina parakeet was quenched.

The second, twentieth-century, wave was a product of industrialization— first of manufacturing, then transportation and agriculture. It rode on oil, concrete, and chemistry, especially in the years following World War II. By 1970, Lake Erie lay almost dead, while the Cuyahoga River burned. By century's end, the old-growth forests of the Rockies and Cascades were devastated, and the bottomland hardwoods of the Mississippi Valley were leveled into soybean fields. Nitrogen-rich farm runoff drained into the Mississippi and Gulf of Mexico, creating a dead zone hundreds of miles from shore. The Everglades, replumbed for the convenience of the sugarcane industry and developers, was dying. Most lakes in the upper Midwest were contaminated with mercury, their fish forbidden to children and pregnant women. The sediments of the Hudson dripped PCBs, eastern forests withered from acidified rain, and thousands of carelessly abandoned toxic waste dumps littered the landscape. Once-mighty schools of salmon beat themselves to death against the great dams that blocked their return to breeding grounds in the inland Pacific Northwest, while radioactive waste from the hyper-contaminated soils of the Hanford nuclear dump seeped inexorably toward the Columbia River.

Our industrial civilization is not as spectacular as the wall of ice that drove this continent's first great herds and forests southward. As avatars of destruction, however, we are nearly its equal. Ice, of course, has no regrets. It grinds and groans, swells where it can, diminishes when it must, unquestioning.

But the American Republic paused and reconsidered. Each great wave of industrial destruction generated a new kind of citizenship to challenge it—the conservation movement of the Progressive Era, and the environmental movement of the late twentieth century. And each of these great public responses encountered fierce resistance from those who had embraced, and profited by, reckless, unconstrained exploitation.

Teddy Roosevelt, Conservation Hero

The conservation movement began in 1892 with the creation of the first national forest and the founding of the Audubon Society on the East Coast and the Sierra Club in the West. The next year, historian Frederick Jackson Turner famously declared, "The frontier is closed." Some Americans were already wondering whether they would be able to pass on to their children the incredible biological and natural wealth that had greeted the early pioneers. Did Americans want their continent to become a second Europe, settled and tamed, flattened and pacified, or did they want to preserve some of its wild glory?

Responding to those early questions were the conservation movement's first leaders, like John Muir, John Burroughs, *Century Magazine* editor Robert Underwood, Sarah Platt Decker, president of the General Federation of Women's Clubs, and Gifford Pinchot, who coined the term "conservation" itself. Conservationism found a home in the broad Progressive movement, with its emphasis on controlling the abuses of industrialism and building a stronger nation-state to safeguard the public interest. Progressivism combined the old populists—southern farmers, western ranchers, and northern workers—with newly alarmed middle-class "goo goos," or good government reformers. "The power of big business alarmed public opinion because its leaders behaved as if they were above the law—fixing prices, driving competitors out of business, neglecting workplace safety and treating workers as if they had no rights," wrote Roosevelt biographer Kathleen Dalton.

The first Progressive president and first champion of the conservation movement, Teddy Roosevelt, convinced the nation that its resources were in fact finite. In 1908 he called a "Conservation Conference" attended by state governors, Supreme Court justices, and cabinet members. "We look upon these resources as a heritage to be made use of in establishing and promoting the comfort, prosperity, and happiness of the American People," the conference concluded, "but not to be wasted, deteriorated, or needlessly destroyed."

Roosevelt signed the Lacey Act, giving the president the power to create national monuments, and promptly used that power to set aside the Grand Canyon—an act initially bitterly denounced by local officials in Arizona. (Later, of course, they put the Grand Canyon on the state's license plates in recognition of its economic benefits.) After camping out in Yosemite with Sierra Club founder John Muir, Roosevelt added the forests of the Sierra to the national park system. When Congress moved to take away his power to create national forests, he sprawled on his office floor with Gifford Pinchot, now head of the Forest Service, setting aside 17 million acres just minutes before his deadline (and, some would say, setting a precedent for eleventh-hour action on the environment by presidents Jimmy Carter and Bill Clinton). Roosevelt also created the first national wildlife refuge at Pelican Island, Florida; the Louisiana black bear he rescued on a hunting trip to Mississippi became the namesake for every "teddy" bear since. Roosevelt supported the Reclamation Act to help western settlers establish homesteads. He established the Tongass National Forest in Alaska over the opposition of his own secretary of the interior, Ethan Hitchcock, and joined Muir in his efforts to save Yosemite's Hetch Hetchy Valley from being dammed.

Roosevelt never had support for his program in Congress or in the business community. The pro-development "boomers" in the West protested his creation of the Forest Service, dubbing its rangers "cossacks" and its chief "Czar Pinchot." Responding to Roosevelt's calls to protect natural resources for posterity, one congressman responded, "What has posterity ever done for me?" So the president turned for support to the Audubon Society, the Boone and Crockett Club, the Sierra Club—and to women, newly enfranchised to vote in half a dozen states. One article claimed that "a million women for conservation" had written letters to Congress. Even the Daughters of the American Revolution were enlisted on behalf of America's natural heritage.

While Roosevelt argued that conservation was important for the economy and the nation's strength, behind his practical-sounding arguments was a fundamental view of the American character. We needed wildness to be Americans, he believed, just as Roosevelt himself had needed his adventurous years in the Black Hills of South Dakota to become the Rough Rider of the Spanish American War.

Neither Woodrow Wilson nor his successors Warren Harding and Calvin Coolidge shared Roosevelt's passion for conservation. The Sierra Club succeeded in creating Sequoia National Park, but only after losing the battle to preserve Hetch Hetchy from being drowned under O'Shaughnessy Dam. Throughout the quiescent 1920s, however, writers like Aldo Leopold, journalists like J. N. "Ding" Darling, and organizations like the Izaak Walton League continued to build a broad base of public support for conservation.

The movement regained its vigor with the onset of the Dust Bowl and the Great Depression. Teddy's second cousin Franklin Delano Roosevelt put hundreds of thousands of Americans to work restoring their landscapes with the Civilian Conservation Corps. His vice president Henry Wallace added badly overcut eastern forests to the national forest system. The Tennessee Valley Authority (TVA) began to restore that region's forests and soils. FDR's interior secretary Harold Ickes battled the timber interests for control of Washington State's Olympic Peninsula and quietly collaborated with John D. Rockefeller, Jr., in creating Jackson Hole National Monument.

The tools of these early conservationists were those of Progressive government. Public lands and waters were retained or acquired as federally managed commons, in the form of national parks, forests, and wildlife refuges; federal dam and reclamation projects were professionally managed by restoration authorities like the TVA or the Bonneville Power Authority. Regulatory agencies were expected to protect the public against monopolistic price gouging by corporations. The government conducted the scientific research needed to improve farming and natural resource management and then funded farmers and communities to help them curb erosion, reduce water pollution, and enhance wildlife habitat. The country was on track to conserve what Muir, the Audubon Society, and Teddy Roosevelt had set out to rescue.

Beyond Blind Progress:
The New Environmentalism

The challenges of the postwar period proved to be beyond the professional management faith of traditional conservationists. The petrochemical and nuclear industries that emerged after World War II created a new kind of devastation, contaminating air, water, and ground with sometimes invisible toxic and radioactive hazards. People were aware that things were amiss (rivers are not supposed to catch fire), but there was a strong predisposition to view dirty air, unswimmable water, and destructive development projects as the price of modern prosperity. The answer to every murmured complaint was always the same: "You can't stop progress."

But you can stop destruction. Remarkably, the birth of the modern environmental movement can be traced to a specific date: the publication in 1962 of Rachel Carson's *Silent Spring*. Carson's exposé of the effects of DDT and other industrial chemicals shocked the nation into action. Membership in the Sierra Club grew from 16,500 in 1961 to 55,000 in 1967; public campaigns persuaded Congress to scrap plans to dam the Grand Canyon; California began major efforts to combat Los Angeles's smog. When Senator Gaylord Nelson and Representative Pete McCloskey issued the call for the first Earth Day in 1970, they were overwhelmed when 20 million people took part in thousands of events around the country.

In the 1960s and 1970s, Congress passed, in rapid succession, a series of bold and farsighted environmental initiatives: the Wilderness Act, the Clean Air Act, the Clean Water Act, the Endangered Species Act, the Resources Conservation and Recovery Act, and the National Environmental Policy Act (NEPA). These actions reflected a shift away from the two Roosevelts' emphasis on production of timber, crops, and minerals for "the comfort, prosperity, and happiness of the American People" and toward the protection of public health and the preservation of natural values for their own sake and for posterity—quality-of-life issues as opposed to economic stewardship. What Teddy Roosevelt had believed, but had to hide behind economic pragmatism, was now at the heart of the public's attitude toward the environment.

Many Progressive Era reforms had been corrupted by Washington's "iron triangle" of industry, regulators, and compliant congressional overseers. The new wave of environmental legislation was informed by knowledge of these forces. As a result, while new regulatory agencies like the Environmental Protection Agency (EPA) were set up to enforce the new laws, ordinary citizens were empowered to intervene in the courts if they did not. James Madison's checks and balances now extended to the citizenry, not just the government. The U.S. Supreme Court, in *Sierra Club v. Morton*, ruled that people who hiked beneath trees had standing to sue (even if, to Justice William O. Douglas's chagrin, the trees themselves did not). But Congress did not leave public power to the courts to decide—law after law, passed in a climate that emphasized "maximum feasible public participation," specified that any citizen could sue if, for example, the EPA failed to carry out its duty to protect the air or water.

During this era Congress was in Democratic hands; the White House was mostly Republican. While the environment remained a bipartisan issue during Richard Nixon's terms, the reforms of the 1970s also represented a revival of the original American concept of a dominant legislative branch. Patrician policy makers like Maine's Senator Edmund Muskie and acerbic street fighters like California's Representative Phillip Burton for the first time made conservation and environmental protection an arena of congressional, not executive, prerogative. Under Burton's gruff handling, for example, the legislative logroll and the discredited congressional pork barrel were forged into the Omnibus Parks Act of 1978—diverse preservation initiatives hammered into one law.

To further empower the people, a Jeffersonian element was added: the knowledge and science of government agencies was laid out for public scrutiny and debate through the processes of NEPA and the Freedom of Information Act. For the first time, concerned citizens would be able to act to protect themselves against the environmental side effects of modern industry as well as sue to protect the places they loved. No longer was pollution, devastation, or extinction to be an acceptable price of progress.

The Plunderers Regroup

The Roosevelts and the early conservation movement encountered fierce resistance from the trusts and robber barons, loath to limit their exploitation of the new nation's fabulous natural wealth. Similarly, after its initial wave of heady triumphs, environmentalism faced a concerted counterattack from corporate America, which soon learned that bold laws passed by Congress could be undermined by a reluctant executive. Claiming goodwill and pleading poverty, business began to assert that compliance should be left to the very industries that had fiercely opposed the standards in the first place. Citizen lawsuits could compel agencies to issue or enforce regulations, but only after lengthy court battles and frequent legislative interference.

A new intellectual enterprise—the "free-enterprise think tank"—was created, with generous funding from polluting industry, to make the best case for toxic chemicals and the rape of natural resources. There is not enough evidence that these chemicals are actually dangerous, they would argue; most of the testing done to establish toxicity was done on animals, but rats are obviously different from humans, so the results are meaningless. (The alternative to lab rats, of course, is lab humans. While no one suggests experimenting on people in labs, allowing untested chemicals into the world effectively makes everyone a guinea pig) Global warming is not really happening, and, even if it is, it might be a good thing, and, even if it's a bad thing, it's not our fault. Clearcuts are actually healthy for forests, and the new growth soaks up a lot of carbon dioxide— if, of course, carbon dioxide is even a problem. Besides which, clearcuts do not burn, and burning releases a lot of carbon dioxide—if, of course, carbon dioxide is a problem. Which it isn't. (Think tanks of the radical right, while continually lamenting that America has too much litigation and too many lawyers, are themselves exactly like defense lawyers: my client didn't do it; if he did do it, no one was hurt; if anyone was hurt, my client was under duress.)

Americans, for the most part, did not buy the arguments for giving corporations free rein to destroy the environment. And whenever they started to be seduced, nature and chance would often conspire to release a grim reminder: the Santa Barbara oil spill, Love Canal, Three Mile Island, the wreck of the *Exxon Valdez*. All of these disasters drummed home the lesson that the stakes of environmental apathy could be large and lethal.

Over the decades, in poll after poll, public support for environmental protection increased. National parks became one of America's most popular and cherished institutions, and citizens tolerated the outrageous logging of the national forest system only because they did not realize that logging was even allowed in the national forests. As the environmental statutes of the 1970s rescued the bald eagle and gray whale, cleaned up the most horrific toxic waste dumps, and started to clear the skies over major cities, the public demanded more environmental progress, not less.

The Environmental Education of Bill Clinton

Bill Clinton and Al Gore came to office in 1993 promising bold environmental reforms. Expectations for them were enormous: Gore, after all, was the author of Earth in the Balance, a powerful case for swift, decisive action on global warming and other issues. (During the campaign, George H. W. Bush ridiculed Gore as "Ozone Man" for speaking out on the dangerous thinning of the earth's layer of protective ozone. Today the reversal of damage to the ozone layer is seen as one of the great environmental success stories of the past century.) Hopes in the new administration initially seemed justified; the new president and vice president met with leaders of the green groups and raided their staffs to fill top positions in the new administration. Many environmentalists saw Clinton's inauguration as the dawn of an environmental golden age.

That optimistic vision crumbled almost immediately. Despite some positive moves and appointments, the environment was clearly not a top-tier issue for Clinton. At the first whisper of opposition to his plan to reduce taxpayer subsidies for grazing, mining, and logging on public lands, for instance, he dropped the issue like a hot branding iron. Against the strong objections of the environmental community, he pushed through the North American Free Trade Agreement (which, as predicted, led to worsened pollution along the border and pressure on the United States to weaken its environmental laws). Worst of all, he signed the disastrous Salvage Logging Rider, a plan written by former timber lobbyist Mark Rey that opened up thousands of acres of pristine forest without being subject to the usual environmental controls or citizen challenges. (Clinton later regretted it, and Gore called signing the bill the "biggest mistake" of Clinton's first term.)

Stumbling badly elsewhere as well, Clinton and the Democrats lost control of the Congress in the midterm election of 1994 to the fiercely anti-environmental Newt Gingrich and his Republican allies. In the wake of that electoral debacle, Clinton slowly came to realize the potency of the environment as a political tool. Gingerly at first, his appointees embraced enforcement of environmental law. Later, Clinton even allowed the entire federal government to be shut down by vetoing a bill that included a provision for opening the Arctic National Wildlife Refuge to oil drilling, saying he was "not prepared to discuss . . . the ravaging of our environment." (The shutdown turned out to be fateful for Clinton's presidency: with regular employees furloughed, a young intern named Monica Lewinsky stepped in to deliver pizza to the president.)

Clinton began to view environmental laws as real laws, to be followed and enforced. He remained cautious and compromising, but so strong was public support, and so robust was the basic legal framework he had inherited from decades of work by the conservation and environmental movements, that even his timid reforms soon bore spectacular fruit.

Under Clinton, the EPA began to bring lawsuits against power plants that had failed to install the required pollution control equipment, with impressive results: the EPA estimated that one-quarter of the nation's total industrial pollution would be cleaned up. Trying to atone for the Salvage Rider, Clinton appointed a new chief of the Forest Service, Mike Dombeck, who determined to restore the agency to its original stewardship mission, and to do so on a solid foundation of administrative, policy, and personnel reforms. Under his leadership, the agency adopted an ecological approach to forest planning, putting the health of the land first. Dombeck put the critical grizzly bear habitat along the Rocky Mountain Front off-limits to oil and gas leasing; he initiated a new "framework" for the management of forests in California's Sierra Nevada, shifting the emphasis from timber production to ecological restoration; and he worked to create the Sequoia National Monument, protecting groves of ancestral sequoias that lay outside the boundaries of Sequoia National Park.

The centerpiece of Dombeck's efforts, however, was the Roadless Area Conservation Rule, an initiative to ban logging on the remaining roadless wildlands in the national forest system—more than 58 million acres. The largest concentrations were in Alaska and Idaho, but almost every state with significant national forest acreage had some jewels in need of protection. Not since Teddy Roosevelt's midnight rescue of the national forest system had there been such a bold land protection initiative. Dombeck knew it would be brutally attacked in court and in Congress by the timber industry and its allies, so he moved methodically, holding more than 600 public hearings and receiving more than a million public comments, over 95 percent of which strongly favored protecting the remaining wild forests. Shortly before Clinton left office in 2001, he put the plan in place, setting aside from logging and road building the nation's most precious remaining old growth and wildlands.

Benchmarks at the Millennium

As America left the twentieth century and entered the new millennium, we were making significant progress on almost every front toward a more environmentally sustainable society. Enormous issues remained, of course—among them global warming, the increasing concentration of persistent poisons in the oceans and biosphere, and the fragmentation or loss of wildlife habitat.

But the efforts of Progressive Era conservationists and post–Earth Day environmentalists constitute one of the great civic success stories of twentieth-century America. Air and water pollution had been dramatically reduced, and society had committed to finishing the job. (In 1977, Los Angeles had 121 days when children could not play outside; by 2000, every day was a play day.) For the first time since the petrochemical industry drilled its first oil well in Pennsylvania in 1859, the number of acres contaminated by toxic industrial wastes appeared to be going down each year. Concentrations of lead in the bloodstreams of urban children fell by 93 percent between 1978 and 2000.

Under the impact of the right-to-know provisions of Superfund legislation, American industries were finding that it was better business to clean up their toxic emissions than to admit to their neighbors just how dirty they were. Total emissions of toxic chemicals declined between 1988 and 1996 by nearly 50 percent, a reduction of more than 1.5 billion pounds.

Because of the efforts of "Ozone Man" Gore and others in banning or severely restricting ozone-destroying chemicals, the hole in the stratospheric ozone layer was healing itself. Sixty percent of the nation's waterways were again safe to swim in, twice as many as when the Clean Water Act was passed. The amount of protected habitat set aside for wildlife was increasing each year; Clinton alone had designated 115 million acres for 50 different species. In addition to the bald eagle, the gray whale, brown pelican, gray wolf, and grizzly bear had recovered—or were on the verge of recovering—sustainable numbers of their historic populations.

For most Americans, environmental progress had ceased to be controversial. Poll after poll revealed that citizens had decided: they wanted America wild (at least in part), they wanted it clean, and they wanted it safe from industrial toxics. They appreciated the progress that had been made thus far and were willing to pay the price to finish the job.

George W. Bush and his supporters had a radically different agenda: first to bring to a conclusive halt the era of environmental progress, and then to turn back the clock.

"When we asked them to pose for pictures to accompany the article, they both said yes; what's more, their representative wanted them to be photographed in outdoor, natural settings. They both look like Sierra Club veterans: [Interior Secretary Gale] Norton in trekking gear and a Patagonia-cum–Smokey the Bear outfit, and [Deputy Interior Secretary J. Steven] Griles on horseback, resembling some latter-day Theodore Roosevelt."

— *Vanity Fair* **editor Graydon Carter on the photo illustrations for "Sale of the Wild," an investigation of conflict of interest and industry favoritism in the Interior Department**

"Cheney, say those who know him, has always had a Hobbesian view of life. The world is a dangerous place; war is the natural state of mankind; enemies lurk."

—*Newsweek,* **November 2003**

"We have the house, we have the Senate, we have the White House. Which means we have the agenda."

— **House Majority Leader Tom DeLay (R-Texas)**

Opening Moves
The Wrecking Crew Goes to Work

In the lame-duck days before George W. Bush's inauguration, after five U.S. Supreme Court justices decided Bush had won the election, President Clinton signed a large number of important environmental rules. Many of these executive orders had been in the administrative pipeline for years; several had been delayed because Republican-controlled Congresses had forbidden federal agencies to work on them. Once signed, their effect was sweeping. For starters, Clinton used Teddy Roosevelt's Antiquities Act to declare a raft of new national monuments. He established new energy efficiency requirements for major appliances, made it harder for the government to contract with companies that had violated environmental laws, lowered the acceptable amounts of arsenic in drinking water, mandated reductions in water pollution from factory farms, and called for a 95 percent reduction in diesel emissions. Clinton's end-of-term actions captured the cutting edge of environmental policy at the dawn of the new century. This was where forward progress was being made.

Bush laid out his environmental intentions within 90 minutes of being sworn in, when his chief of staff, Andrew Card (formerly the top lobbyist for General Motors) sent out a memorandum putting 371 of Clinton's pending rules on hold. An important principle was in play: before you change direction, you must first apply the brakes. "Actions like this, undertaken at the very end of an administration, carry . . . the risk that they were ill-conceived or ill-intentioned, or both," said Office of Management and Budget Director Mitch Daniels. The Bush spin was that the orders were whimsical, despite the many years of preparation that had gone into them, so Bush was merely "reinterpreting" rules and regulations, and "reconsidering" enforcement actions and budgets—all moves designed to be seen as modest corrections to Clinton's supposed "environmental extremism."

Bush's moderate-sounding facade was quickly stripped away in the uproar over his blocking of the new arsenic standard. (See chapter 4 for details.) It quickly became apparent that, despite his promises to govern as a healer and a uniter, Bush and his advisers viewed his one-vote margin on the Supreme Court as a popular mandate to pursue a hard right-wing agenda. His administration since then has pursued winner-take-all with a vengeance.

By mid-March 2001, Bush had largely got past reacting to the land mines left by Clinton and started throwing bombs of his own. He retreated from his campaign promise to regulate carbon dioxide (the primary contributor to global warming), announced that he would consider all public lands fair game for oil and gas drilling, and delayed application of the Roadless Area Conservation Rule, which protected 58 million acres of public lands from logging, mining, and development. These were only the first steps. The list went on and on, and goes on to this day.

Bush's Brain and the Sultan of Spin

Bush's presidency was the radical right's third opportunity to dismantle America's environmental heritage. The first was the comparatively clumsy effort by the Reagan administration, the second Newt Gingrich's vainglorious "Contract with America" (a.k.a. the "War on the Environment"), begun after the Republican ascendancy in the House in 1994. Both efforts failed, and the right dedicated itself to learning from its mistakes—no one more zealously than

Bush's longtime political guru, Karl Rove, and pollster Frank Luntz. Together they perfected a strategy for dragging environmental policy backward, all the while allowing the president to appear to govern from the moderate center.

Rove may or may not be "Bush's brain," as the title of James Moore's book about him asserts, but he certainly plays the role of consigliere. Rove grew up on the seamier streets of American politics; as a college Republican, he ran workshops on how to carry out dirty tricks. Early in his political career, in an Illinois state race, he printed fake invitations promising "free beer, free food, girls, and a good time" on an opponent's campaign stationery. Moving to Texas, he helped gubernatorial candidate Bill Clements by printing fake newspapers accusing Clements's Democratic opponent of having wrecked a car while drunk. In a later race, Rove "discovered" that an electronic bug had been found in Clements's office, just hours before he was to debate his opponent. The FBI investigated and found no trace of foul play. "We were the first on the scene and concluded that Rove had hired a company to debug his office, and that the same company had planted the bug," said a source involved in the Travis County district attorney's investigation.

Rove was fired from George H. W. Bush's 1992 presidential campaign when he was found to have leaked disparaging stories about the campaign (to columnist Robert Novak) to get even with his rival, campaign chair Robert Mosbacher, Jr. He bounced back, however, to become the strategist behind George W. Bush's 1994 victory over Ann Richards for the Texas governorship. The return to the Bush family's graces apparently did not require any change in Rove's methods: in Bush's 2000 campaign, Rove was widely believed to be behind the whisper campaigns questioning rival John McCain's mental stability (because of the torture he had endured while a prisoner of war in Vietnam) and hinting that he had fathered illegitimate children by a black woman. On a book tour in 2002, McCain told audiences that "Karl Rove will stop at nothing, absolutely nothing, to keep power—and George Bush will let him get away with it."

Yet the disconnect between Rove's viciousness and Bush's affability and seeming decency provided just the cover Rove needed for the very dirty campaign he orchestrated for Bush in 2000. That gap is revealed, perhaps, in Bush's two nicknames for his adviser: "Boy Genius" and "Turd Blossom."

Frank Luntz is a boyish, gee-whiz, all-American enthusiast who has spent years analyzing American attitudes on environmental protection. Rather than seeking to help his candidates align themselves with public values, Luntz saw his job as helping to find innocuous language to describe programs most people would find radical and, frankly, terrifying. This is what Bush means when he says he doesn't pay attention to polls. He doesn't, in deciding what he wants to do. Rather, he uses them to figure out how he can get away with doing it, and how to talk about it so no one gets upset.

Back in 1994, Luntz had advised Gingrich on his Contract with America, a collection of ten bills the GOP vowed to push through in its first 100 days in power. These included bills like the Private Property Rights Protection and Compensation Act, which would have forced the federal government to reimburse anyone who claimed that environmental protections had reduced the value of their property by 10 percent or more. The attacks on the Contract by the Sierra Club and others for its anti-environmental provisions were instrumental in its eventual defeat.

Luntz saw it coming, reported the *Cleveland Plain Dealer*. "Republican pollster Frank Luntz, whose work steered much of the 'Contract' campaign, warned GOP leaders in a memo . . . that 62 percent of American voters—and even 54 percent of Republican voters—would prefer to see Congress do more to protect the environment than cut regulations."

Eight years later, with the popularity of environmental protection unchanged and with the new Bush administration planning even more drastic rollbacks, Luntz had his work cut out for him.

The Wrecking Crew

If Bush's immediate reversals of Clinton's late executive orders left any doubt about his intentions, his appointments to the environmental bureaucracy removed them. Time and again, top agency posts were filled with top lobbyists from the affected industries, ideologues from the right-wing think tanks, or a combination of the two. The fox was not just guarding the chicken coop; the fox saw to it that all chicken coops would be run by foxes, declared that any suggestions to the contrary were anti-fox and possibly treasonous, and made sure that the chickens would have no right of appeal.

Here, then, are some of the president's foxes, along with a few of their cousins in Congress:

John Ashcroft, Attorney General

Bush's choice of John Ashcroft for attorney general was a genuine act of compassionate conservatism, since at the time of his appointment the former Republican senator from Missouri was unemployed, having just lost his re-election bid to a dead man. His challenger, Mel Carnahan, had died in a plane crash weeks before the election, but Missouri voters chose him anyway over the right-wing scold Ashcroft.

As a senator, Ashcroft had maintained a perfect environmental voting record—a big fat zero in the major environmental votes tabulated by the League of Conservation Voters from 1997 to 2000. In every major environmental vote that came along in the 105th and 106th Congresses, Ashcroft took the anti-environmental position. Despite a professed deference to states' rights, he had also voted to allow developers to skip past state courts and take their appeals of local planning and zoning ordinances straight to federal court. In addition, he tried to browbeat the Clinton administration into approving lead-mining permits for the notorious Doe Run Co., attempting an end run around environmental safeguards on Missouri's Eleven Point National Scenic River.

But America is a country built upon the possibility of personal redemption, and Ashcroft was duly confirmed as attorney general—though not before suspicious Democratic senators questioned him closely on whether his Justice Department would vigorously defend the Clinton administration's setting aside 58 million acres of wild forest from logging and road building. Ashcroft promised that he would "support and enforce" the rule. He did neither.

Andrew Card, White House Chief of Staff

In addition to the political acumen needed to survive as a Republican lawmaker in the heavily Democratic Massachusetts House of Representatives, Andrew Card possessed the essential prerequisite for service in a Bush White House: a history of absolute loyalty to the Bush family. Card goes back with the Bushes as far as 1980, when he was George H. W. Bush's driver in his failed campaign for the Republican presidential nomination. Card returned eight years later to run Bush the elder's successful primary campaign in New Hampshire, and he subsequently joined the White House as deputy chief of staff to John Sununu.

During the Clinton interregnum, Card found gainful employment as a lobbyist, first for the U.S. Chamber of Commerce, then as CEO and president of the American Automobile Manufacturer's Association, and finally as chief lobbyist for General Motors, which threw him a grateful farewell party on the roof of the Kennedy Center just before Bush's inauguration.

Dick Cheney, Vice President

Back when Dick Cheney represented Wyoming in Congress, he still had a working relationship with the environmental community, even if some found him a bit of a Jekyll-and-Hyde figure. At one moment he would sit down constructively and work out the details of a wilderness bill for his state (which preserved nearly a million acres of national forest land); at the next he would bitterly denounce environmentalists and all their works.

As the years went by, Dr. Jekyll lost control more and more often. Cheney repeatedly stood against the majority of even his own party. He was one of only sixteen members of Congress to vote against the Endangered Species Act, and one of twenty-six voting to sustain President Reagan's veto of amendments to the Clean Water Act. He opposed reauthorization of the Superfund, opposed funding the Safe Drinking Water Act, opposed allowing citizens to sue to protect themselves from pollution, and voted to cut funding for environmental research and development. Cheney went on to become CEO of the Halliburton Company, by which time he was solidly in line with the radical right wing of the Republican Party.

Tom DeLay (R-Tex.), House Majority Leader

The hard, bitter, winner-take-all right finds its apogee in Tom DeLay. The son of an oilman, DeLay started his career as a pest exterminator in Houston and was propelled into politics partly by anger at the Environmental Protection Agency (EPA), which banned several of his favorite pesticides. He has since argued for the return of DDT ("not harmful"), chlordane, and other toxic substances.

Environmental protections have remained at the top of DeLay's hit list. He calls the EPA "the Gestapo of government, pure and simply . . . one of the major claw hooks that the government maintains on the backs of our constituents."

He tried to abolish the Clean Air Act, arguing that the cancer danger from gargling with mouthwash is worse than that from airborne soot. "It has never been proven that air toxics are hazardous to people," he claims, insisting that Clinton's EPA administrator, Carol Browner, was "misrepresenting" the science. ("I'm a scientist myself," DeLay boasted—he got a BS degree from the University of Houston in 1970.)

DeLay does not believe in acid rain; if lakes in the Northeast are too acidic, he says, just add lime. In 1995, when the Nobel Prize went to Paul J. Crutzen, Mario Molina, and F. Sherwood Rowland for establishing the link between chlorofluorocarbons and ozone depletion, DeLay termed it the "Nobel Appeasement Prize," noting for the record that Sweden is an "extremist environmental country." Nor does he believe in global warming: "It's the arrogance of man to think that man can change the climate of the world. Only nature can change the climate. A volcano, for instance." DeLay also does not believe that we can know what the climate was like hundreds of thousands of years ago, because he does not believe the earth is that old, opting for 6,000 years per the biblical calculations of Bishop James Usher of Armagh (1581–1656).

DeLay may be a caricature of a know-nothing politician, but he is a caricature with unparalleled political clout. Not for nothing is his nickname on Capitol Hill "the Hammer." DeLay knows how to reward his friends, punish his enemies, and accomplish his goals. And in 2000 he had all the tools he needed. Even before the Supreme Court had awarded the presidency to George Bush, DeLay declared: "We have the House, we have the Senate, we have the White House. Which means we have the agenda."

John Graham, Administrator, Office of Information and Regulatory Affairs

A bespectacled theoretician, John Graham came to the Bush administration from Harvard, where he ran the Harvard Center for Risk Analysis (with generous funding from corporate donors including Dow, Exxon, General Electric, Monsanto, and Union Carbide). Graham made his mark with elaborate statistical studies assessing how much it "cost" to save a human life through a variety of "governmental interventions"—that is, environmental and public health initiatives. Spending money on seeing that women got regular mammograms, he argued, was cost-effective at $17,000 per life, whereas reducing air emissions of benzene would cost $19 million per averted death. Rather than concluding that America should invest more in women's health programs, Graham went on to claim that the regulation of benzene was causing the "statistical murder" of 60,000 people—a number he derived by assuming that, if benzene regulations were relaxed, the money the oil industry would save would somehow be devoted to paying for mammograms.

Early in his career, Graham was something of an enfant terrible. He even hit up Philip Morris for a $25,000 contribution to his Harvard center, noting that he was working on classifying carcinogens and mentioning, "It is important for me to learn more about the risk-related challenges that you face." In 1979 he wrote in the journal *Public Interest* that America was suffering from "a hypochondria raging among various consumer advocates and public interest groups." He attributed the regulation of everything from nuclear power to PCBs to saccharin to this "flustered hypochondria." Graham had opposed federal regulation of dioxin, even when EPA studies indicated that as many as one in a hundred Americans might get cancer from exposure to the chemical, because this risk was no higher than that of dying in an automobile accident and was thus "normal." He also opposed regulating the use of mobile phones while driving, because the risk—a fourfold increase in the fatal accident rate—was counterbalanced by the increased profitability of employees' being able to work while driving.

By 1996, Graham had learned better than to flatly promote the weakening of health and safety regulations, telling the Heritage Foundation, "I think our message should be that we want smarter, more efficient regulation in order to get more protection at lower cost." Frank Luntz could not have put it better.

J. Steven Griles, Deputy Secretary of the Interior

The environmental history of the Bush administration could have been far different; an early candidate for the deputy secretary position was conservationist John Turner, former CEO of the Conservation Fund and an old friend of Vice President Cheney. But right-wing "property-rights" groups mounted a concerted lobbying effort against his nomination. ("Tell the Transition Team and your Senators," advised the American Land Rights Association, "No John Turner, No Land Grabs, Leave My Property Alone!") As a result of the hue and cry from the administration's zealot base, Turner was dropped in favor of someone much more aligned with their thinking: J. Steven Griles.

They do not come much more wired in Washington than Griles. He was a central figure in Reagan's Interior Department under James Watt, where he undertook to gut federal strip-mining laws, aggressively promote oil drilling off Florida and California, and support a controversial 1986 giveaway of oil-shale lands for $2.50 an acre. (According to Friends of the Earth, one lucky buyer purchased "17,000 acres of the land in question for $42,500, and then sold the same land for $37 million.")

During the Clinton years, Griles was a vice president for National Environmental Strategies, a D.C. lobbying firm serving the coal, utility, and oil industries. Through a separate private lobbying firm, he represented the Coal Bed Methane Ad Hoc Committee as well as the energy company Dominion Resources. Even though he promised not to deal with his former clients' business once he took office, Griles continued to meet with them, starting immediately after his confirmation. (Griles called the meetings "social and informational.") As detailed in *Vanity Fair,* upon becoming deputy secretary of the interior, Griles secured a commitment from National Environmental Strategies to give him four annual payments of $284,000 for the client base he built during his tenure there. *Vanity Fair* concluded: "So the deputy secretary is receiving a major outside income from his former business colleague, who continues to represent Griles' former clients. Those clients are principally coal, oil, and gas companies."

James Hansen (R-Utah), Chairman, House Committee on Resources, 2000–2002

Since James Hansen was first elected to Congress from Utah in 1980, his environmental rating from the League of Conservation Voters has seldom risen above the single digits. For years, Hansen pushed legislation to allow states to veto federally approved wilderness areas and to run a highway wherever a trail of any sort once existed. He supported the decommissioning of national parks he deemed to be "not worthy," like Nevada's Great Basin National Park. ("If you have been there once, you don't need to go again," he said.) Hansen opposed Clinton's designation of the Grand Staircase–Escalante National Monument and did his best to abolish or eviscerate it.

Hansen's most enduring hobbyhorse was trying to cap the total amount of wilderness in Utah at 1.8 million acres. (Conservationists support protecting more than 9 million acres.) Seventy-nine percent of Utahans support increasing the state's wilderness.

With the election of Bush, Hansen saw an opportunity to advance his agenda on a national level. In a letter to the young administration, he proposed changes to the management of public lands that would, in many ways, take our parks, monuments, forests, rivers, and wilderness back to the era before Teddy Roosevelt. (See chapter 7.)

Jeffrey Holmstead, Assistant EPA Administrator for Air and Radiation

Jeffrey Holmstead cut his legal teeth representing corporations on pesticide issues, especially as they were affected by the Clean Air Act. He worked in the EPA in the first Bush administration on clean air issues and was attached to Citizens for the Environment, a libertarian offshoot of Citizens for a Sound Economy, funded by General Motors, Shell Oil, and David Koch—generous moneybags to a large number of right-wing think tanks.

Gale Norton, Secretary of the Interior

Gale Norton comes from the so-called wise use wing of western Republicanism. The successor movement to the Reagan-era "Sagebrush Rebellion," wise use was (and to some extent still is) a loose association of groups representing natural resource exploiters: oil and gas interests, mining companies, the timber industry, and off-road-vehicle riders, plus a thin layer of small ranchers and businesspeople caught in the collapse of the commodity economy. Norton got her start working under James Watt at the Mountain States Legal Foundation, the "litigating arm of the Wise Use Movement." Moving to Washington, D.C., she worked in Reagan's Interior Department, attempting to open up the Arctic National Wildlife Refuge to oil drilling. She has also worked as a lobbyist for a large lead company that faced numerous lawsuits regarding Superfund sites and children poisoned by lead paint.

Norton has been an important supporter of the "property rights" movement, which seeks to expand the takings clause of the Fifth Amendment to require the government to pay property owners when it imposes new environmental restrictions. "We might even go so far as to recognize a homesteading right to pollute or make noise in an area," Norton once wrote. (She later thought better of the notion and repudiated it.) She got herself in a heap of trouble in 1996 when she seemed to excuse slavery as a matter of "bad facts" and lamented that "we lost too much" in the Civil War vis-à-vis states' rights.

As Colorado attorney general, Norton "measure[d] her words with the care of a laboratory scientist pouring chemicals into a beaker." As interior secretary, she has hewn to the gospel according to Luntz and carefully avoided making inflammatory statements in the manner of her mentor, James Watt. According to the profile in *Vanity Fair,* "no Watt-like battle cries emanated from the secretary's corner office at 18th and C Streets. Norton just smiled and invoked her new catchphrase—'the four C's': 'consultation, cooperation, and communication, all in the name of conservation.' She repeated it so often than it began to madden even her own staffers."

Mark Rey, Undersecretary for Natural Resources and the Environment, Department of Agriculture

The Forest Service has a term for officials who are concerned with "getting out the cut" at all costs: they are called "timber beasts." Mark Rey is the archetype. He has spent his entire career, both in and out of public employment, in the service of the timber industry. After stints with the National Forest Products Association, the American Paper Institute, and the American Forest and Paper Association, and as executive director of the American Forest Resources Alliance, he worked with anti-environmental senators Frank Murkowski (R-Ala.) and Larry Craig (R-Idaho). Rey authored the infamous Salvage Rider, which set aside environmental laws on thousands of acres in the Pacific Northwest. In 1992, he was a featured speaker at a wise use convention, and he has branded defenders of endangered species as "the radical environmental legal terrorism campaign ... taking direct aim at private property rights."

The timber industry and timber unions were thrilled with Rey. "We have lost members by the thousands, and it is time we get a little balance back in the equation," said Mike Draper, vice president of the Western District of the Brotherhood of Carpenters, representing mill workers. Environmentalists were appalled. Defending Rey's integrity, former Clinton administration deputy forest chief Chris Wood insisted that "he's not Darth Vader. He's maybe Darth Vader Lite." For Rey, environmental concerns are the "antics" of "well-heeled special interests," whereas opposition to the same represents "the interests of thousands of logging families and communities." Clearcutting, he says, while perhaps "not aesthetically uplifting," is compatible with rain forest ecology and "relatively comparable" to windstorms.

Rey proceeded, once confirmed, to bluntly signal the agency that he was determined to return to its past. He listed ten personal traits his new staff should keep in mind. Number two was a reminder that he had some scores to pay and expected his staff to support him. "Perhaps you have heard the old Sicilian phrase: 'Revenge is a dish best served cold,'" Rey told a ballroom full of Forest Service managers who had crossed swords with him in the Clinton era. "Unfortunately, no matter how hard I try to avoid it, this is part of my personal genome. I humbly request that you try to avoid encouraging that shortcoming."

Thomas L. Sansonetti, Assistant Attorney General for Environmental and Natural Resources

Thomas Sansonetti's previous experience with natural resources had been in expediting their cheap and unsupervised extraction. His legal practice in Wyoming, as detailed by the *National Journal*, "included cases dealing with water law, extractive minerals, endangered species lists and exemptions, surface mining reclamation regulations, natural resource damage assessments, coal permitting and siting controversies, private property rights cases, grazing and timbering on public lands, mineral royalty disputes, and Superfund sites involving federal facilities."

As a coal lobbyist, Sansonetti had petitioned Congress to increase the amount of land available for coal leasing by 50 percent. He represented, at various times, Peabody Coal, the National Mining Association, Kennecott Energy, and Arch Coal. He was also very active in the Wyoming Republican Party and close to then representative Dick Cheney.

At his confirmation hearing, Sansonetti was grilled by Senator Patrick Leahy (D-Vt.), then chair of the Judiciary Committee. Leahy noted that Sansonetti's former client the National Mining Association had opposed pending lawsuits seeking to enforce the Clean Air Act against outmoded coal-fired power plants, and he asked whether Sansonetti would vigorously pursue the suits. "The law is the law is the law," Sansonetti shot back, adding that, if his former clients didn't like it, they could seek to change it. Once Sansonetti was installed, they promptly did so.

Lynn Scarlett, Assistant Interior Secretary for Policy, Management, and Budget

In Lynn Scarlett the Bush administration found a real True Believer. Scarlett was past president of the libertarian, industry-funded Reason Public Policy Institute, which takes a dim view of most forms of government regulation. Scarlett had opposed curbside recycling, a national bottle bill, nutritional labeling, pesticide restrictions, and consumer right-to-know laws. Environmentalism, she once wrote, "is a coherent ideology that rivals Marxism in its challenge to the classical liberal view of government as protector of individual rights."

Scarlett, a quintessential free-market environmentalist, served on the board of directors of the Thoreau Institute, which believes that the public should be willing to pay market rate for its wilderness experiences: "Given market value user fees, some recreation—such as visiting Yosemite Valley, hiking in popular wilderness areas, or hunting trophy elk . . . will be expensive," the institute's Web site admits. "If fees in some areas deny access to some people, the solution is to help people out of poverty, not to destroy the areas by giving them away. Free recreation will do little to help people out of poverty."

This land is my land, Scarlett concludes, but it might not be your land.

Christie Whitman, Administrator, EPA

Former New Jersey governor Christie Todd Whitman fits uncomfortably with the rest of the wrecking crew. She came to the Bush administration as the picture of moderate Republican environmentalism: pro-choice, non-ideological, from a privileged background in Short Hills, where she had raised horses. One of her major accomplishments as governor had been to pass bond measures designed to dramatically increase New Jersey's permanent open space by a million acres.

Yet she had also initiated her term as governor by announcing that "New Jersey is open for business." When Bush nominated her, the *Bergen Record* editorialized, "In New Jersey, Mrs. Whitman made heavy staff and budget cutbacks at the Department of Environmental Protection. She ended what had been a war on polluters in one of the most heavily polluted states in the nation. She bent over backward to accommodate industry, easing rules, cutting red tape, and lowering fines. . . . It would be better if Mrs. Whitman stood up to

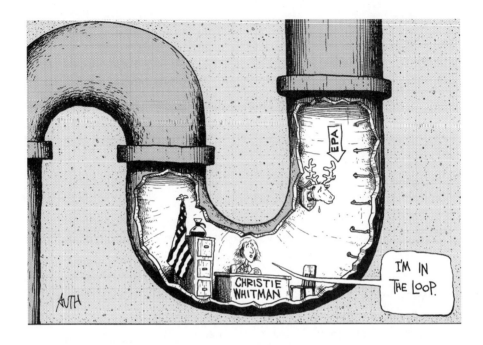

business interests from the beginning, telling them that she wants to help them comply with federal anti-pollution rules, but that she won't be bulldozed."

Nevertheless, Whitman was seen as the model of "compassionate conservativsm." She was easily confirmed, especially after announcing her support for a court decision that gave the EPA the power to set air pollution standards without formally consulting John Graham's cost-benefit wizardry shop.

Once in office, Whitman's role quickly changed. Secretary of State Colin Powell was later to call her the administration's "wind dummy," referring to the device pushed out of an aircraft to determine the wind direction. Instead of moderate environmental leader, Whitman found herself in the role of fall guy.

This list is incomplete. Scores of other Bush appointees were drawn from the ranks of lobbyists and officials in the very companies they now regulate. And Congress is full of anti-environmental ideologues whose views would be comical were their holders not in a position to put them into law. At the start of Bush's term in office, the hard right had the presidency, the House, and the Senate. They had the agenda, and they wasted no time.

"Pervading all nature we may see at work a stern discipline which is a little cruel that it may be very kind. That state of universal warfare . . . is at bottom the most merciful provision which the circumstances admit of."

— **Herbert Spencer, social Darwinist, 1851**

"Don't you know that if people could bottle the air, they would? . . . [T]here would be an American Air-Bottling Association. . . . [T]hey would let millions die for want of breath, if they could not pay for the air."

— **Robert G. Ingersoll, prominent Republican and attorney general of Illinois, 1896**

"I will not wait on events while dangers gather. I will not stand by as peril draws closer and closer."

— **President George W. Bush, State of the Union message, January 28, 2003**

4

Let the Breather Beware
The Right's Romance with Risk

T he president picks and chooses his perils. George Bush announced that he would not tolerate the risk of leaving Iraq's regime in power, even though it had no ties to al Qaeda and (apparently) no weapons of mass destruction. Yet he and his administration ignore very real risks much closer to home—the risks posed by America's own industrial economy.

The twentieth century had rejected the old laissez-faire notion of caveat emptor: let the buyer beware. That idea may have made sense in a Roman spice market but does not in a technologically advanced continental nation, where people eat meat butchered not in front of their eyes but in a distant city, and where the medicines they take are produced and marketed by strangers.

By the 1960s, the growing price Americans were paying in death and disease for air and water pollution made laissez-faire seem truly foolish. "Let the buyer beware" implies a choice of whether to buy or not; but "caveat spiror"— let the breather beware—is a doctrine of despair. Over the course of the past century, a regulatory framework has been built up to protect us from quack medicines and tainted meat. Even today, periodic recalls of drugs like Fen-phen and outbreaks of *E. coli* remind us that the framework is still under construction.

Under cover of the Bush administration, however, the radical right is seeking to drag us back to the laissez-faire days of wary buyers and worried breathers, back to the social Darwinism of the nineteenth century. Its leading philosopher, Herbert Spencer, believed that "under the natural order of things society is constantly excreting its unhealthy, imbecile, slow, vacillating, faithless members." Today's neo–social Darwinists apply this misreading of evolutionary theory to suggest that nature is, perhaps, simply finished with some endangered species. (As one speaker at a Fresno, California, Farm Bureau meeting on endangered species put it, "If the critters can't live on 50 percent of the land, then God is calling them home.") By the same reasoning, regulation designed to protect society's most vulnerable only stops what Spencer called "the purifying process" and holds back the winners. Emphasizing safety is not just economically inefficient but morally corrosive. America needs to abandon its fetish for safety and embrace the thrill of living dangerously, on terms established by Exxon and General Atomics. Endangered frogs, chemically sensitive kids, or people who insist on driving little cars cannot be allowed to hold the rest of us back.

New York Times columnist Maureen Dowd captured the flavor of the new order in Washington: "We want big. We want fast. We want far. We want now. We want 345 horsepower in a V-8 engine and 15 miles per gallon on the highway. . . . We don't have limits. We have liberties. . . . If rising seas obliterate the coasts, our marine geologists will sculpt new ones and Hollywood will get bright new ideas for disaster movies. If we get charred by the sun, our dermatologists will replace our skin." (Dowd's model must surely have been Thomas DiLorenzo, a scholar with the libertarian Ludwig von Mises Institute. In his essay "Airbag Murders," decrying the supposed "carnage" caused by mandatory airbags and vehicles with greater fuel efficiency, DiLorenzo concludes: "This is why I experience such a sense of gratification in owning both a large sports utility vehicle and a Camaro Z-28 convertible with an eight-cylinder, 305 horsepower engine. The sight of me in my Z-28, puffing on a cigar, must drive the environmental busybodies and petty tyrants crazy.")

Rather than the caution one might expect of conservatism, the right's new ideal is to be bold, even reckless—albeit with other people's lives. Angela Logomasini of the Competitive Enterprise Institute recently attacked the banning of DDT as an assault on freedom: "Thirty years ago this month, the government launched an assault on a basic liberty—the liberty to protect one's own health using a pesticide." (She never got to the question of where DDT users had obtained the right to put it in the fish that our children eat.)

Mary Sheila Gall, Bush's nominee to the Consumer Product Safety Commission, qualified for the job by bemoaning what she called the "federal nanny state." (The metaphor is instructive: preventing risks is wimpy and feminine; taking them is macho and desirable.) As a commissioner, Gall had distinguished herself by voting against federal safety standards for baby bath seats, which were later implicated in at least 78 deaths. Her nomination foundered for the brief period in 2001 during which Vermont Senator Jim Jeffords's defection deprived the GOP of a Senate majority. Yet the slur "nanny state" found a home in the right-wing lexicon. Over the years, the list of evidence for its supposedly stultifying embrace has included seatbelts, bike helmets, trigger locks, and the Occupational Safety and Health Administration. More recently, the anti-nannies have taken to complaining about product labels on organic food, claiming that they might create anxiety about the health risks of pesticides.

The Wizard of Risk

In foreign policy, the Bush administration's desire to make Americans tough again required purging the last remnants of the anti-interventionist "Vietnam syndrome." In environmental policy, it was the "nanny state" that had to go. Sending Nanny packing required getting people to reevaluate their perceptions of risk, which is where Wizard of Risk John Graham came in. (See profile in the preceding chapter.) Graham was nominated as head of the Office of Information and Regulatory Assessment (OIRA), a 50-person unit hidden within the Office of Management and Budget. The office had been created during the Reagan administration, in corporate America's first intense effort to make America comfortable with environmental risk. Its original charge was to ensure that every federal regulation, before it was published in the *Federal Register,* was analyzed to see if its benefits were justified by its costs.

Graham had to be confirmed by the Senate, at the time controlled by a one-vote Democratic margin. He allowed under questioning that he planned a much more vigorous role than his predecessors in shaping the approach federal regulations took toward risk. His toughest critic was Senator Joseph Lieberman (D-Conn.). "Dr. Graham acknowledged his opposition to the assumptions underlying our landmark environmental laws, that every American has a right to drink safe water and breathe clean air," said Lieberman. "When it comes to specific measures, Dr. Graham has said society's resources might be better spent on bicycle helmets or violence prevention programs than on reducing children's exposure to pesticide residues or on cutting back toxic pollution from oil refineries. Bicycle helmets save lives. But . . . Dr. Graham's provocative theorizing fails to answer the question of how to protect the health of, for instance, the family that lives next to the oil refinery. His rational priority setting may be so rational that it becomes, to those who don't make it past the cost-benefit analysis, cruel or inhumane."

Nevertheless, enough Democrats followed the typical courtesy of approving a qualified appointee, whatever his views, and Graham was confirmed. His vigor in shaping federal regulation was soon revealed. Graham got to decide whether agencies could publish regulations. He even had the power to ask agencies to repeal them. In one year under Ronald Reagan, OIRA rejected 58 proposed agency regulations. In eight years under Bill Clinton, it sent back 16. In 2002, Graham's office considered rejecting or softening 316 rules—more than four times as many as in 2001, with most of the suggested revisions coming from industry lobbying groups and right-wing think tanks.

Such was Graham's power that he undertook to remedy America's hypochondria concerning dioxin. Health studies showed that dioxin—the active ingredient in the Vietnam-era defoliant Agent Orange—has no safe level. Graham and the administration, however, proposed allowing dioxin-contaminated wastes to be used as fertilizer on food crops, with no subsequent testing or monitoring. Graham's reasoning was classic. Since the sources of dioxin—principally incinerators—had been successfully regulated, levels of the poison in the environment were declining. Rather than be content with such success, Graham viewed it as an opportunity. Recycling dioxin-contaminated wastes as fertilizers might increase risk but probably not to levels Graham worried about—and since we were not going to measure them, no one would even be alarmed.

No small amount of wizardry is involved in Graham's calculations, since the actual costs of health and safety regulations are often highly speculative, and corporations, which often have a monopoly on key information, tend to overestimate costs dramatically. (Industry claimed, for example, that getting vinyl chloride out of factories would cost a billion dollars; the real bill was $278 million. And estimates that it would cost $4.6 billion to clean up sulfur oxides from power plants turned out to be exaggerated by 500 percent.)

The benefits of regulations are also tricky to quantify. Graham's economists might have to put a dollar figure, for instance, on how much it was worth to protect children in low-income urban neighborhoods from lead poisoning that might lower their IQ scores by three or four points. The arbitrary, even imaginary, quality of some of these calculations means that OIRA has enormous discretion to make the numbers come out any way it wants. These calculations are also very difficult to explain to the press or public. Reporters' eyes would inevitably glaze over when public health advocates tried to explain exactly what was wrong with the methodology that OIRA's economists were using to "discount" future costs. Of course, the best wizardry always involves diverting the audience's eyes from what is really happening.

What's in Your Water? Whitman and Arsenic

Regulations also require implementation. And the main implementer, the tough cop on the environmental beat, was EPA Administrator Christie Todd Whitman. One of the administration's token moderates, Whitman had the uncomfortable responsibility for a significant number of late-Clinton-era regulatory actions that were temporarily frozen by White House Chief of Staff Andrew Card. Key among these was a move to lower the level of arsenic allowed in drinking water. The old standard, established in 1942, was 50 parts per billion (ppb). More modern studies have shown that this level still poses significant risk of cancer of the bladder, lung, and skin, and perhaps of the kidney and liver as well. In a 1999 study, the National Academy of Sciences found that arsenic harms the central and peripheral nervous systems as well as the heart and blood vessels, and that it causes serious skin problems. It may also cause birth defects and reproductive problems.

Despite these dangers, only 25 of the 50 states were even reporting on arsenic levels in their drinking water. In those states, a 2000 study by the Natural Resources Defense Council found that between 34 million and 56 million Americans were drinking water with unsafe levels of arsenic. Clinton's EPA administrator, Carol Browner, had tried to lower the standard to 5 ppb, but Republicans in the Congress made her conduct an additional round of studies before she could take any action. In the waning days of the Clinton administration, a 10 ppb standard was adopted. As governor of New Jersey, Whitman had urged homeowners using private wells to take action to remove arsenic from their drinking water if it exceeded 5 ppb—twice as stringent as the level finally proposed by Browner. But as EPA chief, Whitman announced that she would not implement the 10 ppb standard but would go back and reexamine the evidence and look for a "more reasonable" number.

Graham's cost-benefit calculations were opaque to most reporters, let alone the public. Allowing more arsenic in drinking water, however, was something everyone could grasp. Bush's decision to stall arsenic reduction rapidly became a defining early moment in his administration—not quite capturing what most Americans thought Bush had meant by compassionate conservatism.

Vice President Dick Cheney gamely struggled to defend the decision on *Meet the Press.* "You look at the arsenic deal, this was in one of the last-minute regulations dumped out by the Clinton administration. . . . A lot of your small communities out there simply won't comply with it, and a lot of them don't have the money to comply with it. So then what happens is people go out and get their own sources of water. They'll go out and drill their own wells, for example. And lots of times, they'll end up with arsenic in the water that's two or three times what the old standard ought to be."

By Cheney's logic, allowing more arsenic in the drinking water would mean that people would actually drink less arsenic. Cheney knew that the government's estimates of the total cost to bring all of the small community water supplies into compliance with the new arsenic standard was only $200 million—easily affordable to a federal government that was still, in May 2001, floating in budget surpluses. But Cheney had never wanted the federal government to set drinking water standards in the first place; as a congressman he had voted against passage of the Safe Drinking Water Act. It turned out that the drinking water in Crawford, Texas, where Bush has his ranch, exceeded the proposed 10 ppb standard by 40 percent, giving environmentalists the delicious opportunity to suggest to the White House press corps that they ask about the safety of the water they were given, and whether Bush himself drank the same tap water as other McLennan County residents.

As the administration continued to be pounded for its arsenic rollback, Whitman scrambled to defend the decision. Asked about Sierra Club ads pointing out that the mining industry, a major arsenic source, had given heavily to Bush's campaign, she got indignant. "I would hope we would all understand that no one, and particularly this administration, would jeopardize the public health because of campaign contributions."

Would it? Former Bush speechwriter David Frum tells how the arsenic issue led to a West Wing conflict between political guru Karl Rove and long-time Bush adviser Karen Hughes. Some urban areas in New Mexico would fail to meet the new safety standard, Rove believed, and compliance would cost them a lot of money. "Rove pressed for reversal," writes Frum. "Bush had come within a few hundred votes of carrying New Mexico in 2000, and the right decision on arsenic might carry the state in 2004. Hughes resisted. Arsenic was scary, arsenic in the water even scarier, and the wrath of the environmentalists scariest of all. Hughes proved to be right: The attempt to shift five electoral votes Bush-ward handed the national Democrats their most devastating anti-Bush message of 2001."

Loyally, the right-wing think tanks did their best to help out. The obliging Angela Logomasini of the Competitive Enterprise Institute explained that not only was the science on arsenic incomplete, but some studies suggested that arsenic was "an essential ingredient" and good for people.

After a National Academy of Sciences review showed that Browner's science was, in fact, quite "sound," the Bush administration retreated, agreeing to an arsenic standard of 10 ppb. By Earth Day 2001, the administration was loudly announcing that not only would there be a new arsenic standard but other Clinton-era rules (requiring tougher reporting of potential exposures to lead and protecting 20,000 additional acres of wetlands) would also be allowed to take effect. White House Press Secretary Ari Fleischer indignantly denied that these decisions were related to the public fiasco: "The President is not concerned about his image. The President is concerned about results."

Partisans of the hard right were appalled. The problem, in their view, was not so much that Bush had lowered the standard from 50 ppb but that he had failed to use the opportunity to educate the public about why no arsenic standard at all would have been even better. Jonathan Adler, then environmental director of the Competitive Enterprise Institute, wrote an internal memo lambasting the administration for caving in. "This should have been a 'gimme,'" Adler wrote. "[T]here was no scientific basis for the new standard. . . . [T]here is no . . . justification for ANY federal arsenic standard as communities can set their own standards. . . . Despite this background, the administration got hammered and will continue to get hammered. The arsenic rule is the centerpiece of a new Sierra Club ad campaign and is drawing commentary from all sorts of pundits. . . . If the arsenic issue cannot be 'won' it will be hard to win anything that matters."

Arsenic won out in the end, but quietly. In November 2003, Bush's Consumer Product Safety Commission voted unanimously not to ban arsenic-treated lumber from use in children's playground equipment. The agency declined action because most manufacturers were phasing out the poison, not because such wood was safe. In fact, the commission conceded that it probably increased children's risk of bladder and lung cancer. But this was a risk the commission was willing to have them take.

John Graham's Little List

Meanwhile, Graham was getting down to work. He enlisted Barbara Kahlow, a former OIRA staffer who had gone to work for then House Whip Tom DeLay, to survey the business community and solicit a hit list of regulations that, in the words of Gilbert and Sullivan's Royal Executioner, "never would be missed"— at least by those who were being regulated. The exercise was carried out, according to a *Washington Post* report, in great secrecy. "This was hush-hush, behind-closed-doors stuff," one of the lobbyists recalled.

The business of preparing regulatory hit lists had a certain seedy tradition within the hard right. Reagan's Commerce Department had prepared such a list in the 1980s, and in the Newt Gingrich years, DeLay had done the same. So even as Graham was telling the *Post* that "trade groups might be surprised if they think they will get 'whatever they want,'" Kahlow was preparing—and sharing in secret with a dozen business lobbyists—a chart featuring "57 of the most paperwork-intensive rules the business community wants to target. The rules, which deal with health, safety and the environment, govern everything from pesticide use to coal-mine ventilation, to standards for blood-borne pathogens. They cover such areas as air and water quality, food labeling, lead-paint disclosure, truck safety inspections, toxic-release reporting, and family and medical leave."

Graham sent 23 rules, including 13 environmental regulations, back to the agencies that originally promulgated them, asking that they be reconsidered. Of the 13 troublesome regulations, 12 had been opposed by regulated industries or industry-supported think tanks. The chemical industry wanted to zing a rule on handling hazardous wastes; the Mercatus Center, a right-wing think tank, opposed restricted snowmobile use in Rocky Mountain National Park; and the American Petroleum Institute suggested that oil and gas companies should no longer be required to inform surrounding communities that hazardous chemicals were being manufactured or stored in their vicinity.

Graham admitted that this level of involvement was new to OIRA. "We've never actually engaged in this kind of activity before," he said. His strategy has been to achieve "reconsideration" either through "informal conversations" or by a new bureaucratic invention called the "prompt letter," a written "suggestion" that the rule be reexamined. "This was a secret campaign to circumvent the process," an anonymous lobbyist told the *Post*. "With Graham in that job, we figured we could get whatever we want."

Devalue Thy Father and Thy Mother: The "Senior Death Discount"

Graham's calculus of risk required setting a dollar value on a human life. If you are writing equations on whether or not to allow a certain number of people per million to die, you need to know how much their lives are worth to society. The essence of cost-benefit analysis is to show mathematically and scientifically why we should allow practices that will kill some of us while making the rest of us—or at least some of the rest of us—richer.

This rather ghoulish exercise would give many people pause, since it leads to obvious and uncomfortable questions, such as: Are some people worth more than others? How much money do shareholders have to earn to make it okay for an industry to kill someone? (We don't pardon a hit man because he gets paid a lot—why a polluter?) And who authorized federal bureaucrats to say how much our lives are worth, anyway?

If asked to perform the same calculation, most of us—right-wing zealots included—would reply: "My life is not for sale at any price." (This aspect of the right-wing agenda caused conflict among its free-thinkers. Libertarian theory absolutely insists that individuals own their own lives and cannot be compelled to sacrifice them for the greater economic good of society. For this reason many principled libertarians reject cost-benefit analysis as an extension of the collectivist state.)

So instead of measuring what people would actually demand for giving up their own lives, economists tried to measure how much it was worth to people to avoid some hypothetical future risk. The problem is that people's willingness to pay to increase their longevity varies dramatically from what they say they would have to be paid to shorten their lives. (You might balk at paying $100 to buy an anti-moose-collision device for your car, but if your car were hurtling toward a moose in the road you would pay a lot more than $100 not to hit it.)

Tellingly, the figures used by the practitioners of cost-benefit legerdemain do not reflect what rich people actually pay to extend their lives or avoid risks. Rather, they are traditionally based on what people with poor occupational choices choose to give themselves a chance of living longer—within the limits they can afford. For years, the standard measure was the differential in wages between more and less hazardous jobs: how much money people would forgo rather than take a job that is likely to dramatically shorten their lives. Such calculations yield a value per human life saved of about $6 million.

Even that figure seemed too big for many cost-benefit advocates. It turned out not to justify their notion that Americans were being sissies about risk and costing society more than it was worth to protect them. Most major environmental regulations have benefits, measured by this calculus, that far exceed their costs.

Then the administration hit on a new approach, based on what a British test panel said it would pay for increased safety—say, in the form of a higher fare for a safer bus. Although these studies were not even based on Americans and used people's opinions, not their behavior, they did have the terrific benefit of yielding a lower figure for the cost of a human life: only $3.7 million. So in analyzing whether it was worthwhile to clean up power plants under the Clean Air Act, the EPA valued lives at $3.7 million, 38 percent lower than the old $6 million estimate.

Yet even reducing the value of an American life by 38 percent was not enough for Graham. He urged the EPA to consider further data from international studies suggesting that the elderly were less inclined to spend money to avoid risks than were younger people. Obligingly, the EPA concluded that, whereas a younger person was worth $3.7 million, an elderly person's life was worth only $2.3 million.

It was a statistical bonanza. Environmental health risks to younger people have a lot of uncertainty; it is hard to measure the number of birth defects 20 or 30 years hence from exposing young girls to a toxic chemical. In contrast, when air pollution hits the lungs of the elderly, hospital admissions and death rates go up within days, and the costs to society are plain to see. But if we put a lower value on seniors' lives, saving them through cleaning up air pollution no longer looks like such a bargain.

Bottom line: using the $6 million–per-life figure and looking at all health effects, cleaning up the air even partially would generate benefits to society of $96 billion—in lives protected, hospital days avoided, and benefits to employers and health insurance companies. Supporting clean air looked like a no-brainer. But using the discounted, $2.3 million, value of a senior's life and looking only at easily measurable health effects, the benefits were only $11 billion.

Graham's cooked numbers still showed a sixfold benefit for every dollar invested in cleaning up power plants, but that was not what outraged the public. The idea that older people were worth less than younger ones was something everyone could understand—especially after the concept became known as the "senior death discount." In six public hearings, the EPA was raked over the coals for its new "valuation" of senior lives. "To consider lessening the value of human life so that corporations can continue to pollute is moral and scientific recklessness," Marilyn Skolnick, a senior citizen and longtime Sierra Club leader, told a panel in Pittsburgh. "I like breathing clean air today as much as I did when I was a young woman."

The EPA quickly distanced itself from the concept, blaming it on OIRA. Whitman firmly declared that, as far as the EPA was concerned, the idea was dead. But Graham insisted that he still wanted to calculate the value of different lives differently. Other cost-benefit necromancers rallied to his side. "They shouldn't throw out the differential just because it upsets people," argued Alan Krupnick, a fellow at Resources for the Future. "This is a teachable moment to move further ahead the debate about how we value programs that save lives." The cost-benefit wizards, in short, continued to believe that they knew what our lives were worth—even if the rest of us did not agree.

Unnoticed in the furor over the "senior death discount" was the fact that the value of all human lives, three years into the Bush administration, had been cut by more than a third. The $3.7 million figure, though based on foreign studies, became the new Bush benchmark for young and old alike.

Kill or Be Killed:
Auto Safety for Social Darwinists

The hard right's infatuation with risking other people's lives is nowhere more starkly visible than in the debate over sport utility vehicles. Over the past 20 years, Detroit has basically given up trying to compete with Far Eastern and European automakers on economy, efficiency, craftsmanship, or style. Today its only edge—and primary moneymaker—is muscle and size. A desperate attempt to maintain that edge has led to a two-decade campaign against improved fuel economy standards for cars, trucks, and SUVs, led by an industry front group called Coalition for Vehicle Choice.

Since it is hard to argue against making cars more efficient—with the benefits of reducing air pollution, global warming, and dependency on oil from overseas—the coalition instead has pushed a spurious safety equation. According to the American auto industry, buyers have only two choices: drive a giant vehicle heavy enough to crush anything in its path, or drive a flimsy, golf cart–sized car destined to be crushed.

Thanks in part to the "bigger is safer" notion—greatly encouraged by the automakers themselves—SUVs and pickup trucks became wildly popular; they now constitute more than half of all vehicles sold in the United States. Their size and power come at the expense of fuel efficiency. While engineering improvements since 1975 have made cars potentially 33 percent more fuel efficient, the Big Three negated that efficiency gain by boosting horsepower and curb weight, so gas mileage did not improve significantly.

Detroit claimed it was merely responding to consumer demand. But as Chuck Frank, the owner of Z Frank Chevrolet, the biggest Chevy dealer in the Midwest, put it in a letter to Massachusetts Senator John Kerry, "American technological innovation can lead the way to safe, fuel-efficient vehicles that sip gas rather than guzzle it. I would like to see General Motors provide me with a competitive, high-mileage vehicle to sell, and we'll sell it."

There is certainly no technological reason why cars, even SUVs, cannot get far better gas mileage. The Center for Auto Safety has demonstrated how the popular Ford Taurus could easily be reengineered to get 42 miles per gallon (mpg) instead of its actual 27.5. Detroit ignored this. The Sierra Club has outlined a "freedom package" of readily achievable technical innovations that could boost a Ford Explorer from 19 mpg to 35 mpg. Detroit ignored that, too.

In May 2000, the new head of Ford Motor Company, William Clay Ford, seemed ready to break ranks. Ford issued a special report on the social impacts of the company's products, admitting that there were "very real conflicts" between Ford's environmental goals and its reliance on inefficient SUVs. The company announced that, even absent new governmental regulations, it would improve the fuel efficiency of its SUVs by 25 percent in five years, and it also committed to reduce emissions of air pollutants other than carbon dioxide. Environmentalists welcomed this initiative, while making clear that they would be watching to see if Ford delivered on its promises.

The other American automakers and their paid megaphones in Washington were aghast at Ford's admission that its SUVs were "directly contributing to rising greenhouse gas levels and global climate change concerns." Leading the counterattack (as ever) was the *Wall Street Journal,* with an op-ed by Brock Yates, editor of *Car and Driver* magazine. Yates did not challenge Ford's science, or the economic feasibility of building a 40 mpg hybrid SUV, as Ford had promised to do by 2003. Instead, he assailed Ford's manhood, claiming in essence that real men are concerned only with protecting themselves and their families, and the rest of society be damned. "My wife, Pamela, whom I cherish, spends many hours a week at the wheel of our Grand Cherokee," Yates wrote. "Neither she nor I fret over the possibility of her rolling some hapless victim in a Geo Metro into a wad of metal. If such fears haunt one, perhaps public transportation is the only solution." Yates concluded by questioning "whether the latest Mr. Ford isn't yet another guilt-ridden rich kid, not a proud tycoon like those who preceded him." No matter that Ford is also vice chairman of the Detroit Lions football team (or that the "proud tycoon" who founded the Ford dynasty, Henry Ford, was a vegetarian peacenik who challenged the radical right of his day by doubling his workers' wages). By calling his company's report "Connecting with Society," the latest Ford had apparently cast both his tycoon-ship and his virility into doubt.

The supposed safety of the SUV turned out to be bogus. A study by the Department of Energy showed that vehicle design is the key safety factor, not sheer mass. Well-designed small cars like the Volkswagen Jetta or Honda Civic are actually safer than many SUVs, and when you take into account the danger posed to the passengers of both vehicles in a crash—known as "combined risk"—most passenger cars turn out to be safer than the average SUV or pickup truck.

Many SUVs were also revealed to be hazards all on their own. The same unwillingness by the automakers to invest in modern technology that made SUVs gas guzzlers also made them unnecessarily dangerous. The root of the problem was the decision to build SUVs on what is essentially a truck chassis while allowing their center of gravity to be much higher than that of a pickup. This, combined with poor engineering, means that they tend to tip over. SUVs have the highest rollover rates of all vehicles: over half of all occupant deaths in SUV accidents involve the car rolling over by itself, with no other vehicle involved. SUVs' height also makes them a hazard to other cars: their bumpers do not mesh with those of other vehicles, which means that, in a collision, they tend to ride up over the other vehicle. And when the insurance industry discovered that Ford Explorers equipped with Firestone tires were enormously susceptible to fatal rollover accidents, Ford had to recall every Explorer so equipped; the costs and damage to its reputation nearly did the company in. Financially devastated by the burden of lawsuits and recalls resulting from the debacle, in early 2003 the Ford Motor Company quietly retreated from William Clay Ford's promised environmental initiatives.

As the evidence piled up against SUVs, dissenting voices even from inside the administration began to be heard. Jeffrey Runge, head of the National High-way Traffic Safety Administration, went to Detroit in January 2003 and read automakers the riot act. Runge had spent his career as an emergency room physician. For him, risk was not a moral abstraction—it was real human carnage. He said that SUVs were not safe, that consumers should think twice before buying one, and that if Detroit did not make them safer, then Washington would have to order them to do so. He called the tendency of SUVs to roll, and the rate of resultant fatalities, "astounding." One-third of all fatalities in auto accidents resulted from rollovers, he said; SUV occupants were three times more likely to die in a rollover than sedan occupants, and the fatality rate from rollovers was increasing by 22 percent a year.

Runge also warned that, in addition to making SUVs safer for their own occupants, Detroit had to redesign them to make them less lethal to the passengers of other cars on the road. He also discounted the "if it's big and heavy it must be safe" mentality. When choosing to buy a vehicle, he said, someone "might go sit in it and say, 'Gee, I feel safe.' Well . . . gut instinct is great for a lot of stuff, but it's not very good for buying a safe automobile." Runge added that he would not buy some models for his family "if it was the last one on earth."

Despite—or perhaps because of—their safety record, SUVs perfectly sym-

"Nice—but my heart's still set on a helicopter gunship."

bolize the right's idea of appropriate risk. Writing in the libertarian *Reason* magazine, Hans Eisenbeis acknowledged that SUVs "contribute to our environmental dilemma; they burn more gas, oil and rubber . . . and continue to pollute disproportionately once they've been scrapped." Even so, Eisenbeis concludes, people should be indulged if they use "these massive trucks" as a "form of escapism . . . a bulwark against harsh realities the rest of the world still faces on a daily basis." (Among those "harsh realities" faced by others are the effects of the global warming that gas-guzzling vehicles are hastening: the flooding of low-lying nations, increased hurricanes, drought, and disease.)

In a bizarre way, the dangers posed by SUVs (both on the road and to the environment) made them all the more desirable. "I don't own an SUV," radical-right commentator David Brooks wrote in his *Wall Street Journal* column, "but now that they've been identified as the locus of evil, I'm thinking of getting one. And if I do, I figure I might as well let the inner wolf out for a rampage and get the most obnoxious SUV I can find. My SUV [will] guzzle so much gas as I walk out to my driveway there will be squads of Saudi princes gaping and applauding. It'll come, when I buy it, with little Hondas and Mazdas already embedded in the front grillwork." Opposition to SUVs, Brooks said, "is part of a pattern, but there's also a more worrisome element. In centuries past, the armies of righteousness tended to at least fret about things that really matter: character, virtue, innocence, sin and depravity. These days moral energies are directed at health, safety and risk."

Here it is in a nutshell: the hard right does not believe that health, safety, and risk are serious priorities. An American's right to drive a high-impact (in every sense) vehicle is sacred; its effects on others are of no consequence, whether they take place on the road today or in the larger world tomorrow. Similarly, we cannot have a "one size fits all" drinking water standard for arsenic, as White House Press Secretary Ari Fleischer adroitly put it. New Mexicans are just as vulnerable to cancer from arsenic as New Yorkers, but the good Lord evidently intended them to drink more of it, since he put it in their aquifer. In the right's view, the cure of a national standard would be worse than the disease. And even if the administration's own calculations show that making us all safer is a good investment, this does not prove that regulation is worthwhile. Rather, to the risk enthusiasts guiding this president's policies, it suggests that we are foolishly overvaluing our own lives.

"A compelling story, even if factually inaccurate, can be more emotionally compelling than a dry recitation of the truth."

—Republican pollster Frank Luntz

Fair is foul, and foul is fair:
Hover through the fog and filthy air.

—William Shakespeare, *Macbeth*

"The President says one thing, but does another. Perhaps this is most apparent when it comes to the environment. With a straight face he talks about protecting resources for our children—even as he abandons the federal protection of land and air and water as fast as he can.
"Does he think we don't notice?"

—Vermont Senator Jim Jeffords

Clear Skies and Healthy Forests

Foul Deeds Behind Fair Words

P oll after poll shows that about two-thirds of the American public—Democrat and Republican, urban and rural—consider environmental progress crucial. Clean air, clean water, wilderness preservation—these are such bedrock values that many polling respondents find it hard to believe that any politician would oppose them.

Where does that leave politicians who wants to roll back clean air, clean water, and wilderness? If they told the truth about their intentions, they would be bounced out of office. So they have got to fudge.

This is where Frank Luntz comes in. Back in 1997, he offered advice to Newt Gingrich and his colleagues: "Remember," he said, "even Republicans have limited faith in your ability to keep their air clean and their water clean. You have a lot to prove." But rather than cleaning up the environment, Luntz prescribed cleaning up the lingo. "Stay away from risk assessment [and] cost-benefit analysis," he advised. "Your constituents don't know what those terms mean, and they will assume that you are pro-business rather than pro-environment." And puh-leez stop talking about rolling back regulations. "If we suggest that the choice is between environmental protection and deregulation, the environment will win consistently."

Other hints from Luntz: Don't attack the Environmental Protection Agency (EPA), even if you agree with Tom DeLay that it is the "Gestapo of government," because most Americans think the agency is doing a good job. Instead, tell your constituents that you support "a sensible environmental policy that preserves all the gains of the past two decades," even if you voted against them. Talk about your "specific environmental concerns, whether they be forests, natural resources, endangered species, or whatever." Above all, "you are arguing that Republicans have a better approach to solving environmental challenges, not that the environment is not a significant issue."

Six years later, the GOP still had a lot to prove. In another epistle to the troops (subsequently leaked to the Environmental Working Group), Luntz called environmental policy "the single biggest vulnerability for the Republicans and especially for George Bush." Again, Luntz advised that all politicians needed to do was talk a good talk, with liberal use of terms like "common sense" and "safe and healthy." As Jennifer 8. Lee noted in the *New York Times,* "In a speech last August introducing an initiative on thinning forests to prevent forest fires, for example, President Bush used the term 'common sense' at least six times."

However loathsome the radical right finds the idea of public ownership, and as stingy as the Bush administration is with funding for the National Park Service, Luntz advised that the "best way to show our citizens that Republicans can be for something positive in the environment" was to pose as "a champion of national parks." Something positive was needed, he noted, because "[b]eing against existing laws or regulations has been translated as being against the environment."

This charade can work only as long as Bush's anti-environmental objectives remain hidden. Although Bush, Luntz, and Karl Rove are careful never to spell out exactly where they are going, not all of their friends are so circumspect. Grover Norquist, the influential president of Americans for Tax Reform, baldly admits that he wants to turn back the clock. The goal, he says, is "the McKinley era, absent the protectionism. You're looking at the history of this country for the first 120 years, up until Teddy Roosevelt, when the socialists took over." Rove also talks fondly of McKinley, and models himself on McKinley's political choreographer, Mark Hannah. William Greider, the national correspondent for *The Nation,* aptly calls their project an effort to "roll back the twentieth century."

So when the administration began rolling out its rollback programs, they were dressed up by Luntz in the language of grandiose progress. Allowing more pollution from old power plants was "Clear Skies." Opening national forests to heavy logging in the guise of fire protection became "Healthy Forests." And the hydrogen-powered car—a vehicle that will not be on the market for another decade or two—was promoted as the "freedom car" and an alternative to cleaning up today's auto fleets. In addition to misleading an inattentive public, Bush's "Luntzspeak" also served to defang the press. As long as Bush kept saying that his policies would clean up pollution, protect parks and forests, and safeguard communities, journalists were compelled, whatever they knew to be true, to issue reports like: "The president announced another new initiative he said would safeguard America's environment."

Luntz's role was to ensure that the language Bush used was soothing, reassuring, and entirely disconnected from the reality of his policies. Bush would say one thing—resolutely, stoutly, and constantly—and then do the opposite. Luntz and Rove understood that Americans were reluctant to believe that their president really would allow more poison in their lakes, fewer birds in the air. They loved owning the national parks and assumed he, too, understood that Yellowstone, Yosemite, the Everglades, and all the rest were great American institutions. They could not understand why any president would be content to leave toxic waste leaking into their neighborhoods. Especially after September 11, 2001, when all Americans were looking to Bush to keep their families safe from terrorism, few imagined that the administration was willing, even eager, to expose their families to risk here at home.

Bush's 2003 State of the Union message, which devoted an impressive amount of time to the environment, was a classic example of say-one-thing-and-do-another. "This country has many challenges," Bush said. "We will not deny, we will not ignore, we will not pass along our problems to other Congresses, to other presidents, and other generations. We will confront them with focus and clarity and courage."

This would have been welcome relief if Bush had meant it—if his administration really was going to confront global warming instead of ignoring it, really intended to clean up the legacy of toxic waste instead of sidestepping it, and really planned to force America's thousands of antiquated power plants to stop pumping mercury into our lakes and soot into our lungs. But within months of his speech, Bush submitted a budget that gave the polluting power plants a permanent exemption from having to meet existing clean air standards, rejected new requirements to increase energy efficiency, and declined to take action on global warming and a host of other environmental challenges. It will now be up to "other Congresses, to other presidents, and other generations" to deal with the shambles left by the most environmentally irresponsible administration in the history of the United States.

Southern's Strategy for Dirty Air

In Macon, Georgia, on a muggy spring evening in 2002, a young African American from the Macon High School Ecology Club drew uproarious applause from an auditorium jammed with 250 local residents when he described how he learned about Georgia Power's role in polluting the state's air and water.

"I fish," said 15-year-old Anthony Dorsey. "You have to read the rules if you fish, so I got the handbook with my fishing license. I was glad to see an ad there from Georgia Power mentioning an award they had gotten from the Georgia Department of Fish and Game. Good to know my power company is taking care of the environment. But then I went back to page 1, where they tell you about fish advisories. And right there they say it's not advisable to eat more than one meal of largemouth bass a month, and pregnant women, nursing mothers, and children aren't supposed to eat any. At the bottom it says that the mercury gets in our rivers from our power plants. So I guess Georgia Power doesn't mind if I catch fish; it just doesn't want my momma to be able to cook them up."

Macon was not the only hot summer evening for Georgia Power that spring. In Savannah, stunned state regulators confronted 200 outraged citizens, and another 80 showed up in Cartersville to protest the pollution from Georgia Power's Plant Bowen. These communities are downwind from some of America's biggest polluters. The uncontrolled boilers and smokestacks of Georgia

Power's Plant Scherer alone pour ten tons of sulfur oxides, nitrogen oxides, and particulates into the air every hour. And while the pollution from these plants hangs like a pall over Georgia communities like Macon and Cartersville, much of the power is actually destined for customers in Florida—a state that does not allow polluting power plants like these to operate.

It was not just fish at stake. Dorsey—as well as the millions of other Americans living near dirty power plants and refineries—is at unnecessary risk for asthma, cancer, and lung disease. Air pollution is far more than unsightly smog obscuring views. It is a killer, leading to as many as 64,000 premature deaths each year—more than 20 times as many as occurred on September 11. Of those lives cut short, 30,000 a year are attributable solely to power plant pollution. Dirty air also results in hundreds of thousands of cases of asthma and tens of thousands of hospitalizations for respiratory and cardiac illnesses. The causes are the enormous amounts of sulfur dioxide and nitrogen oxides belched out of industrial smokestacks as well as from motor vehicles.

Dorsey's air was supposed to be clean by now, and Georgia's catfish edible. In 1977, Congress revisited the promise it had made in the Clean Air Act of 1970—that every polluting smokestack would eventually be cleaned up, and no community would have to worry about poison from the sky. But while Congress considered strengthening the popular legislation, the Southern Company, which owns Georgia Power, was scheming to maintain business as usual. It led a coalition of public utilities and coal companies that asked Congress to let them delay cleaning up their older plants until they were either shut down or modernized. It made no economic sense, the utilities argued, to install expensive scrubbers in outmoded facilities that were just a step away from the scrap heap. Ultimately a compromise was reached, stating that when the units were significantly upgraded, they would be treated as "new sources" of pollution and would be subject to the full weight of the Clean Air Act. In Beltway lingo, this was known as "new source review."

Although Congress was told that these plants would be retired soon, Southern's chief lobbyist, Dwight Evans, later described even 30-year-old plants like Bowen as middle-aged, far from retirement. "Power plants run for a long time," Evans explained. For 20 years, Southern and other utilities had replaced their units piece by piece without installing pollution control equipment. The foot-dragging paid off big: by 1996, when the Clinton administration finally got around to taking action against the recalcitrant plants in a series of lawsuits, utilities were pocketing about $3.6 billion in savings annually—including an estimated $852 million annually for Southern alone. Under Clinton, the EPA began enforcement actions against dozens of scofflaw industrial plants, including ones owned by ExxonMobil and Southern.

Breaking with the Clean Air Consensus

Ever since Richard Nixon signed the original Clean Air Act, reducing air pollution had been a bipartisan conservation goal. In the 1988 presidential campaign, George H. W. Bush competed with Democratic challenger Michael Dukakis over who had the toughest air pollution plan. When the Clean Air Act was significantly amended in 1990 to phase out leaded gasoline and reduce acid rain, Bush proudly signed the bill. "We sent to Congress the first major overhaul of the Clean Air Act in over a decade," he boasted to a Republican congressional fund-raising dinner on June 12, 1990, "because we must protect our planet for our children and their children."

In the 2000 presidential campaign, George W. Bush sometimes seemed to follow in his father's footsteps, calling for "mandatory reduction targets for emissions of four major pollutants," including carbon dioxide. "With the help of Congress, environmental groups and industry," he said in a September 29, 2000, speech, "we will require all power plants to meet clean air standards in order to reduce emissions of sulfur dioxide, nitrogen oxide, mercury and carbon dioxide within a reasonable period of time." But he simultaneously signaled that he was not disposed to be a tough enforcer, boasting about his voluntary approach to cleaning up old factories and power plants in Texas that had been "grandfathered" in under federal and state clean air laws, because they were already built, and dirty, when those laws were passed. (Actually, the program was not much to boast about: two years after Bush installed his voluntary program, Texas abandoned it as a failure after only 1 of 800 grandfathered plants had applied for a permit to clean up.)

Once installed in Washington, Bush's administration displayed the same schizoid split. On one side were Vice President Dick Cheney and Energy Secretary Spencer Abraham, who opposed the mandatory cleanup of old power plants. When Cheney asked Attorney General John Ashcroft to "review" the EPA's enforcement actions against dirty power plants, the person charged with overseeing environmental and natural-resources cases at the Justice Department was none other than Cheney's son-in-law, Philip Perry. Although he recused himself from work on that particular issue, Perry had come to Justice from the very law firm that represented two of the defendants, Cinergy and American Electric Power, in the very clean-air-enforcement litigation he was now to examine. On the other side was EPA Administrator Christie Whitman, a strong advocate of mandatory cleanup because her home state of New Jersey was downwind of outmoded and highly polluting power plants in Pennsylvania and Ohio.

In summer 2001, Whitman held four public hearings, which strongly opposed weakening the Clean Air Act. In Cincinnati, asthmatic kids and their parents showed up in force. "I've been hospitalized twice with asthma," Mike Sinclair told the *Cincinnati Post,* describing the half-dozen medications he had to take. "Dirty air makes it worse." Whitman circulated draft legislation that would substantially reduce pollution from mercury, nitrogen, and sulfur, but privately, Cheney made it clear that her cleanup goals were far more than he would accept.

Bush cast his lot with Cheney and the power industry on February 14, 2002, when he announced his new air pollution plan with the Orwellian title "Clear Skies." Bush promised, "We will cut sulfur dioxide emissions by 73 percent from current levels. We will cut nitrogen oxide emissions by 67 percent. And, for the first time ever, we will cap emissions of mercury, cutting them by 69 percent."

While those numbers sound impressive, they actually represent a major *retreat* from existing requirements. Bush's numbers ignore cleanups already required and under way; rather, they compare his plan with pollution levels that would exist if every grandfathered power plant and refinery in the country simply ignored the Clean Air Act. Clear Skies eliminates the current requirement that every industrial facility clean up, and postpones standards for meeting public health goals by nearly 25 years. Instead, it proposes a series of national "caps" on how much pollution power plants, overall, can emit. This means that, as long as the national caps are being met, communities near Southern's Bowen and Scherer plants can continue to breathe polluted air for decades, perhaps forever.

Clear Skies also coddles emitters of toxic mercury. Under a current consent decree, mercury emissions from power plants have to be reduced by up to 90 percent by December 2007. Clear Skies, however, does not require any mercury reductions until 2010; even by 2018 there would still be more toxic mercury raining down on our rivers and lakes than current law would allow in 2007. Even that was not enough for Republican Senator James Inhofe, chairman of the Environment and Public Works Committee, who tried to raise the "acceptable" levels of mercury pollution in Clear Skies from 26 tons of mercury per year to 34 tons. In January 2003, the implications of this laxness came into much sharper focus, when, after six months of stalling, the EPA reluctantly reported that 8 percent of American women of childbearing age carry potentially toxic levels of mercury in their bodies.

An immediate effect of the Bush plan was the resignation of the EPA's head of regulatory enforcement, Eric Schaeffer. A career EPA official and former staffer to Republican Representative Claudine Schneider, Schaeffer said that he had finally given up fighting "a White House that seems determined to weaken the rules we are trying to enforce." Schaeffer was particularly alarmed about Clear Skies' effect on the nine lawsuits filed in the last year of the Clinton administration against power companies that had flouted the Clean Air Act. "The companies named in our lawsuits emit an incredible 5 million tons of sulfur dioxide every year," Schaeffer wrote, "a quarter of the emissions in the entire country." The EPA had already negotiated settlements with four power companies, "yet today we seem about to snatch defeat from the jaws of victory." Previously negotiated settlements were falling apart, he said, and "other companies with whom we were close to settlement walked away from the table. . . . We have filed no new lawsuits against utility companies since this Administration took office. We obviously cannot settle cases with defendants who think we are still rewriting the law."

In July 2003, it was discovered that for months the EPA had been withholding from Congress its own analysis showing that proposals by moderate Senator Thomas Carper (D-Del.) would be more effective than Clear Skies in reducing pollutants—and only marginally more expensive. A leaked memo obtained by the *Washington Post* showed that, by 2020, the Carper plan (which was cosponsored by two Republican senators) "would result in 17,800 fewer premature deaths from power-plant air pollution than would Clear Skies. That would save $140 billion a year in health benefits—about $50 billion more than Clear Skies." This information, however, was withheld from Senator Carper. "All we're interested in is having a full and honest debate so we can make a well-informed decision," he later told the *Post*. "I don't believe that's too much to ask."

A full and honest debate, however, was not what Bush's EPA had in mind. The *New York Times* described a meeting at which EPA air programs czar Jeffrey Holmstead was briefed by career staff on the merits of the competing pollution reduction plan: "At a meeting on May 2, employees who attended it said, Mr. Holmstead of the E.P.A. wondered aloud, 'How can we justify Clear Skies if this gets out?'" Even the OIRA risk wizards could not help to justify Clear Skies. A major OIRA study showed that the economic benefits of tougher clean air regulations implemented by the Clinton administration were five to seven times greater than the costs, for a net economic gain to American society of at least $100 billion. John Graham released the report with the terse comment, "The data shows that the EPA's clean-air office has issued some highly beneficial rules." Highly beneficial, but apparently not beneficial enough to warrant keeping.

Ultimately, the EPA stopped worrying about justifying Clear Skies and simply eliminated the existing requirements. Instead of making plants modernize whenever they made substantial changes, the agency specified that cleanup was required only if 20 percent of the total cost of a plant was spent at one time—a level that is almost never reached in upgrading an old facility. California's legislature promptly rejected application of the new rules to plants within its jurisdiction; eastern states that were victims of pollution from upwind states did not have that option.

A few months later, in November 2003, Schaeffer's nightmare came true: the EPA announced that it was going to drop investigations of 50 power plants for past violations of the Clean Air Act. This meant that the weakened rules were going to be applied retroactively as well, not only increasing pollution in the future but excusing it in the past. The EPA discouraged its staff from discussing this unprecedented decision to grant power plants a retroactive waiver of the law. On the same day the agency abandoned its cases, it also warned employees in the firmest terms not to communicate with members of Congress, the press, or the public about this change—using as its excuse the need to preserve secrecy while prosecuting wrongdoers—even though it had decided to abandon the prosecution!

The *New York Times* reported that "the change grew out of a recommendation by Vice President Dick Cheney's energy task force. . . . Representatives of the utility industry have been among President Bush's biggest campaign donors, and a change in the enforcement policies has been a top priority of the industry's lobbyists."

Clearcut Forests Don't Burn

Joe Dorst laid the tinder, Smokey Bear placed the kindling, and the timber industry poured on the kerosene.

Captain Dorst of the Fourth Cavalry, U.S. Army, was effectively the first supervisor of Sequoia National Park. He was reprimanded by the secretary of the interior for failing to stop an 1892 blaze in the park's Grant Grove. Chagrined, Dorst ordered his horse soldiers to put down, and prevent, all future fires. According to the eminent fire historian Stephen J. Pyne, this military template—fire as the enemy, prompt and vigorous suppression as the strategy—became that by which "all wild and forested lands would be managed" by the federal government.

Starting in 1945, a singed bear cub helped transform the Forest Service's policy of "every fire down by 10 A.M." into a national creed of total prevention. But stopping all fires left forests choked with the brush and downed limbs that had in earlier times been regularly cleared out by low-intensity burns.

To make matters worse, decades of ruthless commercial logging had eliminated all but 5 percent of the oldest, thick-barked, fire-resistant trees. Replacing them were thickets of highly flammable, small, even-age trees, as well as piles of "slash," the detritus left behind by the loggers. By the late 1990s, years of drought—a condition consistent with predictions of global warming—caused the moisture content in even green trees to drop far below normal.

The stage was thus set for the inferno that George Bush would manipulate into a last great giveaway of the nation's forests to the timber industry.

Representative Sam Farr (D-Calif.) once summed up the battle over management of the national forests as one between those who liked their forests vertical, and those who liked them horizontal. Most Americans sided with the vertical axis. Polls and focus groups revealed that most Americans, in fact, did not even realize that national forests were being logged; they assumed that the forests, like the national parks, were being managed for their own health, not for the timber industry. (A marketing consultant hired by California's timber industry had warned that Americans view trees almost like people and associate the very word "timber" with the death of something precious. Consequently, the California Timber Association became the California Forest Products Association.)

Mark Rey, the timber industry leader to whom Bush had entrusted the national forests, decided that the solution was to redefine what it meant to cut down a tree. It would no longer be about clearcuts, or robbing spotted owls of their nests, or turning old growth into toilet paper. Rey decided that, henceforth, cutting trees would mean protecting the forest from fire. Every tree hauled out of the forest on the back of a logging truck was one less tree to burn.

Crucial to Rey's strategy was the discredited but enduring Smokey Bear ethos, etched into the popular consciousness by years of "Only you can prevent forest fires" propaganda. For years, fire ecologists had vainly warned that the buildup of excessive fuels on some western forest lands was a serious problem that could not be solved by thinning trees alone. Logging, they insisted, had helped create the problem. The solution was to restore fire to the landscape: to allow low-intensity natural fires to burn, to set controlled burns in other situations, and to accept that some forest types, like lodgepole and jack-pine, were fated by ecological design for big, intense, "stand replacement" fires, like those in Yellowstone in 1999 and again in 2002.

Ecologists did allow that in some situations, where young stands of fire-tolerant species like ponderosa pine were too closely bunched for controlled burning, thinning the young trees *might* improve the situation, largely by allowing low-intensity fire to be returned to the landscape. But such thinning, they warned, was expensive and poorly tested and should be used on a careful and experimental basis. They also recognized that settlements nested in or near fire-prone forests would need a half-mile community protection zone perimeter of thinned forest, so that even if high-intensity fires arrived on the wind, there would not be enough fuel to sustain them, and firefighters could put down individual spot fires as they broke out.

"Putting fire back into the landscape is not the simple reverse of taking it out," warned fire historian Pyne. "It is more like reintroducing a lost species. . . . The fires we introduce deliberately must be set where we have readied the landscape for them, by clearing thickets and brush, for example, and restoring some natural grasses."

But this was scientific thinking about fire. It was not Bush's—or Rey's. Rey designed for Bush what Karl Rove cynically dubbed "Healthy Forests." Quite simply, it consisted of taking commercial timber sales, renaming them "fuels treatments," and then arguing that, because they were being done in the interest of fire safety, they should be immune from environmental objection or legal review. And he bided his time.

The summer of 2002 capped years of drought that had left the West drier than at any time in living memory, with trees in some places as dry as kiln-dried lumber. Flames exploded all across the region, beginning with the Rodeo-Chediski fire, which scorched nearly half a million heavily logged acres in Arizona before burning itself out.

The Bush administration and its allies seized the moment. Arizona's then governor, Jane Hull, blamed the fire on environmentalists, claiming that their opposition to fuel reduction efforts by the Forest Service had created the hazard. But it was Hull's own administration, not the Sierra Club, that had opposed controlled burning, leading the *Arizona Republic* to accuse her of "burning tree

huggers at the stake." (The proximate cause of the blaze was an unemployed firefighter, who looked forward to earning $8 an hour fighting it.) Arizona Senator Jon Kyl (R) and Colorado Representative Scott McInnis (R) alleged that the Forest Service had failed to avert the risks because of "analysis paralysis" stemming from repeated environmental challenges to fire prevention proposals. The General Accounting Office pricked this hot-air balloon by doing some simple counting: of 1,671 fuel reduction projects it studied, only 20 had faced administrative appeals, and none had been held up by litigation.

It turned out that one of the biggest obstacles to reducing fire risk was the Forest Service bureaucracy itself, which kept finding better uses for funds appropriated to prevent fires. In Montana's Bitterroot National Forest, for example, the Agriculture Department inspector general found that forest managers diverted $1.8 million in restoration funds to start new commercial timber sales. In 2002, the Forest Service's inspector general revealed that the agency had "misplaced" $215 million intended for fire prevention. "Either the Forest Service has been using an abacus to account for its wildfire funds," said Eric Lynch of Taxpayers for Common Sense, "or they are employing a few accountants at Arthur Andersen."

Fireproofing Profits, Not Communities

The tinder thus stacked, when the huge Biscuit fire struck in Oregon in the summer of 2002, Rove and Bush prepared to unveil Healthy Forests in Portland. If fully implemented, Healthy Forests would accelerate aggressive logging across millions of acres of backcountry forests, miles away from communities at risk for forest fires. It would limit environmental analysis and public scrutiny of these cuts. Finally, it would pay for the program using "goods for services." That is, the Forest Service would pay logging companies for "thinning" by allowing them to take large, fire-resistant, high-value, old-growth trees—exactly the situation that in the past has led to intensely flammable forests.

Alerted to the Bush move by a Bureau of Land Management employee who happened to be sitting next to a Sierra Club staffer on a plane, environmentalists scooped the president. The day before Bush's arrival, the Sierra Club, the Wilderness Society, and other groups released, also in Portland, their Community Protection Plan. It called for annual appropriations of $2 billion, enough to fireproof every community at risk from forest fire, within five years, by cleaning out excess fuels within 500 yards of homes. The plan also provided for expedited review and rapid approval of projects in the vicinity of forest communities.

Its basic approach had been validated earlier that summer. The Associated Press reported from Colorado about homeowner Vern Vinson, who simply pruned low branches from his trees, raked up the pine needles and dried grass from around his house, and laid out a circle of gravel around it. When the huge Heyman fire raged through, he fled with his neighbors. When he returned, his neighbors' houses were cinders, while his stood out "like an oasis in the blackened, barren landscape."

Frank Johnson's neighborhood escaped the same Heyman fire because of a previous 8,000-acre controlled burn. As Johnson told ABC, "At the time, we didn't think much of it. It wasn't very pleasant and nobody was excited about it." But when the Heyman blaze came to the ridge above his house, he says, it ran out of fuel and just "lay down." "We're all being re-educated about the value of doing prescribed burns," Johnson said.

Bush and Rey, however, proved resistant to the lesson. Their Healthy Forests initiative included no new money for community protection services, nor was there any assurance that more of its funds would be spent on the highest-priority areas. (In 2002, only 40 percent of the money spent by the Forest Service for fire prevention treatment actually went to Community Protection Zones.)

It soon became clear that the Forest Service spent its firefighting dollars to protect timber companies, not communities. In California, the forest closest to the most people—the Angeles National Forest adjacent to Los Angeles—was budgeted for less hazardous-fuels reduction than any other forest, just enough to send a herd of sheep to graze on the chaparral. The bulk of the state's fire funds went to remote forests with very few neighbors but substantial commercial timber industries. Northern California's Plumas National Forest, for example, located in a county of 21,000 people, got $9.8 million—more than 20 times as much as the Angeles. A few rural townships in Alaska, in fact, received more fire prevention funding than all of Southern California, the region with by far the largest number of people at risk.

The Fire This Time

Healthy Forests won instant acclaim from the timber industry and the Forest Service's "timber beasts." According to the *Portland Oregonian,* "Top national forest managers from across the West" said that "they hope to meet annual logging goals for the first time in more than five years." Part of the problem was that logging the remaining national forest land required expensive road building and site preparation—all costs that were paid by the Forest Service. Between 1992 and 1997 alone, the Forest Service lost $2 billion on its commercial-timber-sale program.

Congress had threatened on several occasions to ban these "below-cost" timber sales, leading Bush to stop releasing information on how much money was being lost on individual sales. Now, however, the bad deals could simply be relabeled as "fire prevention" programs, thus assuaging public anger toward the idea of paying timber companies to cut down the national patrimony. In the words of James Connaughton, chair of the White House's Council on Environmental Quality, "If you're interested in getting thinning done, and there's an interest in getting commercial grade timber, the best place to get commercial grade timber is in the context of these thinning projects. . . . [T]hat's really what this is about."

Fire ecologists testified in federal court that what Rey called "fuels reduction salvage logging" was actually going to leave behind "landscape scale bonfires." A study showed that thinning just 1.6 million acres in the Klamath Mountains of southwestern Oregon was going to cost $2.7 billion, or $1,685 per acre. "The costs are enormous. It's hard to see where that money will come from," said Jeremy Fried, team leader on the study for the Pacific Northwest Research Station's forest inventory analysis program.

Not from the federal government, apparently. In 2003, the Forest Service announced that it had already "spent out" its firefighting budget by August 8— the earliest date ever. It promptly began raiding other accounts, including those designed to fund fire research and fire prevention. In its 2004 budget, the Bush administration actually decreased the total funding for fire prevention in real dollars, asking for only $416 million nationally. Senate Democrats added $500 million to their version of the Forest Service budget for firefighting and prevention; House Republicans stripped the increase away in conference committee, even though Rey had admitted in testimony that the agency was going to face a billion-dollar deficit in its fire accounts.

In Arizona, Governor Janet Napolitano was forced to declare an emergency because of the threat of drought and wildfire, asking for $232 million—more than half of what Bush had appropriated nationally to clear brush and smaller trees from more than 230,000 acres in and around the most threatened communities and utility and transportation corridors. In California, in April 2003, Governor Gray Davis requested $430 million in emergency funds from the federal government to remove dead and diseased trees from 415,000 acres of forests. Twenty people died in the fires that erupted that autumn, and three-quarters of a million acres and 2,400 houses burned. The embers were still smoldering when the answer to the funding request finally arrived: Denied.

Despite the better instincts of many legislators, political heat from the California inferno led Congress to give Bush what he wanted. California Senator Dianne Feinstein was able to insert a provision requiring that half of the $760 million annual budget be spent in areas surrounding communities at risk, but otherwise the bill removed citizen participation, limited judicial appeals, and greatly increased commercial logging. The tinder and kindling had been set and the kerosene poured, and Bush, Rove, and Luntz finally got the blaze they needed. Healthy Forests never would have gone through as "Horizontal Forests," just as Clear Skies would not have got anywhere as "Dirty Lungs." By saying one thing and doing another, Bush did the dirty work for his campaign contributors and radical-right supporters while keeping his political hands out of the muck and ash.

"The biggest challenge is going to be how to best utilize taxpayer dollars to the benefit of industry."

—Mike Smith, assistant secretary for
fossil fuels at the Department of Energy

"You have a solar panel on your house, you get tax relief. If you drive a solar-powered car, you get tax relief. It's goofy."

—Vice President Dick Cheney, speaking at a
recreational-vehicle assembly plant in Washington

"A taint of imbecile rapacity blew through it all, like a whiff from some corpse."

—Joseph Conrad, *Heart of Darkness*

Share the Spoils,
Postpone the Future
Throwing Good Money After Bad Ideas

The effort to get George W. Bush into the White House and give him a compliant Republican Congress was the costliest in history. It took nearly half a billion dollars, donated to both Bush himself and the Republican congressional committees, with four dollars out of five coming from corporations or corporate executives. These businessmen and -women, naturally, expected something for their money. In 2002, for example, the Kansas-based Westar Energy company was seeking a change in regulations that would allow it to charge up to $3 billion in debt to its customers. To do so, it needed to curry favor with House Majority Leader Tom DeLay. In a memo that subsequently became public, a Westar vice president wrote to his colleagues, "We have a plan for participation to get a seat at the table, which has been approved. The total of the package will be $31,500 in hard money (individual), and $25,000 in soft money (corporate)." The donation did the trick: the change Westar desired was approved (although it was later withdrawn after a grand jury started investigating the company for securities fraud). DeLay struck an aggrieved tone at the subsequent scandal: "It never ceases to amaze me," he said, "that people are so cynical they want to tie money to issues, money to bills, money to amendments." (On another occasion, in a less jejune mood, DeLay wrote, "Money is not the root of all evil in politics. In fact, money is the lifeblood of politics.")

In terms of return on investment, only drug running or a lucky night at the blackjack table can rival investing in a winning candidate. In the 2000 and 2002 election cycles, for example, the coal industry handed out over $7.3 million in contributions to congressional candidates and President Bush. Depending on which version of the Energy Bill you look at, it might still reap between $1.9 and $3.3 billion. Not bad for a legal transaction. Agribusiness is another big winner; it has already harvested $180 billion in subsidies over the ten years of the 2002 Farm Bill. These gifts from the public purse often reward the most environmentally harmful elements in industry and leave the best begging. For example, even though the Farm Bill is justified to the public as supporting family farms, 70 percent of its funds went to the top 10 percent of the nation's largest farms—all corporate agribusinesses.

Back when the federal government was presumed to be a force for shaping an orderly society to the benefit of its citizens, its enormous financial power was often directed at redressing the mistakes of the past, cleaning up after disasters, and channeling economic and social growth in a generally progressive direction. Thus the Works Progress Administration put millions of Americans back to work during the Depression, the Marshall Plan helped Europe recover after World War II, Head Start provided preschool for disadvantaged kids, and farm bills passed as recently as 1995 rewarded farmers for preserving wetlands and providing wildlife habitat. Even during the Cold War, federal research and development dollars initially targeted for the military ended up accelerating the development of new technologies that helped speed the economy's transition away from old, environmentally damaging production techniques.

But for the hard right, using public resources to advance environmental or societal goals is anathema. Subsidies to favored business sectors are another story. (The libertarian right parts company at this point, eschewing all subsidies. Its allies listen politely and then vote for the subsidies anyway.) Besides, to the extent that payoffs to campaign contributors cement anti-government prejudice in the public mind, so much the better as far as the hard right is concerned. Thus, an anti-government administration can reward its friends and patrons and simultaneously increase public cynicism, making its lowered expectations a self-fulfilling prophecy, and corruption its own reward.

Affirmative Action for Dinosaurs

Bush's beneficence to the business sectors that financed his election goes beyond campaign payola: federal subsidies are being used to prop up the dirty old economy and slow the transition to a new, cleaner future. Bush's biggest supporters represent lagging sectors of the American economy: the hewers of wood and drawers of coal, oil, and minerals. Even within these industries, Bush tended to be supported by the "bottom feeders"—companies that specialized in cutting corners and driving down their prices, rather than being the first to offer newer and better products or production techniques. In finance, Bush found support among those who sought a toughening of federal bankruptcy law so they could more safely sell credit cards to high-risk customers. High-end industries, on the other hand, went Democratic; Silicon Valley was Al Gore country, as was the securities industry. And where cutting-edge industries did support Bush, they often turned out to be elaborate Ponzi schemes—Enron being the signal example.

In the past decade, green technologies like solar, wind, energy-efficient building technologies, integrated pest management in agriculture, recycled paper and construction materials, hybrid autos, organically based industrial solvents, and compact fluorescent light bulbs (to name just a few) have emerged as fully mature, reliable technologies. Each has managed to obtain a respectable share of the potential market. But their rate of growth is dramatically slowed by the fact that their older and dirtier competitors who supported Bush are receiving substantial public subsidies and regulatory favors.

Hybrid cars, for example, were scoffed at by many of the old-line auto executives at Chrysler, Ford, and General Motors who supported Bush. They argued that hybrids cost too much and that gas prices in the United States were so low (in 2001, lower even than the cost of bottled water) that consumers would never pay the modest price premium required to equip a car or SUV with hybrid technology. But if the oil industry were not so heavily subsidized, if American drivers were paying the real price of oil at the pump, the logic of hybrids would have been immediately apparent.

Even without that boost, hybrid technology is penetrating the marketplace on the strength of Toyota's and Honda's marketing it as the cool new thing—part of the actual coolness being that the driver is helping to break our dependence on fossil fuel. As usual, U.S. automakers are the last to catch on, as a *Los Angeles Times* automotive critic notes: "If you ever despair that the U.S. auto industry is whirling, slowly but with gathering momentum, down the tubes of history, the second-generation Toyota Prius will give you no comfort. This is a car Detroit assures us cannot be built. No way. No how. A spacious, safe and well-appointed mid-size four-door with practical performance while returning more than 60 miles per gallon? For $20,000? Are you, like, high?" *Motor Trend* magazine named the second-generation Prius its "2004 Car of the Year."

A Special Pull on President Bush's Affections

In a pre-election analysis with the forthright title "Bush's Donors Have a Long Wish-List and Expect Results," the *Wall Street Journal* noted on July 31, 2000, that "[o]il companies feel particularly confident that a President Bush will take care of them and have provided generous financial support. Kenneth Lay . . . whose executives have been Mr. Bush's most reliable supporters throughout his political career, will have a special pull on a President Bush's affections."

Other companies also had great expectations. The oil industry had been lusting after the hypothetical bonanza under the Arctic National Wildlife Refuge for 20 years, only to be beaten back time and again by environmentalists. But, said Roger Herrera of Arctic Power, the lead oil lobby, "all the stars are aligned this year."

Others stood to cash in. Ralph Reed, the baby-faced, erstwhile Christian soldier of the hard right and now Republican party chief in Georgia, offered to deploy conservative talk shows, leaders of the religious right, anti-abortion groups, and right-wing think tanks in the service of Enron, in return for a modest $380,000. It did not matter that Reed knew very little about electricity. "There are certain people—a friend of family member, key party person, civic or business leader, or major donor—whose correspondence must be presented to the [elected] official for his personal reading and response," Reed wrote Enron. Enron hired him—until it ran out of money.

Publicly, Bush and Cheney started out posing as frontier legislators rolling up their sleeves to do the public business for a few weeks before returning to the ranch to clear brush. But the conceit paled quickly, with every news story about the administration's drill-mine-burn energy policy noting Bush's (failed) career as an oilman and Cheney's (extremely lucrative) leadership of the oil supply company Halliburton. The constant repetition eventually got on Cheney's nerves. "I take a certain amount of pride in my private-sector career," he whiffed defensively on *Face the Nation*. "That gives me, I think, a lot of experience that's relevant in this particular case." (His former employer continues to pay him, every year, $150,000 in "deferred compensation.") In 2003, Halliburton was awarded a $1.7 billion no-bid contract to rebuild the infrastructure in Iraq—with the promise of more to come. It is also the beneficiary of a sweetheart provision in the final Bush energy policy, which exempted a dirty but effective drilling technique called "hydraulic fracturing" from the provisions of the Clean Water Act. Hydraulic fracturing is a major potential profit center for Halliburton.

Industry did not mind the checks slipped under the door but disliked the public attention. "It may well be that companies have found it in their interest to make more money than less," groused Luke Popovich, spokesman for an industry coalition called the Alliance for Energy and Economic Growth, to the *Chicago Tribune*. "That's what businesses do. And it's true that industry people are active in the administration, with Vice President Cheney being one. If we want to have economic growth in the future, we can't conserve our way to get there." (President Bush used a startling similar formulation just a month later: "We can't conserve our way to energy independence, folks," he told an appreciative crowd at the Electronics Industries Alliance. Meanwhile, a detailed report by the five U.S. national laboratories had just demonstrated that conservation, efficiency, and incentives for new technologies could obviate the need for nearly half of the 1,300 new power plants the vice president said the nation needed in the next 20 years.)

Bush and Cheney's efforts to arrange for their friends in the energy industry to make more money than less began early. Immediately after their inaugural (to which the CEO of Peabody Coal graciously kicked in $100,000), Cheney convened his energy task force, officially intended to provide advice on the finer points of a new national energy policy. The members of the task force spanned the U.S. energy field from A to B. (Writer Rob Reiner joked that the GOP's idea of diversity was "two guys heading the ticket from two different oil companies.") In addition to Cheney, the task force included Commerce Secretary Don Evans (former chair and CEO of Tom Brown Inc.; a Denver-based oil company), White House economic adviser Lawrence Lindsay (a former adviser to Enron), and Federal Emergency Management Agency chief Joe Allbaugh, a Bush friend from Texas. During the time that Allbaugh served on the task force, three giant electric companies each paid his lobbyist wife, Diane, $20,000 for—well, apparently for being the wife of the guy on the energy task force.

Meanwhile, administration officials were sending out billets-doux to industry officials and lobbyists, inviting them to draw up the new rules. Take, for example, the e-mail (subject line: "national energy policy") from Energy Department senior policy adviser Joseph Kelliher to lobbyist Dana Contratto: "If you were King, or Il Duce, what would you include in a national policy, especially with respect to natural gas issues?" The memo was pried out of the administration by the conservative watchdog group Judicial Watch. Such embarrassing communications may explain, at least in part, why the White House has been so hesitant to turn over energy task force documents.

While Cheney's task force was drawing up its list of energy industry executives to interview, Enron and the other new energy trading firms were at the height of their fortunes—and the lights were going off in California. Having newly deregulated its energy system (at the behest of Pacific Gas and Electric, a state utility monopoly), California was suffering an unprecedented energy crisis in which the price of a kilowatt hour of electricity zoomed from $50 per megawatt hour in 1999 to a high of $2,500. The state's enormous budget surplus, amassed during the go-go 1990s, was rapidly draining away to energy firms mostly located in Houston. State politicians begged the White House and the Federal Energy Regulatory Commission (FERC) for emergency price controls but were repeatedly rebuffed. Instead, administration officials blamed the state's environmental regulations and alleged lack of capacity. "The real problem in California," Cheney said on *Meet the Press,* "is a screwy regulatory scheme and the fact they didn't build any new power plants for 10 years." (It turned out that environmental groups had actually supported more power plants in California than had the utilities or Enron, and that FERC itself had blocked more power plants than anyone else.)

The real problem in California, in fact, was brazen market manipulation by the same energy company officials who were providing advice to Cheney's task force, a finding documented by FERC in 2003. "There's no longer any doubt," wrote economist Paul Krugman in the *New York Times*. "California's power shortages were largely artificial, created by energy companies to drive up prices and profits." No apologies were forthcoming from the White House.

We Almost Lost Toledo

There has not been a new nuclear power plant built in the United States since the near catastrophe at Three Mile Island in 1979. The nuclear plants built before that time, for the most part, produce electricity at such a high cost that many of them had to be bailed out by electricity consumers. No satisfactory solution has been found—after more than 20 years of looking—to the problem of where to store nuclear waste permanently. Although many of the plants have worked out their initial operating bugs, more and more maintenance-related safety problems are cropping up as they age. Globally, it has become clear that the "peaceful atom" of nuclear power plants is serving as the entering wedge for the unpeaceful atom of nuclear weapons proliferation. India, Pakistan, North Korea, Israel, and potentially Iran either have exploded nuclear weapons developed out of their civilian reactor programs or are believed capable of doing so.

In late 2001, the Nuclear Regulatory Commission (NRC) received alarming information that at least one and as many as nine metal sleeves on the reactor cooling vessel at the Davis-Besse nuclear plant near Toledo, Ohio, had corroded and were leaking. When the inspectors began their work, they found not mere cracks but a "pineapple-sized" pit six inches deep, where corrosion had eaten away 70 pounds of steel, leaving only a quarter-inch to keep radiation inside the core cooling vessel of the reactor. Had the liner burst, vital cooling water would have drained away, threatening the reactor's emergency shutdown system. FirstEnergy admitted that, in such a case, the emergency core cooling system at Davis-Besse "would not have worked as it's designed to work." Former NRC commissioner Victor Gilinsky called the incident the nation's "closest brush with disaster since the 1979 Three Mile Island accident." Cleveland Congressman Dennis Kucinich blasted the NRC, saying, "FirstEnergy and the NRC worked together to put profits above public safety. It's unacceptable."

In a subsequent investigative report, the *Cleveland Plain Dealer* provided a chilling view of the state of safety in America's nuclear industry: "For more than two years, the radiation detectors at the Davis-Besse nuclear power plant insistently signaled that something was wrong inside the hulking gray bunker that houses the reactor. . . . Although they suspected a coolant leak somewhere, Davis-Besse personnel couldn't find one. Instead of pursuing its cause, they moved the monitors' intakes to a different spot. They even bypassed one of the devices' three sensors because it kept triggering alarms."

The NRC acknowledged that this attitude was a problem. In a classic bureaucratic understatement, NRC Chairman Richard Meserve observed, "There clearly were some issues with safety culture at that plant that had not been recognized by us, and not recognized by the top-most management of FirstEnergy." Even so, the nuclear industry continues to argue that no additional safety regulations were needed and that the near-disaster at Davis-Besse—like each of the other 20 "near misses" the nuclear industry has maintained on a quiet list of serious nuclear mishaps—was "unique." While President Carter had responded to Three Mile Island by appointing a presidential commission, Bush and Cheney were never asked about Davis-Besse and never publicly commented.

The lesson Bush's NRC drew from Davis-Besse was that reactor standards needed to be laxer, not tougher. A major safety problem plaguing reactors is that, in many cases, all the cables connecting the control room with the shutdown and safety systems run together, where a fire could disable them. The NRC required fire suppression equipment, or redundant cables, so that no single blaze could eliminate an operator's ability to shut the plant down.

Many plant operators, however, advocated a thriller-movie solution: in the event of a fire or other disaster, designated heroic technicians would run through the plant and operate the equipment by hand if the control cables burned away. The Bush NRC reversed itself, permitting so-called "operator manual actions" as a substitute for safety equipment. Dana A. Powers, vice chairman of the NRC's Advisory Committee on Reactor Safety, was aghast. "Is there any hope? It's not like you can set up a simulator," he said. "How do you simulate smoke, light, fire, ringing bells, fire engines, crazy people running around?" While NRC staff admitted that the change would cause "increases in risks from fires," it did not think it constituted "a safety issue." Staff member Eva Brown suggested to Powers that drills could be made more realistic by turning off the lights.

And just in case the Harrison Ford stand-in does not run fast enough, the National Research Council in December 2003 endorsed passing out potassium iodide pills to people who live near nuclear power plants, so that at least they would not die of thyroid cancer.

Nuclear power is a technology no one needs and many fear. But that has not stopped the Bush administration from making the industry's revival a high priority. Bush's energy secretary, former Michigan Senator Spencer Abraham, had consistently supported subsidies for nuclear power while in the Senate. Abraham was a firm advocate of "solving" the nuclear waste problem by dumping the wastes at the politically convenient but geologically suspect Yucca Mountain site in the Nevada desert. The independent Nuclear Waste Technical Review Board warned that the canisters designed to store the waste could corrode in less than 1,000 years—that is, in less than .04 percent of the toxic lifetime of the waste stored within them. Bush had promised that science, not politics, would decide where the waste went, but Cheney conceded that, if the administration's vision was to materialize, the waste had to be put somewhere. Bush strongly promoted the Yucca Mountain site through the regulatory and legislative processes, against the wishes of Nevada's legislators and citizens.

The waste storage and safety problems thus disposed of, Bush's budgets proposed new subsidies for a new generation of nuclear power plants. Observers knew, however, that this was not enough to lure public utilities to invest the billions required—especially in a deregulated energy landscape where prices were volatile and there was no guaranteed way to recover capital costs. Enter Dick Cheney and his energy task force to the rescue.

Love Letter to Dirty Energy

When Cheney's task force released its recommendations on May 16, 2001, the Public Interest Research Group offered this précis: "Dirty energy wins, and taxpayers pay." Columnist Mary McGrory referred to it as "the love letter to the oil, coal and nuclear interests that they call an energy policy." Cheney called for everything on the energy industry's wish list: drilling in the Arctic National

Wildlife Refuge, a return to nuclear power, looser governmental regulations all around, and easier access to the petrochemicals beneath public lands. Memorialized by the DeLay-controlled House of Representatives as the Energy Policy Act of 2003, the Bush policy includes $38 billion in tax breaks and subsidies for polluters—very nearly as much as the amount appropriated for cleanup and recovery in the wake of the September 11 attacks. Balanced against the $18.4 million contributed to federal candidates in the 1999–2000 election cycle by the oil and gas, mining, auto, and electric utility industries, the Public Interest Research Group calculated a more than 2,000-fold rate of return on investment from this one bill alone.

Here is how Bush proposed to distribute the spoils: Oil and gas would get $47.5 billion in tax incentives and subsidies. Coal and electric utilities would reap $9.3 billion, mostly to continue their quixotic (but highly profitable), decades-old search for "clean coal." The nuclear industry would pocket $9.2 billion in tax breaks and subsidies, including $1.1 billion toward producing hydrogen from nuclear plants—a cruel slap to those who saw hydrogen as the clean fuel of the future. It would also provide $865 million for the reprocess-

ing of spent nuclear fuels, a step previously denied it for fear of nuclear prolif-eration (because if other countries followed our lead, it would vastly increase the availability of fuel for nuclear weapons).

Even the Bush-friendly *Wall Street Journal* editorialized against the last part: "Commercial use of plutonium is a gift to the world's terrorists and rogue states," the paper wrote. "It would be folly for the U.S. to head any further down this path." The nuclear industry got another gift too: reauthorization of the Price Anderson Act, which shields the industry from the financial risks of catastrophic accidents—leaving those risks, as usual, to be shouldered by the taxpayers.

The Bush plan also provides about $2.4 billion for renewable energy—fine as far as it goes, but essentially canceled out by larger tax credits that companies could use if they converted relatively clean natural gas–burning plants to dirty coal-fired ones. Funding both, says the Natural Resources Defense Council, "is like driving with your foot on the gas and the brake at the same time."

In addition to outright payments, the Bush energy policy saves industry untold billions in lowered standards and greased processes. For example, it pro-poses a laughably tiny improvement in gasoline fuel economy for American cars, and it strips tax credits from truly efficient hybrids in order to reward SUVs that have made minuscule improvements in gas mileage. And it takes away authority over oil and gas leasing from local forest supervisors and gives it to Washington. (So much for local control.)

A slightly more responsible version of the bill came out of the Senate, but it still proved the rule that, when politicians lack the courage to solve problems, the path of least resistance is to subsidize politically potent industries that seem to offer a solution. Despite the near-disaster at Davis-Besse, nuclear energy turned out to be a particular favorite of the Senate leadership, which pledged it $19 billion in subsidies—far beyond anything anyone had suggested for the industry before. Even with previous sweetheart deals and liability waivers, no public utility had stepped forward to build a new nuke, so the bill authorized the Department of Energy to provide loan guarantees worth $14 to $16 billion to pay 50 percent of the construction costs of seven new nuclear power plants.

In justifying the nuclear subsidies, Senate Energy Committee chair Pete Domenici (R-N.M.) explained, "This provision allows industry to build advanced lightwater nuclear reactors that are smaller, safer and more efficient than the plants we built 30 years ago. The electricity they produce costs less than electricity from coal or natural gas." But if that were the case, why would the industry need to be subsidized?

This "if you pay them, they will build" approach obviously turned on its head the administration's theoretical commitment to the free market. The Congressional Budget Office, even under new leadership appointed by Republicans, acerbically commented that the risk of these loans defaulting was "very high—well above 50 percent." The CBO also noted that these new plants would be "uneconomic to operate because of [their] high construction costs relative to other electricity generation sources." Even the pro-nuclear *Chicago Tribune* called the bill "a risky and expensive subsidy for the nuclear industry" that only "papered over" the remaining issues with nuclear power. Britain's free-market *Economist* magazine pointed out that there is "little case for throwing good public money after bad to build new nuclear plants."

Who *Are* Those Guys? Secrets of the Task Force

Oddly for a policy-making body, the workings of the energy task force were treated as clandestine, a secret as closely guarded as Cheney's post–September 11 "undisclosed location." Information as mundane as who advised the vice president, how many times, and to what end was elevated to the level of state secret. The vice president steadfastly refused to divulge this information, sometimes citing executive privilege, more often simply refusing. ("Cheney is protecting the presidency itself, wrote McGrory. "It will be weakened if ordinary citizens are allowed to know how come the country has an energy policy that sounds as if it were written in the executive suite of Enron.")

In an attempt to pry out the data, the General Accounting Office took Cheney to court, as did the Sierra Club and Judicial Watch in a separate action. After a long, unprecedented battle, the GAO finally caved and gave up its statutory right to know where and how money appropriated by Congress was being spent. The other suit was still pending at the time of this writing. Federal courts repeatedly called upon Cheney to release the information, but the vice president chose to take the case all the way to the Supreme Court.

The frantic effort at secrecy has sparked lively speculation about exactly what the vice president might be hiding. Secret agreements with Enron? Pre-war oil company designs on Iraq? Cheney's lawyers claimed that, if the details of the making of public policy were made public, important sources (like major oil companies) would be too shy to offer their opinions.

This was news to oil company execs, not generally of the shrinking-violet sort. When *New York Times* reporter Don Van Natta queried the Republican Party's 25 largest energy campaign contributors, 18 cheerfully acknowledged that the Cheney task force had consulted them. Many of the companies expressed surprise that the administration was resisting releasing the information, noting that their recommendations to the task force could be found on their public Web sites. As an example of industry access, the *New York Times* reported, "Officials from Exelon, the nation's largest nuclear energy company . . . were among a group of about 75 energy executives who met with Mr. Cheney in March 2001."

As the *Los Angeles Times'* Judy Pasternak reported, "Many of the executives at the White House meetings were generous donors to the Republican party, and some of their key lobbyists were freshly hired from the Bush presidential campaign." On March 1, 2001, the CEO and vice president of Peabody Coal, the world's largest coal company, met with Cheney. Peabody and its affiliates had given the GOP $900,000 in the previous two years. Five days after the task force's final report appeared on May 16, 2001, calling for additional coal production, Peabody was ready with a stock offering that raised $420 million, $60 million more than analysts had expected. Peabody vice president Fred Palmer gave the task force credit: it "affected the valuation of the stock," he told the *Los Angeles Times.* What stock analyst would factor into his or her projections a company's inside track in formulating the country's energy policy? Was it possible that Cheney was hiding not what the energy industry had told him but what he had told them? Just knowing when the report was going to come out might easily have been worth millions to the inside traders who made up the Bush-Cheney energy circle. Treasury Secretary Paul O'Neill, who had promised to sell his stock in Alcoa on taking office, in fact waited until after the energy plan was released and Alcoa's stock value increased by 30 percent.

While we do not know exactly who did construct the nation's energy policy, we know for certain whose ideas were *not* taken into account: the nation's energy conservation experts, the environmental organizations, the citizen consumer groups. But they can't say they weren't consulted! Late in the afternoon of March 21, 2001, an Energy Department staffer phoned the Sierra Club's

Washington office, soliciting thoughts on energy and the environment—within 48 hours, please. (A subsequent letter from the Department of Energy to the General Accounting Office complained about environmentalists' "lack of responsiveness.") In that same week, Energy Secretary Abraham met with executives from Duke Energy, Westinghouse Electric, Entergy, Exelon, and various nuclear industry officials.

On April 4, task force energy director Andrew Lundquist actually met for an hour with fifteen representatives from various environmental groups. Unfortunately, by the time the participants had finished introducing themselves, the allotted time was up, and attendees were hustled out the door—where, unlike any other energy task force advisers, they were ushered into the arms of the waiting press corps.

The White House was not ashamed of being seen with the Sierra Club—but it was ashamed of being seen with Exelon and Enron. Nonetheless, Enron was able to score, by the White House's own acknowledgment, six meetings with the task force, including one between three top Enron officials and Vice President Cheney. Ken Lay got his own tête-à-tête with the VP in April 2001 and gave him a memo (later leaked to the *San Francisco Chronicle*) with eight energy policy recommendations—of which Cheney's final report adopted seven.

Cheney repeatedly boasted on national television that the administration had adopted eleven of the Sierra Club's twelve key energy planks. When this boast led to a June 1 meeting with the vice president, environmental groups asked exactly where in the administration's published energy policy were such Sierra Club initiatives as major reliance on renewable energy and enhanced fuel efficiency. In a bizarre scene, administration officials pointed to the thick energy policy volumes it had just published—with $135,000 pilfered from the renewable energy budget—and shrugged them off. "These are not our policy," they said to the startled environmentalists. "These are the status quo." (No subsequent document, of course, ever embodied the Sierra Club's planks, or challenged the status quo, but Cheney stopped making his strange claim.)

The White House liked to claim that it was simply listening to industry because industry had expertise. But not all "experts" were consulted equally. Kurt Yeager, chief economist for the electrical utility industry, told the Sierra Club that the task force had rebuffed his recommendations about modernizing the nation's electric power grid. Bush chose instead an Enron-backed proposal giving the federal government the power of eminent domain to force states to allow the construction of new transmission lines. Yeager said he had warned Cheney that eminent domain would make modernization controversial and prevent it from happening—which is exactly how the issue played out. Enron, it developed, had a reason for its recommendation; it was using the antiquated and clumsy structure of the electrical grid to manipulate the California electricity market, making billions in unearned profits.

This particular example of Bush's coziness with backward-looking industry was to prove expensive indeed. The failure, at Enron's behest, to install modern digital switches on the grid left the nation vulnerable to the worst blackout in its history in the summer of 2003, the proximate cause of which was ineptitude on the part of FirstEnergy, the Ohio energy company and major Bush campaign giver also responsible for the near disaster at Davis-Besse. Even then, Bush and his allies in Congress still delayed legislation designed to modernize the grid, insisting that it could not be allowed to pass unless the administration also got drilling in the Arctic and oil leases off California, the Northwest, Florida, and the East coast, plus billions for the oil, coal, and nuclear industries.

Old Daniels Midland Had a Farm

As scandalous as the subsidies to outmoded energy industries might be, they almost pale in comparison to the bushels of money piled up at the door of agribusiness. The Farm Bill of 2002 actually started out attempting, under Agriculture Secretary Ann Veneman, to stabilize rural livelihoods, enhance rural environments, and end crop subsidies. Veneman called it "a thoughtful piece of legislation that was in keeping with the president's principles."

The core idea was to refocus farm spending on small farmers—something the 1996 Farm Bill, cynically titled "Freedom to Farm," had spectacularly failed to do. The GAO reported that the percentage of payments to small farms had steadily decreased since the bill took effect. In 1995, small farms received 29 percent of all federal support; four years later, they were down to 14 percent, even though they made up 76 percent of all farms nationwide. This was the situation Veneman meant to address, along with Indiana Republican Senator Richard Lugar, her main congressional ally.

But before long Veneman and Lugar's vision was hijacked by the usual agribusiness interests (with bipartisan support from senators in the farm belt up for reelection), and Bush ended up signing a bloated grotesquerie of subsidies totaling $180 billion, with 70 percent still going to "farmers" like Cargill, J. G. Boswell, and Archer Daniels Midland. The Environmental Quality Incentives Program, originally designed to help farmers protect drinking water, was turned into a multibillion-dollar giveaway subsidizing the expansion of industrial feedlots. The net effect is that the taxpayers will finance Big Corn, Big Pig, and their big brethren in driving the remaining family farmers out of business.

While advocates of big farm subsidies like to claim that these payments deserve credit for the efficiency and productivity of American agriculture, the numbers show the opposite. Major beneficiaries of farm subsidies include big sugar interests like Alex Fanjul's Atlantic Sugar Association, one of the biggest contributors in American politics. What Big Sugar got from the federal government was not new technology or greater efficiency but price supports and protectionist barriers against cheaper imported sugar. The Bush administration also teamed up with the president's brother, Florida Governor Jeb Bush, to propose an Everglades "restoration" plan that shifted the burden of cleaning up Big Sugar's phosphorous pollution of the Everglades to the people of Florida. The striking virtue of the Bush brothers' plan was to keep uncompetitive U.S. sugar growers in the business of polluting the Everglades.

Greed Cometh Before a Fall

The energy bill moved to its endgame in the fall of 2003. On the table was a House-passed version that included drilling in the Arctic Refuge, exploring for oil in previously off-limits coastal areas, and weakening clean air standards. In conference committee, a handful of Republicans, led by DeLay, Domenici, and Billy Tauzin of Louisiana, sat down with the administration to put together an enormous giveaway: $25.7 billion in subsidies hidden in 1,700 pages. Moderate Senate Republicans were able to keep drilling in the Arctic and off the coasts out of the final bill but paid for it with funding for new power plants in Minnesota, North Dakota, Alaska, Louisiana, and West Virginia, plus a huge ethanol subsidy for the farm states. Purchasers of Hummers got a $100,000 tax break. The bill that came out of conference even provided federal funding for shopping centers to reward key backers in several states. Domenici was clear about his strategy; he wanted a bill "that is tough to walk away from."

In one final payoff, DeLay and Bush teamed up to protect DeLay's largest campaign contributor, Lyondell Chemical, the nation's biggest manufacturer of MTBE, a gasoline additive that had left a devastating legacy of water pollution across the nation. (Lake Tahoe on the California/Nevada border, for example, lost a third of its water supply to MTBE.) The chemical was going to be phased out, but DeLay wanted to keep it on the market as long as possible, as well as shield his patrons from lawsuits over the damage MTBE had caused. DeLay's proposal deeply angered states facing MTBE problems, but the administration stood by the rules of the game: reward your friends. DeLay was allowed to hold the energy bill hostage, and Lyondell got its get-out-of-jail-free card.

A wave of revulsion shook the nation's editorial pages. (Even Domenici admitted that "as soon as you start reading the language, we're in duck soup.") The *Wall Street Journal* said the GOP leadership "has greased more wheels than a Nascar pit crew." The *Detroit News* called the bill "an oinking mastodon." The Heritage Foundation joined the Cato Institute in a libertarian assault on the bill. Senators John McCain (R-Ariz.) and Charles Schumer (D-N.Y.) organized a filibuster of non–farm state Democrats and moderate Republicans; New Hampshire Republican senators John Sununu and Judd Gregg, whose state would be badly damaged by the MTBE exemption, signed up. The loss of the two normally loyal New Hampshire senators left the White House unable to muster the 60 votes needed to break a filibuster. Only 58 senators could bring themselves to vote for Domenici's grotesquely larded product, in what Fox News called the biggest domestic defeat yet suffered by the Bush administration.

Congress went home for the holidays without having passed any energy legislation at all. But the administration promised that, when Congress reconvened in 2004, the bill would be back—just in time to raise more campaign money. Because economic dinosaurs—companies that cannot clean up, cannot innovate, cannot compete in the twenty-first century—can still make campaign contributions. And when those contributions are followed by ample federal subsidies, it really does not matter how competitive the companies are in the marketplace. What counts, as Ralph Reed told Enron, is how well connected they are in the White House and on Capitol Hill.

"On America's long march towards the welfare state, retention of the public lands was the first milestone. Let's demolish that milestone."

—Professor Robert L. Nelson, chair, Department of Sociology, Northwestern University, in *Forbes*

"I'm able to clear my mind, and it helps me put it all into perspective. Problems don't go away when we're here, but you can see them in a different light."

—President George W. Bush, about his Texas ranch

"I've heard cynics describe Bush's sun-scorched ranch as something of a faux cowboy prop that he uses to maintain down-to-earth distance from his old-money East Coast heritage. The truth, I think, is the opposite. These 1,600 acres are not a retreat from elitism, but rather an open-arms embrace of the most uncharitable kind of elitism: the belief that nature belongs to those who can afford it. That nature is a privilege for the privileged. That nature is another free-market commodity for high bidders."

—John Balzar, *Los Angeles Times*

This Land Was Your Land
Auctioning Off the Commons

At its heart, the Bush administration has always thought of itself as cowboy. The vice president, after all, is from Wyoming, a state that greeted Franklin Roosevelt's creation of Jackson Hole National Monument by getting itself exempted from the Antiquities Act. Although the president bought his ranch in Crawford, Texas, only just in time to sit out the ballot counting and court shenanigans in Florida, there is no doubt that he considers himself someone who has always belonged on a ranch.

Ranching, like mining and logging, is not what it used to be. In the 1960s and 1970s, the American economy shifted away from resource extraction. The best old trees had already been cut, the richest lodes tapped out. Commodity communities, even those with heavy federal support, could no longer hold young people or generate new jobs. Global market shifts drove down prices for timber, beef, wheat, and minerals, because it was cheaper to produce them in Siberia, Argentina, Australia, or Indonesia. Recreation, retirement, and preservation became the growth sectors of the western economy. As veteran western writer Ray Ring pointed out in explaining the new realities of the Mountain West, "The pillars that had always held up Montana—agriculture, mining and logging—cracked all at once, as a national recession cut demand for raw materials, and global competition kicked in. Average per capita income plunged relative to other states, down to 45th by 1990."

It looked like the dying gasp of the "boomer" West. Author Wallace Stegner decades ago distinguished between two types of western settlers. On the one hand were the "boomers," who saw the West as treasure to be felled from the hills or dug out of the soil, turned into money, and shipped far away. Boomers were not interested in sticking around: once the hillsides were bare or the mines played out, they moved on. On the other hand were the "nesters," those who came west seeking a new home and community, who planned to work hard and stay. Farmers and small ranchers, mostly, were nesters; big ranchers (initially, at least) along with loggers and miners were boomers. Salt Lake City, with its Mormon vision of the valley as Zion, inspired Stegner's image of nester heaven. Idaho's Coeur d'Alene Valley—scene of the bloody silver strikes of the early twentieth century, the assassination of Governor Frank Steubenberg, and the stronghold of Joe Hill and the Wobblies—was boomer hell.

Nesters and boomers generally loathed each other. Brigham Young did everything he could to keep the miners out of, and away from, Salt Lake City. The conflict was reflected in those treacly lines from *Oklahoma*, "The farmer and the cowman should be friends." "Should," perhaps, because mostly they weren't.

By 1980, the small-town, rural voters of the West were feeling desperate, dispossessed, and unappreciated. The boomers, and Republican Party operatives who wanted to separate the Mountain West from its historic New Deal loyalty to the Democratic Party, saw their chance. Mining and timber corporations learned to blame environmentalists for layoffs, shaft shutdowns, and mill closings, even when automation or globalization was obviously to blame. (In the small northeastern California community of Loyalton, in the early 1990s, laid-off workers at the newly modernized Sierra Pacific sawmill strewed the landscape with yellow ribbons proclaiming that limitations on logging were costing jobs. In fact, the mill was working three shifts and cutting every board foot its laser-guided saws could juggle—precisely so that Sierra Pacific could close it a few years later, having taken out all the timber in the immediate vicinity.)

Many nesters were induced to throw in with the boomers to form the "wise use movement," a name worthy of master spinner Frank Luntz. Rather than see the West's future in a new economy of recreation, retirement, and high-tech jobs—all attracted by natural values and intact ecosystems—the wise users preached that if only the heavy hand of Washington were removed, the bustling, blue-collar, commodity-based economies of the 1940s and 1950s would return. ("Removing the heavy hand of Washington" was always understood not to mean removing the substantial federal subsidies showered on western resource extractors. Western historian Bernard DeVoto captured the sentiment nicely: "Get out, and send more money.")

But even twelve years of Ronald Reagan and George H. W. Bush could not bring back the good old days. Reagan doubled logging in the national forests, only accelerating the collapse of the timber economy. Pockets of timber and petroleum and minerals remained, but technology had made humans almost incidental to their extraction. Still the boomers kept at it, intent on pumping the last barrel of oil, cutting the last board foot of cedar, and heap-leach mining the last ounce of gold. Resistance came now from the new nesters of the New West: retirees, river-rafting companies, and computer programmers working only minutes from their favorite trailhead.

During the 2000 campaign, George W. Bush sometimes seemed to be leaning toward the New West. He promised to increase funding for park acquisition through the Federal Land and Water Conservation Fund and to take care of the national park system by eliminating its backlog of maintenance projects. He even took Al Gore to task for his supposed neglect of the national parks. (The "best way to show our citizens that Republicans can be for something positive in the environment," Luntz had advised, was to pose as "a champion of national parks.") But the boomers always understood that Bush was one of their own; the timber industry gave him an unprecedented million dollars in campaign contributions at a single event. They understood that he shared their extractive vision of the West—and it did not include taking tourists on llama pack trips.

Why Not Sell the Grand Canyon?

To help shape his wildlands policy, President-elect Bush brought to his transition team Terry Anderson, a libertarian economist who heads a Montana think tank called the Political Economy Research Center (PERC) and author of a "blueprint for auctioning off all public lands over 20 to 40 years." Instead of retaining large ecosystems for wildlife, Anderson urged that we "partition" our forests and wilderness areas into individual tracts and allow them to be auctioned off. And he strongly urged that we sell all the parks, too, leaving conservation to the wisdom of the market. "What special provisions, if any, should the divestiture plan make for the Grand Canyon and similar national parks, monuments, forests, and wilderness areas?" Anderson wondered rhetorically. "One possibility would be to specify no restrictions at all. . . . The greater the willingness to pay for preservation, the greater the incentive of a private owner to negotiate restrictions on the development of subsurface, grazing, or timber rights." So Anderson sought a future where there might, or might not, be restrictions on logging or mining the Grand Canyon and Yellowstone—depending on the high bidder at the auction.

Stegner once called the national park system "the best idea we ever had." Anderson's might have been the worst. Transferring public lands to the private interests who thought they could make money off of them was not exactly new; it had happened with public timberland in the nineteenth century. Once timber companies had obtained control of most of our most productive forest lands, they typically clearcut them. And the practice did not end in the 1800s: timberlands granted to Burlington Northern were tied up for almost a century in legal wrangling left over from the days of financier Jay Gould. The moment the wrangle was resolved, Plum Creek Timber Company emerged as their owner and promptly admitted that it was liquidating them, not managing them for sustained yield.

Even given this bitter history, ancient and recent, Anderson insisted that if ARCO or Disney were willing to pay enough, they should have a shot at Yellowstone or Yosemite. It does not seem that he dislikes wild places—it is just that he and the libertarians and social Darwinists who are making policy in the Bush administration cannot stand the idea that such lands belong to everyone— or (worse yet) no one. For those whose model for public recreation is Disneyland, the public parks and public forests are a nightmare.

There may be no concept more loathed by Bush and his wrecking crew than that of the commons: the air, ocean, rivers, forests, and other resources held in common by every citizen. Starting in seventeenth-century England, this concept of common property, common bounty, and common responsibility was already under assault in the process known as "enclosure"—originally, British landlords putting up fences around what had previously been common pastures. (Those pastures were not privatized because commons management had failed but because landlords wanted to monopolize them for their own gain.)

Here in America, our commons are our national forests and grasslands as well as our rivers, shores, and oceans. The goal of Anderson and his free-market environmentalists is to enclose these last commons, on the theory that the resources will be better cared for by private landowners than by public stewards. While it is true that our national forests have been poorly managed, that is the result of allowing commercial logging inside them. Old-growth forests in private hands have been almost totally liquidated. The western forest type with the least remaining old growth is the coastal redwoods, the one forest that passed most completely into private hands.

Although Anderson did not remain with the Bush administration, he helped usher into its fold another reliable free-marketeer, his good friend (and a fellow at PERC) Gale Norton. Norton had become a libertarian after reading Ayn Rand's *Fountainhead* novels in college and had learned the right-wing approach to public lands management at the knee of James Watt at the Mountain States Legal Foundation. During Senate confirmation hearings, Washington Senator Maria Cantwell (D) asked Norton if she would commit to consulting with the congressional delegation before changing the state's new national monuments. Norton replied (placid smile): "Well, I again look forward to learning more about that. . . . I'll look forward to learning more about it." When Cantwell pressed, Norton slithered away again. "We would certainly look at providing some comments for the record on that, some written comments." Cantwell's concern was justified, for no sooner was Norton in office than she contacted state officials about the nineteen national monuments declared by Bill Clinton—to find out how much the officials wanted to shrink their boundaries and what kinds of commercial exploitation should be allowed. Mining? Logging? Both?

Now that they were in charge, the boomers needed a plan, and Utah Congressman James Hansen had one ready. Hansen, who had fiercely opposed his state's new Escalante–Grand Staircase National Monument (along with every other effort to protect wilderness in his wilderness-rich state), found himself the new chair of the House Resources Committee. Even before the new administration's installation, he fired off an eight-page letter to Bush and Cheney, bemoaning "the Clinton administration's unreasoned and frequently absurd interpretation of law and Congressional intent" in managing natural resources, and outlining his plan to convert public lands to private profit. Some key features of Hansen's back-to-the-past plan:

- Get snowmobiles back in the national parks, especially Yellowstone; abandon the Clinton-era preference for "natural quiet" in the Grand Canyon and increase the number of tourist aircraft; turn lose personal watercraft (Jetskis) in the park system's lakes and beaches.

- Resubmit Clinton's national monument designations to Congress to be overturned. This would effectively revoke presidents' ability to use the Antiquities Act to protect special places like the Sequoia National Forest and the Escalante redrock country.

- Repeal Clinton-era regulations that required mining companies to restore public lands they destroyed and that prohibited them from dumping spoils without a permit.

- Remove "ecological integrity" as a reason to block mining, logging, and other commercial uses of the wildlife refuges, since ecological integrity "had no basis in law."

- Most important, undo Clinton's Roadless Area Conservation Rule, which protected the last 58 million acres of roadless and unlogged forest in the national forest system.

While other administrations would have filed Hansen's letter away in the crank file, the Bush administration dutifully cut-and-pasted it into its "to-do" list and went to work.

Timber Beasts in the National Forests

One of President Clinton's final acts was to put in place a comprehensive plan to protect the nation's remaining wild forests. Little is now left of the magnificent old-growth forests that once blanketed our country, but three-quarters of what remains lies within the national forests, where it constitutes prime habitat for endangered species and a model for future restoration efforts. But more than half of the total area of the national forests has been degraded by logging, mining, and the 440,000 miles of publicly funded roads that make that industrial resource extraction possible. To protect the precious remnants, Clinton's Forest Service chief, Mike Dombeck, devised the Roadless Area Conservation Rule. Simply put, it prohibits new roads from being built in virgin forests, of which nearly 60 million acres remain. Two vast national forests in Alaska, the Tongass and the Chugach, account for a quarter of that total.

This was no hasty midnight action. Rather, it was the result of one of the most extensive public rule-making processes in American history. It took three years, hundreds of public hearings, and a million public comments to put the Roadless Rule in place. Subsequent efforts to back up the rule added another 1.2 million comments to the record. Of the 2.2 million total, 95 percent were in favor of strong wilderness protection. The need for conservation was clear, the science was sound, public support was overwhelming. Bush immediately began working to tear it down.

This was a job for Mark Rey, former chief lobbyist for the American Forest and Paper Association. Rey came to the task with experience in opening up vast swaths of forest for the timber industry; he was the architect of the disastrous 1995 Salvage Logging Rider, which allowed the Forest Service and Bureau of Land Management to sell off the nation's forests without regard to environmental laws or even whether the sale made any money. Two years later he tried to push through a wholesale revision of the National Forest Management Act (NFMA), using language virtually identical to the recommendations of his former employer. His revisions would have made timber sales mandatory and environmental laws optional, would have relieved the Forest Service of having to consult with federal fisheries agencies on the likely impacts of timber sales, and, for good measure, would have levied $10,000 fines on anyone who sued to hold up a timber sale for "improper purposes."

Once confirmed as the Agriculture Department official in charge of the Forest Service, Rey picked up where he had left off (see his profile in chapter 3), only now working from a position of power. Testifying before the House Subcommittee on Forests and Forest Health, Rey made clear that all of the fundamental environmental laws governing the forests—the NFMA, the Endangered Species Act, and the National Environmental Policy Act—needed to be "re-examined," "reviewed," and "re-opened." The Roadless Rule, he testified, also needed to be made more "balanced." Despite the million-plus comments that had been solicited during its formulation, Rey claimed that local forest communities were somehow excluded. He also stated that "protecting roadless values does not mean protecting every roadless acre we have out there now."

The first forest to suffer Rey's review was the mighty Tongass. In June 2003, the Forest Service announced that it would allow individual states to "seek relief for exceptional circumstances." Alaska had sued over the protections given the Tongass, and (as they did in many other cases) John Ashcroft's lawyers simply caved, allowing the first exemption from the Roadless Rule. Western governors were invited to join Alaska in seeking exclusions for their states as well.

Bush and Rey soon found a more expedient way around the rule. In July, U.S. District Court Judge Clarence Brimmer in Wyoming struck down the Roadless Rule, claiming that the three-year, multimillion-comment process had been rushed and that there had been confusion about which areas were covered by the ruling. (The ones without roads, Your Honor?) Despite the obvious objections, and despite promises made by Attorney General Ashcroft (see chapter 3) that he would "support and enforce" the rule, the administration said that it would not appeal Brimmer's decision. Eight environmental groups stepped in to defend the rule in the government's stead. The Justice Department argued that the groups had no "direct stake in defending the regulations" and thus could not defend it in court.

Even Anderson has had a hard time defending Rey's tenure. He gave Norton and Rey a C-minus on their overall performance, saying that the administration "did a really poor job selling" its forest programs. "They are emphasizing over and over again what everyone expects from a Republican administration: They are rolling back regulations."

Coal-Bed Methane: Return to Boomer Hell

Despite Bush and Cheney's cowboy boots and big belt buckles, any real westerner would immediately peg them as classic boomers. They are the guys building trophy homes where the kids used to learn to hunt; the ones fighting zoning regulations so they can put up some more strip malls; the guys whose oil drilling venture spoils the town swimming hole and who just say "That's progress!" Boomers' hearts are stirred less by big skies and rolling range than by the roar of compressors and cavalcades of tanker trucks. And both wildlands and the working homesteads beloved by nesters were to be victims of their assault on the Rocky Mountain West.

Hansen's to-do list was not enough. The White House appointed James Connaughton, chairman of the Council on Environmental Quality, to head a Task Force on Energy Project Streamlining. Its mission was to collect a wish list of places the petroleum industry would like to drill. Many of these were places that previous administrations had preserved as "off-limits" but that Bush sacrificed on the altar of "energy independence." On Padre Island National Seashore in Texas, for example, BNP Petroleum secured exclusive oil and gas lease options covering 36,000 acres of the barrier island. It planned an "aggressive drilling campaign," and the administration promptly began issuing permits for converting the national seashore into a national sacrifice zone.

Some might quail at the prospect of eighteen-wheelers making 40 trips a day along a fourteen-mile stretch of beach where endangered sea turtles nest, or the rest of the Bush energy development agenda. For those faint of heart, Interior Department assistant secretary of land and minerals management Rebecca Watson had some blunt words, delivered at the September 2003 meeting of the Western Governors' Conference in Big Sky, Montana. "This isn't for sissies," said Watson. "We have to get serious about this because it's critical to our economy and our quality of life."

Local communities in the Rocky Mountain West turned out to have decidedly different views about what intensive energy development is doing to their quality of life. One of the ugliest fights centers on eastern Wyoming, the historic scene of the bloody Johnson County War between nesters and boomers. Back in the nineteenth century, big, often foreign ranch interests in the Powder River basin tried to drive smaller ranchers out of business by denying them the right to participate in the roundup and bringing in hired gunmen from Texas. (In that respect, not much has changed.) When the nesters fought back, President William Henry Harrison sent in the Sixth Cavalry to protect the invaders. In the next election, Wyoming voted the Republicans out.

Today there is a new range war, this time over the methane gas that lies trapped in coal seams underneath eastern Wyoming (and Montana and New Mexico as well). Much of the coal is not economical to mine, but the methane, which is dissolved in subsurface water, can be brought to the surface and released as natural gas. Unfortunately, this process leaves behind huge quantities of saline water far too toxic to use for irrigation or livestock. It could be reinjected back into the aquifer, but that would raise the price of the gas by five to seven cents per cubic foot—and, as a typical gas firm's spokesman commented, "We're a bottom-line kind of company." And Bush's White House is a bottom-line kind of administration. When Bush came to office, some 5,000 wells were spread out across the 25,000-square-mile Powder River basin. Bush permitted thousands more, and Wyoming has estimated that by 2010 there could be as many as 50,000 wells.

Some farmers and ranchers, particularly those who owned their mineral rights, favored letting the gas companies drill—if they would take responsibility for the water. Others are unalterably opposed to the disruption to their livestock operations and land by the extensive road building, noise, and pollution that accompanies drilling. Some, like Tweeti Blancett—who had run the Bush campaign in Garfield County, New Mexico—were deeply radicalized by the experience.

"I once believed that if the President knew about the damage done to our land by the energy industry, the damage would cease," she says. Blancett went to Washington, D.C., and met with Watson and the New Mexico congressional staffs, among others. "I told them all that gas drilling could be done right but that it was being done wrong. I begged them to enforce existing regulations. I came home to the small town of Aztec, New Mexico, and waited for change. I'm still waiting.

"We once ran 600 cows on those 35,000 acres. Today, we can barely keep 100 cows. Grass and shrubs are now roads, drill pads, or scars left by pipeline paths. We have trouble keeping our few cows alive because they get run over by trucks servicing wells each day, or they get poisoned when they lap up the sweet anti-freeze leaking out of unfenced compressor engines. . . . At times it seems hopeless. Then I hear from people facing similar situations in Colorado, in Montana, in Wyoming, in Utah. Many are like us—conservative, Republican, pro–free enterprise people. Others are environmentalists, or just care about land and animals." Soon, Blancett warned, "there will be a huge natural gas explosion, but it won't be pipelines or gas wells that blow. The explosion will come from the average Westerner, who is tired of being used by the oil and gas industry, with the help of state and federal officials."

A similar sentiment was voiced by Stoney Burk, a conservative Bush supporter in Choteau, Montana, who was quoted in the *Los Angeles Times:* "I'm not an environmentalist; I've never liked people with long hair sitting in trees smoking a pipe. But I would consider anyone who would violate this [Rocky Mountain] front my enemy. I guarantee you that if this thing goes through, there will be a lot of us lying down in front of bulldozers and not moving."

A foreshock of Blancett's promised explosion came in the midterm elections of 2002. Widely hailed as a triumph for Bush, the returns were oddly muted in the reliably "red-state" Mountain West. Republicans lost the statehouses in Arizona, New Mexico, and, stunningly, Cheney's home state of Wyoming. Eli Bebout, the Republican candidate there, ran a textbook Karl Rove campaign, blasting the Endangered Species Act and claiming that protection of the Preble meadow jumping mouse would devastate the state's ranchers. He also said that coal-bed methane development was good for the state.

Dave Freudenthal, his underdog Democratic opponent, ran against the foreigners and Texans who were running the coal-bed methane operations. He called for a "Wyoming way" of mineral development, emphasizing not only production but environmental and community protection. His classic nester vs. boomer campaign swept him into office. Six months later Judy Martz, Montana's notoriously pro-methane, boomer governor, announced that she would not even run for re-election—her favorability ratings had dropped to 20 percent.

Taking the "Wild" out of Wildlife

Conservatives are divided about big wildlife. Traditionalists like it. Libertarians such as Terry Anderson do not have any intrinsic objection to wildlife or wildlands—as long as private owners want to finance them. But the boomer corporatists who funded George Bush do. For one thing, extensive public wildlands tend to foster large animals whose presence can complicate resource extraction projects. Since Richard Nixon signed the Endangered Species Act in 1973, many species had made amazing recoveries from near extinction. Bald eagles, brown pelicans, and gray whales all fought their way back, thanks to federal support. Grizzly bears were listed as a threatened species, and an extensive recovery program was initiated. And the gray wolf, eradicated from the West in the 1920s, made its way back into the northern Rockies in the mid-1990s, with a little human help and with spectacular success.

Who's Afraid of the Big Bad Wolf?

Wolves remain an enormous symbolic issue for the Bush boomer constituency in the West. Ranchers who think of themselves as having "tamed" their land hate wolves, even if the number of livestock they kill pales in comparison to that of animals taken down by domestic dogs. Defenders of Wildlife maintains a bounty program to compensate ranchers who lose stock to wolves, but over six years only 180 ranchers have documented losses.

While remnants of the old wolf hatred still persist in pockets of the Mountain West, they are quickly becoming anachronistic. With the passing at last of the Little Red Riding Hood stereotype (there is no documented case of a wolf in North America killing a human), a generation of Americans raised on television nature programs thrills to a distant howl. The wolf reintroduction program in Yellowstone in particular has been a great tourist draw, generating a Web site where tens of thousands of people have logged on to find where they could most likely see a wolf during their visit to the park.

Wolf reintroduction in Yellowstone proved ecologically valuable as well. As the elk population was brought into better balance with forage, the riparian willows, critical habitat for dozens of other species, rebounded, and coyote numbers went down.

Whereas wolves were once found across most of the United States, they are now limited to 3 percent of their former range. If they are protected from hunting, however, full recovery seems likely. "A lot of groups and a lot of people want more wolves in more places," commented Ed Bangs, wolf recovery coordinator for the Fish and Wildlife Service in Helena, Montana.

The Bush administration, however, had a cynical plan to make sure that this will not happen. The Fish and Wildlife Service simply declared its job done and the wolf recovered, ordering that it be downlisted from "endangered" to "threatened." This means that further management of the species is turned over to state fish and game agencies, which have historically been hostile to large predators. Wyoming's management plan, for example, classifies any wolf found outside Yellowstone or Grand Teton national park as a "predator" that can be shot on sight. Such plans virtually guarantee that wolves will remain penned up in isolated pockets and will never spread to other states in their original range. "The Endangered Species Act was intended to put species on the road to recovery," said Brian Vincent of the California-based Animal Protection Institute, "but the Bush plan will load wolves on the express train to extinction."

Say Good-bye to the Grizz

Even worse off than the gray wolf is the grizzly bear. Unlike with wolves, bear/human interactions often end badly for both parties. Grizzlies need unfragmented habitat, far from humans; habituation to human settlements and garbage is a certain death sentence for a bear. Of an original population estimated at 100,000, only 1,100 grizzlies remain in the lower 48 states, more than half of them in and around Yellowstone National Park. Much of the best remaining grizzly habitat lies in the million-acre backcountry of the Bridger and Shoshone national forests along the Rocky Mountain Front—exactly where oil and gas interests want to develop their spiderweb of new roads and wells that would spell the end of any grizzly recovery. On the slopes of Ramshorn Peak in Wyoming's Absaroka Mountains, for example, fifteen grizzlies have been tracked along with wolves, lynx, and the northern goshawk. The Forest Service is now considering allowing both an exploratory oil well and a major timber sale in the area.

Bringing back healthy grizzly populations in the West means retaining or even restoring contiguous wild habitat with minimal human intrusion—more wilderness, or at least more wildness. The Bush administration, however, is philosophically opposed to both. And so a decades-long scientific planning effort to reintroduce grizzlies to the Bitterroot Mountains has been abandoned, most directly in response to pressure from Idaho Governor Dirk Kempthorne. "I oppose bringing these massive, flesh-eating carnivores into Idaho," he declared. (Observers wryly noted that the biggest population of such creatures in Idaho included the governor and his fellow Idahoans.) The Fish and Wildlife

Service concedes that the Bitterroot reintroduction is key to grizzly recovery; Interior Secretary Norton admits that, without reintroduction, recovery of the population would not occur within the next 50 years. Which is to say, it will probably never happen. Defenders of Wildlife President Rodger Schlickeisen noted that, on the same day that Norton announced her decision, "even Terry Anderson—the free-market economist and western property-rights advocate from Bush's transition team who championed her appointment—was praising the Selway-Bitterroot grizzly plan in Washington, D.C. Dr. Anderson devoted special attention to the grizzly plan because of its innovative, collaborative approach and consideration of local concerns."

Just to drive home its point, the administration announced that it would no longer designate critical habitat under the Endangered Species Act for grizzly recovery. The act requires that such areas, which do not currently contain endangered species but which would be necessary to their full recovery, be protected from oil and gas development, logging, mining, or other development threats. Since the act was passed, however, the Fish and Wildlife Service has designated critical habitat for less than 10 percent of the 1,200 listed species, and basically does so only when under court order. The Bush administration has whittled down the size of already-designated areas by more than half over the past three years, declaring that critical habitat "provides little additional protection to species." Craig Manson, the Interior Department assistant secretary for fish and wildlife and parks, the official in charge of protecting wildlife, even questioned whether extinction is such a bad thing after all: "If we are saying that the loss of species in and of itself is inherently bad—I don't think we know enough about how the world works to say that," he told the *Los Angeles Times*. The purpose of the Endangered Species Act, he went on, "is not to create a perpetual hospice for threatened or endangered species."

The Second Buffalo Slaughter

The saddest, most unnecessary, and most revealing battle in the Bush administration's war on the West's remaining megafauna is the slaughter of the Yellowstone bison. The near extinction of bison in the late nineteenth century was one of the bleakest moments in the European conquest of the West. But bison numbers gradually rebounded from Yellowstone's tiny remnant herd, and now, in addition to the large herd at Yellowstone/Grand Teton, bison are found on ranches all over the West. Ranchers have found them better suited to grazing western lands than cattle, better able to take care of themselves, especially in harsh weather, and their meat is lower in fat than beef. Sociologists Deborah and Frank Popper have even argued that the steady depopulation of the northern Great Plains shows that those lands are unsuited to agriculture and cattle grazing and would be better off turned into a great "buffalo common."

After Newt Gingrich and the Republican right seized control of Congress in 1994, ranchers who grazed their cows on the public lands surrounding Yellowstone began to agitate against the Yellowstone bison that left the park in the winter in search of lower-elevation fodder. The ranchers argued that the bison, some of which carry a disease caused brucellosis, might pass it on to their cattle—even though there is no evidence that such transmission has ever occurred, and even though elk, which are far more numerous and pass through a much greater area of cattle-grazing land, also carry the disease. Nevertheless, in order to protect 2,200 cattle grazing in the vicinity of the park, Montana game officials and the Park Service have killed 3,000 bison.

"The National Park Service killing bison is akin to a doctor killing his patients," said Charles Clusen, director of the Natural Resources Defense Council's National Parks Program. "Congress mandated the park service to be the steward, not the executioner, of our last free-roaming buffalo herd."

The End of Wilderness

In 1893, historian Frederick Jackson Turner declared the "closing of the American West." In 2003, Bush's Interior Secretary, Gale Norton, bolted the door, declaring that America had as much wilderness as it would ever need: the current 22.8 million acres, and not an acre more.

As the twentieth century wound down, the radical right fought new wilderness designations tooth and nail. In 1993, when California's senators advocated wilderness protection for areas in the California desert, Senate Republicans mounted a filibuster. The bill passed by a single vote on the last day of the session. Once Gingrich became House Speaker, the radicals in the House leadership made sure that big wilderness bills, even those with local support, never came to the floor for a vote.

By law, however, Congress was required to decide what to do about areas that could, because of their remoteness or outstanding recreational value, qualify as wilderness but had been neither formally rejected nor accepted into the wilderness system. Such lands are called Wilderness Study Areas, and while awaiting congressional action they are largely protected from commercial exploitation. By 2003, many states had well-organized citizen groups lobbying to make them official wilderness.

To avert that abhorrent possibility, the Bush administration encouraged yet another lawsuit against itself. The state of Utah went to court, ostensibly to protest the 2.6 million acres of Wilderness Study Areas designated by Clinton's Interior secretary, Bruce Babbitt, in Utah's redrock canyon country. Utah had already sued over these acres, only to be rebuffed by federal judges. This time, Norton simply threw in the towel, agreeing to withdraw protection from the 2.6 million acres. She also volunteered to preclude protection of as much as 220 million more acres in other states—caribou habitat in Alaska, sequoia forests in California, Vermillion Basin in Colorado. This ended a 25-year-old practice by the Bureau of Land Management of considering wilderness qualities before allowing logging, mining, or other anti-wilderness activities. Norton simply signed a court settlement promising that never again would she or any other secretary of the interior protect wilderness-quality areas that Congress had not yet acted on.

It was the largest single loss of public land protection in American history. It came, like so many of Bush's environmental attacks, late on a Friday afternoon, this one before a long weekend while the nation was intensely focused on the war in Iraq. As Karl Rove planned, almost no one noticed—except the miners, contractors, off-road-vehicle manufacturers, oil companies, and timber interests who now had the right to despoil an area of the public domain as large as Oregon, Washington, and Idaho combined. Beneath the radar of public attention, Bush had given up on the promise of America's common heritage of wilderness.

As Congress went home at the end of 2003, Jim Hansen had nailed a lot of coyote skins to the fence—trophies from his checklist to the incoming administration. The Roadless Rule had been abandoned, Yellowstone opened briefly to snowmobiles (Judge Emmet Sullivan of the Federal District Court, District of Columbia, soon restored the Clinton ban), mining companies freed of their obligation to keep toxic mining spoils off the public lands, and the Interior

Department and Forest Service excused from public scrutiny of their faithfulness to the ecological charters given to them by Congress. Clinton's national monuments remained as lines on a map, but with logging trucks regularly rolling out of Giant Sequoia National Monument, that seemed less painful to the radical right than it had three years earlier.

George Bush has not (yet) been able to scrap all of Theodore Roosevelt's legacy. But that says more about the size of TR's legacy—about 230 million acres—than it does about the intensity of the administration's efforts. Indeed, Bush has stripped protections from more of the American landscape than any other American president, including Roosevelt, ever managed to protect—some 234 million acres and still stripping.

"It will be a grand triumph for America if we can preserve the Arctic Refuge in its pure, untrammeled state."

—President Jimmy Carter, in original caption for an exhibition by photographer Subhankar Banerjee at the Smithsonian Institution, censored because it might be "construed as advocacy"

"An area of flat, white nothingness."

—Gale Norton, describing the Arctic National Wildlife Refuge

"We feel very, very confident we will be able to crack the backs of radical environmentalists."

— House Majority Whip Tom DeLay, on the prospects for opening the Arctic Refuge to oil drilling. (He was wrong.)

"It's never decided until we win."

— Senator Ted Stevens (R-Alaska)

8

Alaska
The Great Land or the Last Welfare State?

At the top of America, within sight of the polar ice cap, the rough peaks of the Brooks Range level out to austere flat tundra swarming with dense clouds of ravenous mosquitoes. There will never be a Club Med on the coastal plain of the Arctic National Wildlife Refuge, but a visit there teaches that human comfort is not the measure of a thriving ecosystem. Vast antlike herds of caribou pour over the mountains to the plains each summer to calve and raise their young; musk oxen form defensive circles, guarding the legacy of the Pleistocene; 180 species of birds fatten for their flight to each of the lower 48 states; grizzlies roam where, in a few short months, polar bears will make their dens. Life goes on, tumultuous, glorious, and heedless of the heartless plans laid 3,000 miles away to turn the region into a petroleum sacrifice zone.

No environmental issue before the American public in the past 20 years has achieved greater symbolic value than preserving the integrity of the Arctic Refuge. Only a few hardy visitors have seen this South Carolina–sized chunk of far northeastern Alaska, but even so nearly everyone has an opinion on whether it should be converted from wildlife refuge to industrial wasteland. In recent years the fate of the refuge has graduated from a political litmus test for environmentalists to a fundamental schism between the American people and those who see this land only as an oil field-in-waiting. For most Americans, the refuge came to be where they drew the line; if the oil industry could spoil this remote, wild region, nothing was safe. For the boomers, George W. Bush's campaign trail declarations that he favored drilling were a clear tip-off that their enormous financial investment in his election might, this time, actually pay off. (His father, after all, had let them down.) And for Bush's right-wing cheering squad, the test of his mettle was his success in taking on and crushing the environmentalists' precious wonderland.

The Arctic National Wildlife Refuge was set aside in 1960 by President Dwight Eisenhower. Under Jimmy Carter, most of it was protected as wilderness. The coastal plain, however, where the oil industry dreamed of finding a jumbo oil field to rival the North Slope, was left in limbo: not protected wilderness but not available for drilling without an act of Congress. Ever since, industry and its congressional allies have fought and clawed to gain access. Environmentalists had saved the refuge once by filibuster and twice by presidential veto (thank you, Bill Clinton). The margins were always narrow, but each time the number of senators willing to defend this far-off wilderness increased. Over the years, polls showed a slow, steady growth in America's commitment to the refuge as a principle worth defending—that pristine, wild places are not only more valuable than oil but are not for sale at any price.

Any Excuse to Drill: Pumping as Panacea

From the earliest days of his administration, Bush and his lieutenants pushed drilling in the Arctic Refuge, zealously but never very convincingly. This may be, as we shall see, because the most noteworthy reasons—preserving Alaska as a welfare state and using refuge drilling as a wedge to exploit other places considered off-limits—were unmentionable. Unable to name the real issues, they sought to attach Arctic drilling to the tail of every passing crisis. First it was touted as the solution to California's electricity woes. Leaving alone the fact that California's crisis was caused by rapacious energy companies, not lack of capacity (see chapter 6), the state does not even generate any electricity from oil. Even if it did, and even if Congress voted immediately to sanction oil exploration, the first tanker full of coastal plain crude could not possibly dock at El Segundo or Richmond for fifteen years.

Next came September 11. The attack on the World Trade Center sobered most members of Congress, but Alaska Senator Frank Murkowski (R) was unchastened. Almost immediately he began beating the drum for opening the refuge, claiming that its oil would protect America from unreliable foreign oil sources. Fellow senators were embarrassed and tried to ignore him, but every day he was out on the Capitol lawn holding another press conference. The administration waited a week and then cautiously picked up Murkowski's pitch. On September 20, however, Murkowski took the Senate floor to hotly deny that he was seeking to attach Arctic drilling to an upcoming defense appropriation bill, saying that doing so "would be inappropriate and in poor taste." The next day, Oklahoma Senator James Inhofe (R) offered just such a measure. "He's always seen energy policy as a national security issue," an aide explained.

Environmentalists argued that Arctic oil was already peculiarly susceptible to terrorist attacks, especially along the Alyeska Pipeline running between the North Slope oil fields and the port of Valdez. Should someone blow up the pipeline in midwinter, they pointed out, 800 miles of oil would freeze into "the world's largest Chapstick" and could not be thawed until the following August, meanwhile cutting off 18 percent of America's oil supplies. Driving home the point, a drunken hunter in 2001 shot a hole in the pipeline, shutting down the flow of oil for a week, fortunately just before the freeze. Energy analyst Amory Lovins, along with the U.S. Army, shuddered at the difficulty of defending the pipeline from terrorists. "Why on earth would the United States want to create another Strait of Hormuz?" Lovins acidly commented. "One is quite enough."

Then the administration claimed that Arctic oil would lead the country to "energy independence." Even Bush's allies at the libertarian Cato Institute mocked this argument as "beyond nonsense. To paraphrase Jeremy Bentham, it's nonsense on stilts." Cato pointed out that "government policies that restrict drilling on attractive public lands in Alaska and off America's coasts aren't primarily responsible for our heavy reliance on imported oil. This is: It costs between $5.00 and $7.50 to produce a barrel of domestic oil versus about $1.50 to produce a barrel of Saudi crude."

Ignoring the cost issue (oddly, for a free-marketeer), Gale Norton told the House Committee on Resources that, according to the U.S. Geological Survey (USGS), the Arctic Refuge has an estimated 10.4 billion barrels of technically recoverable oil. "The potential daily production . . . is larger than the current daily onshore oil production of any of the lower 48 states," she said, calling the refuge our "nation's single greatest onshore prospect for future oil." But her 10.4 billion figure is disingenuous; "technically recoverable" means how much oil could be extracted using modern methods "without regard to cost." The more telling figure is the "economically recoverable" amount; at today's oil prices, the USGS's mean estimate is about 6 billion barrels. (If prices fell to $16 a barrel, the figure would drop to zero.) Since the United States uses about 20 million barrels of oil a day, 6 billion barrels works out to a 300-day supply—hardly "energy independence."

("Even at its peak," writes economist Paul Krugman, "oil production from the Arctic National Wildlife Refuge would reduce imports by no more than would a 3-mile-per-gallon increase in fuel efficiency—something easily achievable, were it not for opposition from special interest groups. . . . Or put it this way: Total world oil production is about 75 million barrels per day, of which the United States consumes almost 20; ANWR would produce, at maximum, a bit more than 1 million." Until it was used up.)

Finally, as manufacturing jobs drained out of the country to Mexico, Latin America, and Southeast Asia, Arctic drilling became the ticket to jobs. A useful byproduct of this attack, from the White House's point of view, was that it might split up the powerful alliance of the environmental lobby and organized labor. The building trades unions, which would build the new facilities, had always supported drilling in the Arctic, but in 2001 the administration recruited one of the biggest and most politically potent unions, the Teamsters, to lead the charge. "This is about jobs in America," said Teamsters President James P. Hoffa, claiming that drilling would produce 750,000 jobs. Drilling foes easily demolished the calculation. After first claiming "they don't know what they are talking about," Teamster Vice President Jerry Hood admitted in a debate before the Senate Democratic caucus, "We don't know how many jobs it will create, but even if it's 50,000, they are good jobs and we want them." Labor leaders noted that Hoffa was hoping the government would end federal oversight of his union for its previous history of corruption, and they hinted at a deal. Other unions, like the service employees and the electrical workers, opposed drilling in the Arctic. Hoffa's pressure produced a narrow majority in the House for drilling but never moved the crucial block of moderate Republicans and Democrats in the Senate.

Snow Job on the Tundra

Accompanying these far-fetched pitches to the public was a truly remarkable set of exercises in legislative sausage making. Bush, Norton, and the Alaska congressional junta tried every trick in the congressional playbook to ram drilling through, and then invented some new ones. In Bush's 2002 budget, for example, he presumed revenues from a lease sale in the refuge that would generate $2.4 billion. Until that check cleared, he proposed taking the money from the amount appropriated for renewable energy—a crude form of blackmail.

The hostage strategy did not work, so the White House tried to purchase a filibuster-proof majority, dangling the promise of federal guarantees for steelworker pensions before Jay Rockefeller (D-W.Va.) and other steel-state senators, in exchange for support on the Arctic. Senate Minority Leader Tom Daschle (D-S.Dak.) called the ploy "a desperation move that shows that they don't have the votes on ANWR, and they're trying to do almost anything, even things they don't believe in, to get it done." After another failed vote in 2003, staffers for Arkansas senators reported that the administration had been inquiring what policy or pork for their home state might bring them around to vote for drilling. And Minnesota's Norm Coleman (R), elected to the Senate after the tragic death of environmental hero Paul Wellstone, hinted in late 2003 that he might vote for drilling in exchange for $800 million in federal loan guarantees for a giant new power plant in northeast Minnesota. The votes still were not there.

In an attempt to pacify Congress, Norton tried to minimize environmental concerns about Arctic drilling. "I believe that we can ensure that any exploration and development of the oil and natural gas reserves in the 1002 Area [the coastal plain] of ANWR can be conducted in a manner that is protective of the environment and minimizes impacts on wildlife in the area," Norton told Congress. That would be a miracle, given that Arctic oil could be profitable only if produced very cheaply. The industry customarily accomplishes this by cutting corners—for example, by blocking plans to have tankers in the Prince William Sound escorted by tugs (the lack of which allowed the *Exxon Valdez* to go on the rocks), or simply by failing to maintain pipes, valves, and flanges at the production fields at Prudhoe Bay. That facility generates twice as much air pollution as Washington, D.C., and suffers more than 400 oil spills a year. Truckers on the haul road fitted their cabs with $2,000 bars to protect them from collisions with moose and caribou. ("Those caribou are just dumb," one trucker said. "A whole herd will run right at you.") In March 2002, two whistle-blowers from BP Exploration met with Senate staffers. One of them, Robert Brian, who had worked at Prudhoe Bay for 22 years, testified that the company was "putting Prudhoe workers and the environment at risk" and that "[w]orking for BP is like working for a drunk driver that is your boss and insists on driving you home."

Norton also had to deal with the bad scientific news that kept threatening to complicate the rosy picture she was painting of caribou frolicking around the pipelines. In March 2001, USGS contract mapmaker Ian Thomas sent out an e-mail that was forwarded widely and reprinted in the *Earth Island Journal*:

> I have been fired for posting to the internet a single web page with some maps showing the distribution of caribou calving areas in the Arctic National Wildlife Refuge (ANWR). My entire website was … removed from the internet. This represents about 3 years worth of work and 20,000 plus maps showing bird, mammal and amphibian distributions, satellite imagery, land cover and vegetation maps for countries and protected areas all around of the globe.

Thomas's offending map showed that the heart of the calving area for the mighty Porcupine caribou herd was smack in the middle of the "1002 Area," the oil-rich coastal plain. Unfortunately for his career, it came at a time when Norton was asserting that caribou calving "occurred primarily outside the 1002 Area in 11 of the last 18 years." It was subsequently revealed that Norton had been supplied with data from the Fish and Wildlife Service that noted "calving concentrations within the 1002 area for 27 of 30 years." Norton also omitted data showing that the caribou calved less frequently than normal in developed areas near Prudhoe Bay. She said there "was no evidence" of adverse effects at the Kaktovik oil field—without mentioning that no research had been done to examine such effects. Public Employees for Environmental Responsibility, a whistle-blowing group of federal employees, blasted the secretary: "It appears Secretary Norton misled Congress and broke her pledge to faithfully convey the best science on the Arctic Refuge." They called for her resignation. The *Washington Post* quoted a Fish and Wildlife official saying, "We tried to present the facts, but she only passed along the ones she liked. And to pass along facts that are false, well, that's obviously inappropriate."

Norton apologized for "mischaracterizing" the data, but that did not stop her from doing the same thing a few months later when presented with a report based on twelve years of research by biologists in the Alaska Science Center of the USGS. The study detailed the damage that Arctic oil development would do to musk oxen, snow geese, caribou, and other wildlife. Norton's press secretary rejected the study as "science fiction," and Norton gave the scientists ten days to produce a new, more agreeable report, which required all of two pages.

Bush and Norton also sought to literally minimize the problem, touting the "smaller footprint" that modern technology would supposedly give to the oil infrastructure on the plain. "The impact will be limited to just 2,000 out of 1.9 million acres of the Refuge," said Norton. It turned out, however, that she was not counting roads linking the drilling rigs spread out across the refuge or even the ground beneath a raised pipeline—just the concrete posts that actually touch the ground. ("By those definitions," wrote Krugman, "my 'impact' is limited to floor areas that literally have stuff resting on them: the bottoms of the legs on my desk and chair, and the soles of my shoes. The rest of my office floor is pristine wilderness.")

Bush's Interior Department promoted the drilling pads at newer North Slope oil fields like the Alpine as the sort of environmentally friendly technology it foresaw for the Arctic Refuge. They urged reporters to go and see; the *Washington Post* did. While conceding that Alpine was unquestionably superior to the older fields at Prudhoe Bay, reporter William Booth warned: "There is, however, no escaping the fact that Alpine is a major industrial complex that can be seen and heard from miles away. It is powered by roaring turbines as loud as jets and visited by a half-dozen flights a day. Its drilling tower rises above the tundra and a gas flare ignites the sky like a Roman candle." Not exactly a quiet nursery for a caribou mom and her calf.

Alaska's Dirty Secret

If drilling in the Arctic Refuge was not needed for national security, would not be economical, and would likely be environmentally devastating, why then did the Bush administration invest so much political capital in its losing Arctic battle? Not even the oil giants were deeply invested in the issue. "Let me put it this way," one oil executive dryly explained. "We spend a lot more time talking about Kazakhstan in board meetings than we do about Alaska." Since refuge oil would be very expensive, no one would ever make a killing on it—and if world oil prices rose high enough to bring the refuge into production, then the amount of money to be made from an Arctic play could be dwarfed by gaining access to cheap Caspian oil at $5 a barrel.

The mystery can be solved by heeding the advice of legendary Watergate source Deep Throat—"Follow the money"—and seeing who has been paying for all the lobbying for Arctic drilling. Almost all of the cash has come from the state of Alaska itself: $8 million over the past ten years. The oil companies do not care where their oil comes from, but Alaskan politicians care desperately— as do the national politicians who rely on the mercurial Alaskan congressional delegation in a narrowly divided Senate.

Alaska votes as if it were filled with rock-ribbed Ayn Randians, fiercely independent opponents of big government. But Alaska's well-kept secret is that it is America's last great welfare state. Unlike other states, Alaska keeps half of the royalties from oil extracted from federal lands, a portion of which is distributed each year in direct payments to every resident: man, woman, or child, rich or poor. Alaskans pay no state sales tax or income tax; instead, the state pays them—in 2003, $1,107.53 each.

Such largesse is unprecedented outside such oil emirates as Brunei and Kuwait. Although most rural Alaskans use the funds to meet subsistence needs, for many urban residents it is "mad money," used to buy toys ranging from snowmobiles to "feather boas, vinyl miniskirts, platform shoes and leather corsets." Alaskans used to this annual handout do not want to give it up. With oil from Prudhoe Bay on the decline, Alaskans (and Alaskan politicians) look to the Arctic National Wildlife Refuge to maintain the standard of living to which they have become accustomed.

(The failure of the Alaskan delegation to deliver the goods may be taking its toll. In January 2003, Frank Murkowski left the U.S. Senate to become governor, appointing his daughter Lisa to his Senate seat. When Congress wisely declined to include refuge drilling in the otherwise horrendous 2003 omnibus energy bill, political observers like Charles Cook, an independent analyst and author of *The Cook Political Report,* concluded that this seat, hitherto safe for the Republicans, was now at risk. Even Alaska Teamsters thought the obsession with the Arctic was hurting them. The first chance they got, they turned Frank Hood out of office as head of his Local 959, with many citing his closeness to Murkowski and the administration over the Arctic as the reason.)

Alaskan politics aside, the radicals in the administration and Congress— particularly the Texans—had another reason for their pursuit of Arctic oil. Tom DeLay, in a closed and (he thought) confidential meeting of House Republicans, spilled the beans. "It's about the precedent," he said. If he could get drilling permitted there, it would happen everywhere else (except, he conceded, "the coast of California").

Republican vote counters, however, knew that the numbers were not there for violating the Arctic Refuge. So Bush took the easy way out: by executive fiat, he ordered in November 2003 the opening of 9 million acres of the National Petroleum Reserve–Alaska to oil and gas development. The strategic reserve, located to the west of the Arctic National Wildlife Refuge on the North Slope, is believed to hold substantial oil reserves, although they are not as easily accessible as on the flat coastal plain of the refuge. It is a breeding ground for caribou and birds, and a source of subsistence hunting and traditional gathering for the Inupiat village of Wainwright. But despoiling it lies within the power of the president alone, and that, in the administration's eyes, is its primary value.

"Eppur si muove." ("And yet it moves.")

—Attributed to Galileo Galilei, as he left the Inquisition hearing
that found him guilty of heresy for believing that the
earth revolves around the sun

"Scientific information is not neutral in a policy context. . . . In a political world, knowledge, whether about species or oil, is a powerful weapon."

—Fred Smith, Competitive Enterprise Institute

"In order to obtain a certain result, you must want to obtain precisely that result. . . . I need only such people as will obtain the results I need."

—Trofim Lysenko, Stalin's favorite scientist

"Science, like any field of endeavor, relies on freedom of inquiry, and one of the hallmarks of that freedom is objectivity. Now more than ever, on issues ranging from climate change to AIDS research to genetic engineering to food additives, government relies on the impartial perspective of science for guidance."

—President George H. W. Bush

Strategic Ignorance
Choosing the Facts That Fit

Why would our government lie to us about something this big?

Immediately after the collapse of the World Trade Center in the attacks of September 11, 2001, scientists at the Environmental Protection Agency gathered as much data as they could on the health risks caused by the fires and airborne debris. Based on that research, the agency quickly drafted a press release warning of high asbestos levels in lower Manhattan and of risks to "sensitive populations" such as the elderly and asthmatics. The EPA also intended to caution property owners that their homes and businesses would need professional cleanup to remove asbestos, heavy metals, and other contaminants. But the White House objected, fearing it would hamper the "return to normalcy." Even while George W. Bush expressed compassion for the victims and support for the rescue workers and residents of lower Manhattan, including a dramatic visit to Ground Zero, his White House spin doctors took their blue pencils to the agency's announcement.

"Our tests show that it is safe for New Yorkers to go back to work in New

York's financial district," announced the rewritten statement, released on September 16. The reference to sensitive populations was deleted. The asbestos warning was replaced with an assurance that "ambient air quality meets OSHA [Occupational Safety and Health Administration] standards and consequently is not a cause for public concern." OSHA standards, however, assume limited hours in a workplace as well as appropriate protective equipment. The need for professional contractors to clean homes and offices was watered down to a general recommendation that people should follow instructions from city officials.

Two years later, in August 2003, the EPA's Office of Inspector General concluded that the findings had been manipulated. "Competing considerations, such as national security concerns and the desire to reopen Wall Street . . . played a role in EPA's air quality statements." (Another "competing interest," apparently, was the desire to downplay New York's need for federal help and to protect the president's cherished tax cuts. When New York officials complained that promised federal aid was slow in coming, White House Budget Director Mitch Daniels accused them of playing "money-grubbing games.") The inspector general's report came too late for thousands of people like Pat Moore, who cleaned up the three feet of dust and debris in her apartment herself because "no one told us about the possible risks." It was too late for the Ground Zero workers, 78 percent of whom, according to Mount Sinai Hospital, suffered from lung ailments after their service at the disaster site.

On September 11, Stuyvesant High School, in the neighborhood of the twin towers, had been evacuated. It reopened October 9, as a symbol of a city that refused to yield to terrorists. Two years later, Jenna Orkin, whose son was at Stuyvesant, thinks that "[a]ll that happened too quickly. School started again, but for months World Trade Center detritus was dumped . . . just behind the school. The ventilation system stayed open and contaminated the whole building. A study showed that 60 percent of teachers were having respiratory problems. But the children have not been tested at all. Yet, many parents report that their children have developed chronic sinusitis or asthma."

A private testing firm found asbestos levels of 850,000 fibers per square centimeter in the Woolworth Building, just across from city hall—more than eight times the level considered "high" by federal standards. Other tests found heavy asbestos loads in a stairwell used by employees of the Securities and Exchange Commission. Robert Gulack, senior counsel for the SEC, who developed bronchitis after the attack, charged that the stairwell had been recontaminated by the failure to clean the exterior of the building. "They rushed us back into contaminated playgrounds and schools and places of business," Gulack said. "They took it upon themselves to decide what we would be told and what might be too upsetting for us to know." When New York City firefighters asked to have their stations tested for toxic contamination, the administration refused.

If Bush and his backers are willing to lie about something as emotionally riveting to the nation as Ground Zero, we are on very shaky ground indeed. Ronald Reagan once said that "facts are stupid things," but Bush feels free to dispense with them altogether when it suits his purposes. This approach has made his the most incurious, anti-scientific presidency in our nation's history. (When asked who he thought was a typical Democrat, Karl Rove suggested "someone with a Ph.D.")

Science has not been so intensely politicized since the quack Soviet agronomist Trofim Lysenko convinced Joseph Stalin that genetics and evolution were "bourgeois science," contrary to the tenets of dialectical materialism. (Today's know-nothings deride results they dislike as "junk science.") Lysenko's pet theory of "vernalization" held that variation within a population was due to environment, not genetics; if seeds were soaked in cold water, he believed, they would grow in cold climates. He did not need much evidence for this view because, as historian Helena Sheehan points out, his research methods "were seriously lacking in rigor, to put it mildly. His habit was to report only successes. His results were based on extremely small samples, inaccurate records, and the almost total absence of control groups.... He was capable of the crudest anti-intellectualism, remarking on one occasion: 'It is better to know less, but to know just what is necessary for practice.'"

Yet Lysenko knew what Stalin wanted to hear, and he quickly advanced to the top rungs of Soviet science—literally over the bodies of genuine biologists, many of whom were exiled to the gulags or even shot as "enemies of the people." When Lysenko's socialist agronomy was put into practice on the collective farms of the Soviet Union (and, later, Maoist China), millions died in the resultant famines.

Politicized science is not quite so crude these days, but it could be as deadly—especially should the more dire global warming scenarios come to pass. Up to now, scientists have enjoyed far greater public credibility than either politicians or the media have, but that could be in jeopardy if manipulated science comes to be seen as just another tool to help the party in power achieve its ends—in this case, a rollback of much of the social and environmental change that took place in the twentieth century. To ideologues, whether of the left or the right, nonpartisan, objective inquiry can be deeply threatening, and scientific findings have often undermined Bush's political efforts. Biology, for example, has shown that wildlife and fish are finite resources that need habitat and clean water; epidemiology, that the burning of coal kills thousands of people; forestry, that big trees are more fire resistant than tree farms; meteorology, that burning fossil fuels contributes to the warming of the earth's atmosphere. The questing, challenging nature of scientific inquiry is not a friend to ideologues longing for a past era of reckless exploitation and weak regulations.

Bush signaled his intentions early on when his new administration removed from government Web sites, particularly the EPA's, scientific reports reflecting the scientific consensus on the seriousness of environmental problems such as global warming. This was accompanied by a dramatic shift in the flow of federal dollars to scientific research. In making a modest 8 percent cut in the budget for the U.S. Geological Survey in 2001, Interior Secretary Gale Norton cut the research and development budget of the National Water Quality Laboratory by 70 percent—even though (or was it because?) the lab had been responsible for ferreting out the biggest drinking water threat of the past decade: the role of MTBE as a water pollutant. The cuts also would largely eliminate the National Biological Information Infrastructure, a program designed to allow researchers to find ecological information easily through a centralized system. EPA STAR (Science to Achieve Results) fellowships, the only federally funded graduate fellowships for environmental research, were eliminated in the president's proposed 2003 budget. When public protest persuaded Congress to restore them, the administration fell back on an effort to cut them by 50 percent in 2004.

"The Politics Dictate What Science Can Be Used"

New to the arena of foreign policy and lacking in international contacts, Bush initially clung fast to his relationship with Mexican President Vicente Fox. One of Mexico's most pressing foreign policy objectives was to find a way for its tuna fleet to break into the lucrative U.S. market. The problem was that the Mexican fleet still caught tuna by chasing the dolphins that often swim above tuna schools, a practice forbidden by "dolphin-safe" U.S. standards.

Rather than persuading the Mexicans to change their fishing methods, the Bush administration sought to change the definition of "dolphin safe." Doing so apparently necessitated shutting down the research of two government scientists affiliated with the Southwest Fisheries Science Center in San Diego, California: Albert Myrick and Sarka Southern, who were demonstrating that the practice of chasing and encircling dolphins to get at tuna subjected the protected mammals to dangerous degrees of stress. These findings could explain why dolphin populations in the Pacific are failing to bounce back, despite the supposed dolphin-safe fishing methods. Their research, which showed that some dolphins are chased more than ten times a year and caught in nets more than three times a year, was suppressed until it was leaked to the press.

Dr. Southern described to the *New York Times* how her supervisor had ordered her to withhold her findings: "He came to my office and said that I have to understand that there's science and there's politics, and the politics dictate what sorts of science can be used." Subsequently, U.S. District Court Judge Thelton Henderson blocked the Bush administration from relaxing the dolphin-safe rule. His reasoning was that the decision to change the dolphin-safe definition appeared to have been influenced more by international trade policies than scientific evidence.

Tell Me What I Want to Hear

In order to craft policy in a complex world, presidents rely on scientific advisory committees, composed of leading experts in a variety of specialized fields. The intention has always been to mobilize the nation's top scientists to provide the best available advice to policy makers. The composition of these committees is governed by the Federal Advisory Committee Act, which requires that they be "fairly balanced in terms of the points of view represented" and not "inappropriately influenced by the appointing authority or any special interest."

Given what Bush has done to the federal advisory committees, that requirement sounds almost naive. He eliminated some committees altogether, like the secretary of health and human services' Advisory Committee on Genetic Testing, which had been formed to deal with the complex issues around the burgeoning gene-testing industry. In September 2002, members were informed that the committee's charter would not be renewed. "We were making real headway with informed-consent issues and with categorizing levels of risk," committee member Wylie Burke told the *Washington Post.* "It would be a shame if that does not get completed."

Since the very nature of the work of the Food and Drug Administration's Reproductive Health Drug Advisory Committee put it at odds with the Christian right, it did not stand a chance. The Department of Health and Human Services nominated as chair of the committee Dr. W. David Hager, a conservative religious activist most known for his opposition to the abortifacient RU-486 and his advice that women suffering from premenstrual syndrome should pray and read the Bible. (Hager ultimately was not appointed chair but does serve on the committee.)

The Advisory Committee to the Director of the National Center for Environmental Health, which had been assessing the effects of low-level exposure to environmental chemicals, was informed that fifteen of its eighteen members

...AND GEORGE CREATED SCIENCE ADVISERS IN HIS OWN IMAGE... AND HE SAW THAT IT WAS GOOD.

were to be replaced. The *Post* detailed the backgrounds of some of the committee's incoming members:

> They include Roger McClellan, former president of the Chemical Industry Institute of Toxicology, a North Carolina research firm supported by chemical company dues; Becky Norton Dunlop, a vice president of the Heritage Foundation [a right-wing think tank] who, as Virginia's secretary of natural resources, fought against environmental regulations; and Lois Swirsky Gold, a University of California risk-assessment specialist who has made a career countering environmentalists' claims of links between pollutants and cancer.
>
> The committee also includes Dennis Paustenbach, the California toxicologist who served as an expert witness for Pacific Gas and Electric when the utility was sued for allowing poisonous chromium to leach into groundwater. The case was made famous in the movie, "Erin Brockovich."

(In thousands of theaters around the nation, audiences cheered when Brockovich bested the polluters' attorneys. In the White House, they said, "We need those guys on our team.")

Even the Centers for Disease Control's Advisory Committee on Childhood Lead Poisoning Prevention was not safe from the administration's meddling. In October 2002, the panel was studying whether to toughen federal standards for lead exposure, last set in 1991. Since then, a wealth of new studies showed that children exposed to even very small amounts of lead could suffer cognitively and suggested that federal standards be tightened. Shortly before the committee took up the issue, however, the Department of Health and Human Services rejected five nominations to the committee by staff scientists. Those named in their places included a consultant to a lead-smelting company, a toxicologist who served as a paid defense witness in lead-paint liability trials (who once denied any connection between lead exposure and cognitive problems in children at all—"I don't think anybody has determined that"), and a hematologist recruited by the lead industry who had opposed the 1991 standards. "Keep in mind," wrote the *New Republic* in its exposé of the committee stacking, "that companies with a significant financial stake in lead-poisoning issues—everybody from Dow Chemical to Dupont to ExxonMobil—all gave disproportionately to the Republicans in the 2000 and 2002 campaigns."

These brazen efforts went far beyond anything the U.S. scientific establishment had previously experienced and led to uncharacteristically harsh denunciations in the leading scientific journals. "Any further right-wing incursions on expert panels' membership," warned *The Lancet*, "will cause a terminal decline in public trust in the advice of scientists." An editorial appeared in *Science*, signed by ten top scientists: "Scientific advisory committees do not exist to tell the secretary [of Health and Human Services] what he wants to hear but to help the secretary, and the nation, address complex issues," they wrote. "Regulatory paralysis appears to be the goal here, rather than the application of honest balanced science."

The *Science* editorial sparked a deluge of comments from other scientists and a follow-up editorial: "The present epidemic, in which advisory committees are shut down and reassembled with new members, and candidates are subjected to loyalty tests, seems old hat to some observers. 'After all, that's fairly standard practice,' we have been told by officials in [Health and Human Services]. Well it isn't—or at least it wasn't."

One nominee to an advisory committee on muscular dystrophy told *Science* of being queried by a White House staffer "about her views on various Bush administration policies, none of them related to the work of the committee." A nominee to the National Council on Drug Abuse was asked if he had voted for Bush, "and on being informed that he had not, asked 'Why didn't you support the president?'"

"What's unusual about the current epidemic is not that the Bush administration examines candidates for compatibility with its 'values,'" concluded *Science*. "It's how deep the practice cuts; in particular, the way it now invades areas once immune to this kind of manipulation."

Fish out of Water: Rove and the Klamath

At her January 2001 confirmation hearing, soon-to-be Interior Secretary Gale Norton made this pledge: "I am absolutely committed to the idea that the decision making should be based on the best science, on the best analysis of environmental issues that we can find."

It soon became evident that the "best science," in the secretary's view, was that which best agreed with the business plans of her boss's corporate sponsors. Speaking perhaps more candidly than he ought, Thomas Sansonetti, part of the Bush-Cheney transition team for the Interior Department, had this praise for the incoming secretary: "She understands the system. She is very good on national park issues and on Endangered Species Act law. There won't be any biologists or botanists . . . to come in and pull the wool over her eyes."

Norton lived up to that praise by repeatedly refusing to let the facts get in the way of her predetermined policy goals. In January 2001, Norton's Interior Department reversed a long-held position, confirmed by studies in 1995 and 1997, that oil drilling in the Arctic would contravene a 1973 international treaty to protect polar bears. "Despite the earlier reports," the Associated Press blandly noted, "Fish and Wildlife scientists more recently concluded that the risks to polar bears are minimal if oil development in the refuge is properly regulated." ("Out with the old 'good' science, in with the new 'bad' science," commented Charles Clusen, the Natural Resources Defense Council's program director for national parks and Alaska.)

In April 2001, using criteria and standards established by the Endangered Species Act, the Fish and Wildlife Service and the National Marine Fisheries Service (NMFS) determined that additional releases of fresh water into Oregon and California's Klamath River were needed to protect threatened salmon and endangered suckerfish. When farmers protested and illegally opened headgates to divert fishery water supplies to irrigate their fields, Interior asked the National Research Council to review the issue, using weaker standards and criteria. The council's review indicated that there was incomplete information on the subject, and therefore the issue remained open. In response to this finding, Interior overturned the decision of its own scientists and allowed farmers to divert fishery water supplies to irrigation. The result was the deaths of 33,000 salmon—the biggest fish kill in the river's history.

In October 2002, a month after the fish kill, Michael Kelley, a biologist with the NMFS, came forward and stated that the Bush administration, through the Bureau of Reclamation, had pressured the NMFS to override its own scientists. "Morale is low among scientists here," Kelley said. "We are under pressure to get the right results. This administration is putting species at risk for political gains—and not just on the Klamath." Meanwhile, a major Interior report on the Klamath, known as the Hardy Phase 2 Report, had been held in final draft form since November 2001, according to the scientists involved in its peer review, because the administration did not like its conclusions. The same fate befell an economic study by the U.S. Geological Survey showing that water released for fisheries generates 30 times the economic benefit per acre-foot of water used for irrigation. Although it has been fully peer reviewed, the study has been kept from public release.

"This government does a better job of hiding data it doesn't like than Saddam Hussein does of hiding his weapons," said Zeke Grader, executive director of the Pacific Coast Federation of Fishermen's Associations. "The stench of the recent fish kill in the Klamath River is permeating to the highest levels of the Bush administration."

It turned out that the Bureau of Reclamation had some expert assistance in managing the science on the Klamath. Three months before the headgates were opened to release water for irrigation, not fisheries, Karl Rove had made one of his PowerPoint presentations to "50 top managers at the U.S. Interior Department," the *Wall Street Journal* reported. Rove had just returned from a swing through Oregon with the president and was worried about the re-election prospects of Senator Gordon Smith. Rove's presentation to the managers spoke not of temperatures or water quality but of "poll results, critical constituencies and water levels in the Klamath." The Interior Department staff defended their professionalism, leading the agency's inspector general to launch an investigation into the possibility of political tampering.

As Trofim Lysenko put it, "I need only such people as will obtain the results I need."

Gale the Goddess

Not every abuse of science began with the Bush administration. Even under Clinton, the White House was knowingly and deliberately starving the Fish and Wildlife Service of the funds and scientists it needs to carry out the Endangered Species Act. The ESA requires the government to identify species at risk for extinction and to map out the habitat they need to recover. Less money means that species go unlisted, which means no protected habitats, which means that strip mines, timber sales, highway projects, shopping centers, and housing developments can proceed unhindered.

Wildlife advocates sued repeatedly, and repeatedly won. In response to dozens of lawsuits brought by the Sierra Club, Earthjustice Legal Defense Fund, Defenders of Wildlife, the Center for Biological Diversity, and the Wilderness Society, federal judges consistently told the Department of the Interior to list species when the science showed they were endangered and to designate habitat once they were listed.

The ESA already had an escape hatch in the event that the president felt there was a serious conflict between the national interest and protecting a species. In such cases, a complex interagency mechanism popularly known as the "God Squad" could make a public and accountable determination that a project should proceed, even at the risk of extinction. In place of the God Squad, Bush proposed making Norton Goddess. Norton alone, the first Bush budget suggested, should be allowed to decide whether or not to list a species as endangered, and whether or not to designate and protect critical habitat once a species was listed. The justification was that citizen lawsuits were preventing Interior from "prioritizing" which species to list and protect. The complaint was not that the lawsuits were frivolous—their success rate, even among conservative federal judges, was overwhelming. California Representative Richard Pombo (R), one of the ESA's most bitter right-wing critics, noted that in 434 such cases judges had awarded attorney's fees to the citizens who sued. (Pombo called them "radical environmentalists.")

Interior attempted to dispense with the need to protect critical habitat by dispensing with the concept. Norton asked Congress to rule that 25 million acres of critical habitat owned by the Defense Department were immune from ESA requirements. And in May 2003, the administration simply declared that designating critical habitat for endangered species had no value for protecting wildlife. In doing so, Norton flatly ignored reports such as one by the National Academy of Sciences in 1995 declaring critical habitat to be "absolutely critical to species survival" and "an essential component of any program to protect endangered species." She also ignored the work of Fish and Wildlife scientists who demonstrated that species with designated critical habitat were much more likely to stabilize their populations and begin to move toward recovery than those for which no habitat had been designated. She suppressed two reports by the Fish and Wildlife Service showing that critical habitat designations dramatically increased the prospects for recovery of endangered species. And she ignored her own "commonsense" standard: how could a failing species be brought back, after all, if it has no place to live?

The Bush Scientific Method

Another trick was simply renaming things. Energy Secretary Spencer Abraham tried to reclassify highly radioactive waste as "incidental waste" so that he could simply abandon it in corroding, underground storage tanks in Idaho, New York, South Carolina, and Washington. The National Academy of Sciences warned Abraham that these hazards "will persist for centuries . . . millennia . . . or essentially forever." When a federal court told him he could not do as he wished, he turned to Congress for an exemption from the order.

By all available evidence, the Bush White House regards scientific findings as the raw material of spin, to be dribbled out, manipulated, or suppressed as suits the political needs of the moment. For example, after the National Association of Home Builders sued the Army Corps of Engineers over its proposed new protections for wetlands, the corps obligingly reversed course and proposed weakening the protections. Scientists at the Fish and Wildlife Service, not so adept at responding to the prevailing political winds, wrote in a report that the new rules would "encourage the destruction of stream channels and lead to increased loss of aquatic functions," and they criticized the corps for its "lack of basic knowledge of the effects of these permitted losses on the environment." This critique failed to reach the corps, however, because Interior Secretary Norton declined to pass it on. The *Washington Post* quoted former Fish and Wildlife Director Jamie Rappaport Clark: "This is just nuts. . . . For Interior to stop Fish and Wildlife from commenting on something of this magnitude and importance, that's really unbelievable."

A similar case of suppression occurred when the Interior Department was formulating new rules for snowmobile use in national parks—especially Yellowstone, where park personnel had taken to wearing gas masks to protect themselves against the fumes. In a draft letter to the EPA on the issue, Interior deleted the comments of its own scientists, who recommended that snowmobile emissions be reduced. Norton ended up recommending an *increase* in snowmobile traffic in the park.

In August 2002, the EPA released a draft report on the effects on groundwater of hydraulic fracturing, a technology used in producing coal-bed methane. The report pretended that the procedure would not pose an unacceptable risk to drinking water supplies, even though it showed estimates of chemical concentrations that exceeded drinking water standards. When this was pointed out, the EPA asked the oil and gas industry to help it rework the numbers. The new data, while inconsistent with the methodology of the earlier report, showed dramatically lower groundwater concentrations of these chemicals. Problem solved.

In an example of "No science is good science," the EPA flatly refused to appraise Clean Air Act proposals that conflicted with Bush's Clear Skies initiative. According to the *New York Times,* "Agency employees say they have been told either not to analyze or not to release information about mercury, carbon dioxide and other air pollutants." (This led Senator Joseph Lieberman [D-Conn.] to charge that "[t]his is an administration that lets its politics and ideology overwhelm and stifle scientific fact.") Specifically, the EPA refused to evaluate the proposed bipartisan substitute to Clear Skies by Senators Thomas Carper (D-Del.) and Lincoln Chaffee (R-R.I.), which a preliminary report showed to have some clear advantages. (See chapter 5.) "Is the analysis flawed? That is a legitimate reason for not releasing it," the *Times* quoted William Ruckelshaus, EPA director under Richard Nixon. "But if you don't like the outcome that might result from the analysis, that is not a legitimate reason."

For the first two years of the Bush administration, EPA scientist Bruce Boler tried to ensure that sprawl in South Florida did not threaten water quality in the state's fastest-growing counties. Boler, the government's top wetlands scientist in the region, was fired after objecting to the administration's use of a developer-funded study that claimed that natural wetlands actually made water pollution problems worse—a finding contradicted by thousands of peer-reviewed scientific studies showing that wetlands are among nature's major clean-up agents. (The developers, of course, used the study to show that, even if their projects destroyed wetlands, they actually improved water quality.)

When Mike Zahn, a Department of Agriculture scientist, discovered that antibiotic-resistant bacteria could migrate from factory feedlots to neighboring farms, he accepted an invitation to speak to family-farm advocates in Iowa. Pork industry lobbyists persuaded the USDA to forbid him to appear and to cancel scheduled appearances before county health commissions.

And when it turned out that some 20 million Americans in 43 states are drawing their water from sources contaminated with perchlorate, a cancer-causing chemical released in the production of rocket fuel, the Bush administration took the easy route: it yanked funding for a study designed to obtain data on whether perchlorate had contaminated the food supply. When the Environmental Working Group did the government's work for it, it found that dangerous levels of the chemical were, in fact, showing up in lettuce on supermarket shelves. The largest dumper of rocket fuel is the military, so Bush then asked that the military be exempted from laws that might have required a perchlorate cleanup and ordered the EPA not to release additional information on the chemical.

Bush and his backers routinely insist that whatever action they are taking is based on "sound science." But doing so must surely involve maintaining a spirit of independent inquiry, of deriving conclusions from the facts, of openness to the possibility that perhaps one is wrong. In the words of Eric Schaeffer, the EPA's head of regulatory enforcement who resigned his job in disgust over the administration's Clear Skies plan, "'Sound science' is a slogan so manipulated that it has lost its meaning. Sound science ought to mean independent, objective research that leads to informed decisions about how best to protect human health and the natural world. Instead, it has come to mean suppressing data that fails to justify desired outcomes and manufacturing data that does."

And that is no longer science at all.

"With all of the hysteria, all of the fear, all of the phony science, could it be that man-made global warming is the greatest hoax ever perpetrated on the American people? It sure sounds like it."

—Senator James Inhofe (R-Okla.)

God gave Noah the rainbow sign
No more water, the fire next time.

—Old spiritual

"The Earth is sending us a message and you don't have to be an environmentalist to read it. The Arctic ice is melting. The Arctic winds are balmy. The Arctic Ocean is rising. . . . In the face of this evidence, the government in Washington has declared war on nature. They have placed religious and political dogma over the facts."

—Journalist Bill Moyers

CHAPTER
10

See No Evil, Hear No Evil, Speak No Evil
Bush and Global Warming

These days, it takes an enormous effort to deny the gathering effects of global warming. The last decade of the twentieth century was the warmest in recorded history; the nine warmest years all occurred after 1990. The hottest year ever was 1998; the second hottest was 2001—until it was replaced by 2002. And 2003 proved to be the third hottest.

Of the 150 glaciers in Montana's Glacier National Park a century ago, only 35 remain. At this rate, within 30 years it will be Glacierless Park. In Tanzania, the snows of Kilimanjaro ("as wide as all the world, great, high, and unbelievably white in the sun," Ernest Hemingway called them) are vanishing and will be gone within 15 years. The tropical-latitude glaciers that crown the Andes are melting so fast that there is fear of flash floods. When they are gone, they will leave millions of people without a water source. In the summer of 2003, melting permafrost on Switzerland's Matterhorn rained huge rocks on climbers, forcing the closure of the mountain.

According to the Environmental Protection Agency, "Arctic temperatures

during the late 20th century appear to have been the warmest in 400 years."
Alaska is more than five degrees warmer than it was 30 years ago. The sea ice
that covers the North Pole has thinned by 40 percent over the past four decades
during late summer and early autumn; the summer of 2002 found it the scant-
iest in half a century at least. Shipping companies are looking forward to the
opening of an ice-free Northwest Passage. Temperatures on the Antarctic
Peninsula have risen four and a half degrees in the past half-century; this is
where a 1,250-square-mile section of the Larsen B ice shelf collapsed in March
2002 in a flurry of giant icebergs.

Tropical diseases like West Nile virus are spreading across the United
States, borne by mosquitoes that range increasingly widely. Warming temperatures are disrupting migration patterns of birds; six states are in danger of losing their state birds. Baltimore may soon be without orioles.

For the Bush White House, the challenge presented by global warming is
primarily rhetorical. Pollster Frank Luntz advised, in his leaked memo, that it
should always be referred to as "climate change," because "while global warming has catastrophic connotations attached to it, climate change sounds a more
controllable and less emotional challenge."

"Should the public come to believe that the scientific issues are settled, their
views about global warming will change accordingly," Luntz went on. "Therefore, you need to continue to make the lack of scientific certainty a primary
issue in the debate. . . . The scientific debate is closing (against us) but not yet
closed. There is still a window of opportunity to challenge the science."

Contrary to Luntz's assertion, the science is, in fact, settled. Greenhouse
gases—carbon dioxide, methane, water vapor, and certain other atmospheric
chemicals—absorb heat from the sun during the day and do not re-radiate it at
night, much as a blanket keeps our body heat in and the night cold out. The greater
the concentration of such gases in the atmosphere, the more heat and energy available to drive winds, storms, and other powerful aspects of global weather. Some
heat gets moved to the ocean, where it causes sea levels to rise (warm water takes
up more space than cold), causes currents to shift, and provides more power
to tropical storms. Melting glaciers also cause waters to rise, and changing
weather patterns bring drought to some areas and deluge to others.

The "debate" that Luntz wanted to keep alive was really a debate about the
details. How much greenhouse pollution was needed to make global climate

really unstable? How long would it take? And which areas would get colder and drier before they got hotter and wetter? Interesting and important scientific questions, but irrelevant to the basic question: Don't we owe it to ourselves and our children to stop overheating the planet?

Never Say "Warming"

Before Luntz's memo, Bush at least sometimes pronounced the words "global warming." (They vanished from his lexicon afterward.) During the 2000 campaign, he consistently attacked the Kyoto Protocol, the 1997 international agreement that requires industrial nations to reduce their emissions of greenhouse gases to 5 percent below 1990 levels. (Kyoto has now been signed by every major industrial country except the United States and Russia.) Even so, Bush stated repeatedly that global warming was a real phenomenon and committed himself to reducing emissions of carbon dioxide from power plants. (U.S. power plants alone account for 10 percent of global carbon dioxide emissions, about one-third of the U.S. total.)

At Bush's very first cabinet meeting, Treasury Secretary Paul O'Neill distributed a paper calling for a government program at the level of the Manhattan Project on climate change. According to syndicated columnist Robert Novak, "O'Neill's paper said: 'For these two issues—nuclear holocaust and global climate change—we may not get a second chance for it.'" O'Neill was joined by EPA Administrator Christie Todd Whitman in asking for a presidential statement. As Bush prepared his first State of the Union message, early drafts reaffirmed his pledge to control carbon dioxide.

Conservative activists heard that the speech was going to commit Bush to action on carbon dioxide, and they sprang into action. Even during the campaign, the oil industry press was calling the pledge "a Bush misstep on CO_2.... Regulation of CO_2 as an air pollutant is a bad idea that belongs on the outer fringes of environmental extremism." Industry and the right flooded the White House with protests. Novak, firmly in their camp, challenged Whitman the day before the State of the Union "and received a surprisingly unequivocal answer. 'George Bush was very clear during the course of the campaign that he believes in a multi-pollutant strategy, and that includes CO_2,' said Whitman. 'He has also been very clear that the science is good on global warming.' She added that 'introducing CO_2 to the discussion' is an 'important step' in confronting a 'real problem.'"

According to Jeremy Symons, at the time a climate policy adviser at the EPA, "[A]s soon as Whitman publicly reiterated the president's pledge in late February 2001, a debate ensued within the administration. White House aides drafted a six-page memorandum to John Bridgeland, who was then the president's deputy assistant for domestic policy. It listed the potential impacts on the coal industry, but devoted only six sentences to global warming."

Whitman and O'Neill expected the president to keep his promise. O'Neill even drafted a second memo: "Energy and the environment are in many ways the same problem," he wrote. "These subjects must be considered together." But the protests from the right prevailed, and Bush's first State of the Union was mum on the state of the atmosphere. While Novak warned that "the issue is far from settled," time would show the contrary. Bush's promise to deal with carbon dioxide was dead.

Only Whitman had not been told yet. At a G8 meeting in Italy, she reassured her fellow environmental ministers that the United States' waffling "does not represent a backing away from Kyoto." Upon her return, however, the White House issued a letter in which Bush reversed his campaign pledge and opined that the science on global warming was "incomplete." (As Luntz advised, "You need to continue to make the lack of scientific certainty a primary issue in the debate.") Days later, Bush formally rejected the Kyoto Protocol.

Given that the United States produces one-quarter of the world's carbon dioxide emissions, this announcement dismayed the international community. "I am horrified that the world's only remaining superpower can be so irresponsible towards the environment," said the environmental spokesperson for Germany's Social Democratic Party. Editorials and cartoonists subsequently depicted Whitman as embarrassingly undermined or out of the loop; Vice President Dick Cheney called her a "good soldier," an opinion seemingly confirmed when Whitman gamely continued to insist that both she and the president "take the issue of climate change very seriously."

Even with the U.S. rejection, the Kyoto Protocol has lingered on, waiting for sufficient signatures to take effect. Myron Ebell, director of global warming policy for the industry-sponsored Competitive Enterprise Institute, called it "a walking corpse," albeit one that he did not want to put to rest completely lest "something far worse" take its place. "We want to keep that corpse walking as long as possible," Ebell said. Regarding the president's action, Ebell predicted, "Bush may have some people who are not fully on board, like Whitman, but at bottom they're going to side with conservatives." On this issue, at least, he was dead right.

How the Pollution Lobby Stifles Science

The Bush administration's desperate attempts to cast doubt on the reality of global warming were ceaselessly buffeted by strongly worded scientific reports from the world's top scientists. Bush's response was to try to stifle the scientists and their inconvenient findings. The foremost international body speaking out on global warming was the Intergovernmental Panel on Climate Change, chaired by Dr. Robert Watson, a top scientist at NASA and the World Bank. Under his leadership, the IPCC had produced a groundbreaking report attributing warming to human activity. After the report came out, ExxonMobil sent a memo to the White House's Council on Environmental Quality (CEQ) asking, "Can Watson be replaced now at the request of the U.S.?" The answer, apparently, was yes: the State Department declined to support Watson's re-election, and he lost his chairmanship.

In June 2002, the EPA issued its "Climate Action 2002 Report," a document required under the Rio Convention on Climate Change (the agreement that Bush's father had signed and that later resulted in the Kyoto Protocol). The report concluded that recent changes to the climate "are likely due mostly to human activities" and that "continuing growth in greenhouse gas emissions is likely to lead to annual average warming over the United States that could be as much as several degrees Celsius (roughly 3 to 9 degrees Fahrenheit) during the 21st century." Such temperature increases, it warned, might be accompanied by "rising seas, melting ice caps and glaciers, ecological system disruption, floods, heat waves and more dangerous storms."

This conclusion, even though unaccompanied with strong prescriptions for how to cut greenhouse gases, alarmed the White House, which entered into an undercover dialogue with the Competitive Enterprise Institute. In a June 3,

2002, memo (later leaked to Greenpeace), Ebell writes to Phil Cooney, a senior CEQ official: "Thanks for calling and asking for our help," he says. "It's nice to know we're needed once in a while."

The "help" the White House was requesting was evidently for Ebell's think tank to undermine the EPA. "It seems to me that the folks at EPA are the obvious fall guys," wrote Ebell, "and we would only hope that the fall guy (or gal) should be as high up as possible. . . . Perhaps tomorrow we will call for Whitman to be fired."

Ebell had a price, though: "I think that what we can do is limited until there is an official statement from the Administration repudiating the report." Two days later, Bush openly dismissed the results of years of work by federal scientists as "the report put out by the bureaucracy." Ebell's group subsequently sued, seeking to invalidate the report by challenging its use of computer models. After Ebell's tête-à-tête with the White House became public, the attorneys general of Connecticut and Maine asked Attorney General John Ashcroft to investigate, saying that "Mr. Ebell's response . . . suggests that CEQ may have been directly involved in efforts to undermine the United States' official reports, as well as the authority of the EPA Administrator." No response from Ashcroft was forthcoming.

What About the Kids?

When Bush rejected Kyoto, he promised to present an alternative plan through which "we can grow our economy and, at the same time, through technologies, improve our environment." He also called for further research to study supposed "scientific uncertainties." Practically, his alternative approach never amounted to anything more than some halfhearted voluntary measures. Having capitulated to his right-wing base, which did not admit global warming was happening at all, Bush was hard put to come up with policies to slow it down.

The most prominent feature of the administration's global warming plan continued to be denial. In September 2002, the White House simply removed the global warming section from the EPA's annual report on air pollution trends, even though the agency had reported on the topic in each of the previous six years. In June 2003, an EPA report billed as "the first-ever national picture of environmental quality and human health in the United States" had to first pass by West Wing censors, who insisted on making "major edits" to the global warming section. According to the *New York Times*, "The editing eliminated references to many studies concluding that warming is at least partly caused by rising concentrations of smokestack and tail-pipe emissions and could threaten health and ecosystems." Blue pencils at the CEQ and John Graham's shop at the Office of Management and Budget "also deleted a reference to a 1999 study showing that global temperatures had risen sharply in the previous decade compared with the last 1,000 years. In its place, administration officials added a reference to a new study, partly financed by the American Petroleum Institute, questioning that conclusion."

An internal memo from EPA staff warned that, as edited by the White House, the section "no longer accurately represents scientific consensus on climate change." To its credit, the EPA simply deleted the section rather than publish spurious information.

In its crusade to keep all heads firmly planted in the sand, the administration even denied information about global warming to Congress. Senators John McCain (R-Ariz.) and Joseph Lieberman (D-Conn.) asked the EPA for an analysis of a global warming plan they were proposing, which included the mandatory measures Bush had rejected. (Lieberman acknowledged that the plan was not even up to the level of Kyoto, "but it's the first realistic U.S. proposal to deal with the problem.") The EPA refused, per its directive to ignore any proposals that conflicted with Clear Skies. Lieberman called the denial "totally unacceptable."

Environmentalists and others who favor action on global warming, Luntz had warned the president, have a very powerful argument—as he paraphrased it, "The future will be a better place if we take the necessary action today." To undermine this message of hope, Luntz advised Republicans to talk about how "unnecessary environmental regulation hurts moms and dads, grandmas and grandpas." What about the kids? It's a notable omission—but one that those who ignore the clear signs of global warming have chosen to make.

"We are not afraid to entrust the American people with unpleasant facts, foreign ideas, alien philosophies, and competitive values. For a nation that is afraid to let its people judge the truth and falsehood in an open market is a nation that is afraid of its own people."

—John F. Kennedy

"There's been a constant, steady erosion of the prerogatives and the power in the Oval Office, a continual encroachment by Congress.... [T]he office is weaker today than it was 30, 35 years ago. What we're committed to is to make sure we preserve the office at least as strong as we found it for our successors."

—Vice President Dick Cheney

"It was fun. When I wanted to build a road up a watershed when I first started out as a ranger in the BLM, all I did was take a bulldozer and start pushing dirt. I didn't have to consult with anyone."

—Ed Hastey, retired California director, Bureau of Land Management, on his early days in the Department of the Interior

11

Behind Closed Doors
Locking Out the Public

Being an environmental lobbyist in 1969 was a far cry from the endless hearings and briefings of today, as Carl Pope can attest from experience. Back then, the business of government took place mostly behind closed doors. Congressional committees drafted and approved legislation in executive sessions. The House of Representatives allowed recorded votes only on final bills, not on amendments. Agency bureaucrats simply told the public what they had decided, revealing neither the reasons for their decision nor the options they had rejected. Highways, power plants, airports, and other major projects were forced down the throats of communities, without their agreement and sometimes even without their knowledge. There was no mechanism by which citizens could contest proposals to dam rivers, log ancient forests, or mine national parks. Business and industry had "standing" before the courts to challenge government orders to clean up air and water pollution, but those being poisoned did not. It might have been government for the people, but it certainly was not by the people.

The reforms of the next decade let light into the backrooms. Congressional committee hearings were opened to the public. Legislative votes were recorded in their entirety. State and local "sunshine" ordinances ended backroom meetings. At the national level, the Freedom of Information Act gave individuals and citizen groups access to the previously secret raw material of policy. The National Environmental Policy Act and other laws mandated environmental review and public participation. And the citizen suit provisions of the Clean Air, Clean Water, Endangered Species, and Superfund acts gave Americans the unprecedented power to go to court to make sure these landmark environmental laws were being followed. For the first time, agencies had to answer to more than wealthy economic interests. Environmental laws became enforceable, largely because citizens could insist that they be enforced.

What You Don't Know Won't Hurt Us

Today the windows that were opened during the 1960s and 1970s are being systematically slammed shut—and bricked over for good measure. The Bush administration always regarded the public's right to know as an irritant, but after September 11 that right was reframed as a threat to national security.

Immediately after the September 11 attacks, the administration ordered the deletion of material from government Web sites regarding risks at nuclear power plants, chemical factories, and refineries, even though right-to-know laws called for them to be publicly posted. The argument was that terrorists might use this information to mount an attack. It seemed plausible to a frightened country, but the administration knew well that the censored Web pages were still available to any diligent terrorist on scores of Web archives. The only parties who would be left in the dark were the Americans living near these facilities, who lost their right to know what risks they faced and what their government was doing (or not) to protect them. (Strikingly, the Bush administration declined to ask industrial facilities to take steps to make themselves less vulnerable to terrorist attack. Asked about enhancing anti-terrorism precautions at such plants, EPA Administrator Christie Whitman said, "I don't know that we're contemplating at this point any changes.")

Attorney General John Ashcroft followed with a full-scale assault on the public's right to know. On Friday of the Columbus Day holiday weekend, 2001, when the fewest possible people would be paying attention, Ashcroft quietly issued an order urging all government agencies to deny, whenever possible, all Freedom of Information Act requests. In the dazed aftermath of September 11, few noticed what had happened. It was not until months later that the *San Francisco Chronicle* editorialized about the extraordinary diminution of public access to the workings of government. "The President didn't ask the networks for television time," the paper wrote. "The attorney general didn't hold a press conference. The media didn't report any dramatic change in governmental policy. As a result, most Americans had no idea that one of their most precious freedoms disappeared on Oct. 12. Yet it happened. In a memo that slipped beneath the political radar, U.S. Attorney General John Ashcroft vigorously urged federal agencies to resist most Freedom of Information Act requests made by American citizens."

Ashcroft used the attack on the World Trade Center as his justification. But the reasons he allowed federal agencies to use in denying information requests from the public were not limited to questions of security: "When you carefully consider FOIA requests and decide to withhold records, in whole or in part, you can be assured that the Department of Justice will defend your decisions unless they lack a sound legal basis or present an unwarranted risk of adverse impact on the ability of other agencies to protect other important records." Secrecy, that is, was the preferred response—unless denying a specific request for information might threaten the entire secrecy enterprise. The only valid reason to provide information was to enhance secrecy.

Public agencies eagerly embraced their restored ability to keep the public in the dark. The Interior Department did not even bother to respond when environmental groups sought information on its communications with the oil industry on drilling in the Arctic National Wildlife Refuge. The EPA passed the gift further down the line, revising its rules so as to allow states to hold secret their regulations governing industry plans to clean up (or not) toxic air pollutants.

Environmentalists seeking information on such seemingly mundane matters as grazing permits on public lands ran into a stone wall. Trying to learn more about a proposed development at Coyote Springs, Nevada, the Center for Biological Diversity could not even find out if the Bureau of Land Management had a file related to the project. Jon Marvel, executive director of the Western Watersheds Project, complained that BLM and Interior officials had simply cut his organization off from public records: "Field offices are obliged to send us, without further request, documents relating to further actions regarding livestock grazing, but a number of field offices have not sent us these documents at all."

Why would the Bush administration limit public access to such rudimentary information? It clearly was not for fear of al Qaeda cattle rustlers or terrorists utilizing information about watershed health. Rather, the White House knew that environmentalists needed access to detailed information in order to rally the public, appeal harmful decisions, or document their case to a federal judge. At a stroke, the right had found a way to put government decision making back where they thought it belonged—in secret backroom deals between bureaucrats and business.

"A Giant Vacuum Cleaner Sucking Up the Public's Right to Know"

Vice President Dick Cheney sought to throw the administration's new cloak of invisibility over the nation's energy policy (see chapter 6), especially the workings of his own energy task force. Members of Congress, the General Accounting Office, and environmental and public policy groups all inquired about how the task force made its decisions—which had, after all, formed the basis for the subsequent energy bill with its multibillion-dollar subsidies to favored industries. The Natural Resources Defense Council (NRDC) filed repeated Freedom of Information Act requests for the minutes of the meetings but received no response.

At first the administration claimed that the task force had consisted entirely of federal employees and that its workings were not subject to congressional or public oversight. Cheney went so far as to assert on *Nightline* that his task force had not brought in any "outsiders" at all.

Eventually, however, the vice president admitted that he had met at least six times with Enron executives, including once with Kenneth Lay himself. As the Texas company went down, almost taking California with it, public outrage built. California Representative Henry Waxman (D) issued a report detailing how the energy task force had advocated huge favors for private companies that met with it. The lawsuits began to roll in: one from the General Accounting Office to obtain the information it had demanded, another from the conservative watchdog group Judicial Watch and the Sierra Club to obtain the internal minutes of the task force under the Federal Advisory Committee Act.

"It's extremely unfortunate that it takes a lawsuit to learn how much influence polluting companies had over a policy affecting all Americans," the Sierra Club commented at the time. "If the White House had conducted their meetings in the light of day, we wouldn't need this lawsuit. The American people were shut out of this process while energy companies and oil industry were given the red-carpet treatment. Americans deserve to know what happened behind those closed doors—and the law requires it."

The NRDC's Freedom of Information Act case was resolved first. A federal judge ordered the Energy Department to release 7,500 pages of documents; when they arrived, the important information in almost all had been blacked out under various claims of privilege devised by Ashcroft.

In the Sierra Club/Judicial Watch suit, federal judge Emmet Sullivan repeatedly ordered the administration to release the records. The administration repeatedly refused. On the eve of the midterm election, an exasperated court demanded that the administration produce the documents immediately. The Justice Department claimed it could not comply—because although it had been asserting in court that releasing the records would seriously damage the government, it admitted that it had not even begun to look at what they contained. Secrecy had now become not a last resort but the operating assumption of the government's lawyers.

In early September 2002, the administration once again refused to comply with Sullivan's orders, claiming that producing the records "would impose upon the Executive unconstitutional burdens." Its assertion was that since the vice president had personal control of the records, they were, by that fact alone, constitutionally protected. Harvard University constitutional scholar Laurence Tribe commented that, if upheld, this claim "would turn the office of the Vice-President into a giant vacuum cleaner, sucking up the public's right to know." And in what the NRDC called "an unprecedented move" in "ramping up its secrecy fight," the administration announced that Solicitor General Theodore Olson would personally argue the case. On October 18, unpersuaded by Olson's arguments, Judge Sullivan told the administration to do one of three things: produce the documents, claim executive privilege, or find itself in contempt of court: "Why should these defendants . . . be excused from doing what everyone else under the law has to do?" Instead of complying, the administration took another extraordinary legal step, seeking an order from the appeals court to quash the legal proceedings.

A three-judge panel on the appeals court slapped Cheney down again, as did the full court when he appealed. Backed into a corner, in September 2003 the Bush team asked the U.S. Supreme Court to intervene. To the astonishment of many legal observers, the high court took the case; arguments will be heard in 2004.

The jury is still out on why Cheney fought so hard to keep the public from seeing how administration policy was made. It is already common knowledge, after all, that his panel met almost exclusively with executives from well-connected polluting industries. One possibility is that the requested documents include a damaging bombshell. (One set of papers released during the course of the court proceedings, for instance, showed that as early as March 2001 his task force had an interest in Iraqi oil. The papers included a detailed map of Iraq's oil fields, terminals, and pipelines as well as a document titled "Foreign Suitors of Iraqi Oilfield Contracts.") Another possibility is that it all may have been for show, to assert the Bush administration's new principle that it does not have to account to the public for its actions. In any event, Cheney managed to maintain the secrecy of his task force for two and a half years and demonstrated that anyone who wanted to know what the Bush administration was doing would have to wage a long, expensive legal war to find out.

Surprise! A New Highway Through Your Backyard

If the Bush administration disliked the Freedom of Information Act, the National Environmental Policy Act was far worse. NEPA requires the government to look at, and document, alternatives to cutting down forests, building unneeded highways, or permitting increased pollution. Not surprisingly, those alternatives often come off looking pretty good. FOIA was the burglar's bar that allowed citizens to pry open the government's filing cabinet. But NEPA was filling those cabinets with damning evidence of citizens left at risk or public lands plundered for private profit. It was like having an agency biologist hand-cuffed to the wrist of every Bush appointee.

In an early, probing move, the administration argued that NEPA should stop at the water's edge. To give itself more discretion to ignore damage to coral reefs, dolphins, and other marine mammals, the administration ruled that the act did not apply to 4.4 million acres of marine habitat lying within the U.S. Exclusive Economic Zone. "That's the equivalent of giving away roughly half of the U.S.," said Tulane University's Oliver Houck. "It's just equivalent to saying everything west of the Mississippi we won't touch. I also think it's flat illegal." The courts agreed, and they rejected Bush's proposal.

Bush also dispensed with public input to a number of key energy decisions, including approval of 77,000 methane wells in Wyoming and Montana and a seismic testing project near Arches National Park in Utah: the Interior Department ignored NEPA and simply turned over public lands to oil and gas development without public comment or review. Long forgotten was Interior Secretary Gale Norton's explicit promise in her confirmation hearing to comply with NEPA, not to amend or attempt to evade it. Soon she was complaining that "[i]t can take six months to prepare environmental planning documents for even the most routine forest treatments. . . . Once completed, these projects are often challenged, leading to lengthy protests, appeals, and litigation." (Since the forests to be "treated" by chainsaw and bulldozer often took hundreds of years to grow, a six-month review of their fate does not seem so much to ask.) Again, the courts had to override those decisions.

Indeed, Bush's record on NEPA cases strongly suggested an administration determined to ignore, not enforce, the law. In Bush's first two years, his administration was sued 94 times for short-circuiting NEPA. The administration lost 73 cases, a 78 percent failure rate, even though federal judges generally give great deference to the White House in such cases. Federal judges ruled that the administration employed "bait-and-switch tactics" and "mystical legal prestidigitation" to "eviscerate" the law.

Despite defeat in the courts, Bush moved on to carve out other loopholes. NEPA regulations allowed communities to speak out about being cut in half by a major transportation facility like a highway or airport. Federal highway planners complained that it could take four to five years to approve a major new highway. "Sometimes you feel a little bit like that small rodent in a maze, trying to complete all these reviews," complained Mary E. Peters, head of the Federal Highway Administration. (That is just a hint of what it feels like to try to stop a highway the FHA wants to build—or to get rid of one that turns out to be a mistake after it is built.) So by executive order in September 2002, the administration allowed the Department of Transportation to cut out much of the analysis previously required in public documents, to speed up the review process, and to establish a "streamlining task force" to identify further ways to reduce or eliminate public involvement.

The record shows, however, that NEPA has repeatedly helped highway agencies build better roads, with less harm to communities and wildlife. The pesky citizens Bush wanted to keep away from the planning process were often far more creative than the highway engineers. Along California's San Mateo County coast, for example, citizens came up with a proposal for a tunnel to bypass a treacherous stretch of highway known as Devil's Slide, in place of the engineers' preferred option: a more expensive multilane freeway through a park. In Colorado, citizens figured out how to reconfigure an expansion of Interstate 70 while minimizing damage to the beauty of Glenwood Canyon. The public suggested that "Alligator Alley," Interstate 75 as it crossed the Florida Everglades, be improved with 24 wildlife underpasses and fencing to reduce collisions between wildlife and autos. In Michigan, a NEPA analysis found cheaper ways to expand U.S. 23, saving $1.3 billion.

But the days of getting good ideas from the public are over. The EPA had twice rejected the proposed "InterCounty Connector" in suburban Maryland because it would do so much damage to forests, wetlands, streams, and wildlife. Now Bush "fast-tracked" the project so that newly elected governor Bob Ehrlich would be able to ignore local residents. "What's past is past," said Tom Voltaggio, the EPA's deputy administrator for the mid-Atlantic region.

The corporate right continued to portray NEPA as "much abused and outdated . . . hijacked by environmental groups that use it to keep federal agencies tied up in legal knots," as the editorial page of the *Wall Street Journal* put it. "Under NEPA, Earth Firsters don't even have to address substantive environmental arguments. Instead, they can demand Bible-length environmental impact statements, endless internal reviews. . . . As a result, environmental agencies today spend so much time guarding against green legal challenges they've largely lost the ability to manage our public lands."

What outdated abuse had provoked this jeremiad from the *Journal*? It was that the administration had to pretend to listen to the American people before ignoring them (and its own wildlife biologists) by turning Yellowstone National Park into a playground for the snowmobile lobby. Eighty percent of 360,000 cards and letters received by the National Park Service favored a ban on snowmobiles, but in announcing its decision to greatly expand snowmobile access at Yellowstone, the Interior Department made clear that, though it might be required to accept and record public comment, it was not going to be influenced by it. "It was not a vote," the administration said. The *Journal* applauded but clearly felt that it would be much tidier if public comment were dispensed with altogether.

Industry urged the administration to go further. The *National Journal* reported that "the Idaho Cattle Association recommended that NEPA lawsuits be limited to 'individuals who have an economic stake in the outcome of a NEPA decision.'"

James Connaughton, head of the White House Council on Environmental Quality, who had presided over the decision to deny the citizens of lower Manhattan accurate information on health risks at Ground Zero (see chapter 9) now stepped in to help developers and other private interests avoid NEPA's mandate that the impacts of their projects be assessed and disclosed. In September 2003, Connaughton assembled a task force that then advised agencies to create broad "categorical exemptions" for developers' projects. While Connaugton had studied Frank Luntz's scripts very well, saying that these exemptions would merely "modernize the paper process," one of his staff was, anonymously, more candid: "creating more exclusions," he told the Associated Press, "could allow more projects to avoid environmental reviews."

Your Voice Doesn't Count

Finally, just as Bush had sought to limit the votes counted in Florida, his administration took aim at rules that gave all Americans a voice in the management of their national forests. When considering the avalanche of public comment

in support of the Roadless Area Conservation Rule, the Forest Service announced that it would no longer count public comments if they were similar or
identical to each other. Thus, a million citizens writing to say that "I like this
watershed the way it is; don't log it" would count as a single comment. "When
the courts have reviewed a final rule, they have focused on whether the rule is
a rational exercise of agency discretion and not on the number of comments
for or against the rule," Mark Rey told Congress.

Forest Service Chief Dale Bosworth defended the new approach. "My
view is that we're not counting votes anway," he said. "People say, 'If you have
1.6 million comments on an issue and 95 percent of them went one way, then
how can you possibly do something different?' It just distorts the picture."
(Especially, it seems, when the result is predetermined.) In late December
2003, however, Bosworth quietly agreed to continue accepting public comment; an agency spokesperson said that the proposal to the contrary had only
been in the interest of saving time.

Teddy Roosevelt had fought vigorously for the public interest on the public lands, declaring: "All the great natural resources which are vital to the welfare of the whole people should be kept either in the hands or under the control
of the whole people." But the Progressive tradition in which he created the
national forests is faltering in the care of an administration that seeks to keep
citizens as far away as possible from the daily management of their property.
Managing that property for the oil and gas industry, the timber companies,
and the mining interests requires shutting out its owners, the American people.
Bush's appointees are genuinely outraged, however, by the accusation that they
are just paying off campaign contributors. In their view, national forests really
ought to be tree farms, rivers are better off dammed to provide reliable irrigation for agribusiness, and, if you want to see wildlife, you can pay your money at
an animal farm or game ranch. If bringing the American people to the decision-
making table is going to get in the way of such sensible decisions, then the
American people do not belong at the table.

Not everyone is going along quietly with the return to secret government.
Many newspapers, including the *New York Times, Seattle Post-Intelligencer,* and
Atlanta Journal-Constitution all editorialized against it. They were joined by
John Cornyn, the new Republican senator from Texas. "Frankly," he com-
mented during his campaign, "if there's one thing I could change, it would be

to try to persuade the administration to be less closed when it comes to what they're doing."

So hermetic has the White House become that the method by which citizens could e-mail the president has changed to an almost comical procedure for weeding out negative comments. Those who do wend their way through the circuitous, multilayered process for sending a message find at the end that they are not free to speak their mind, only to indicate whether or not they agree with various positions of the president.

Dissenting voices from Congress are hardly more welcome, especially if they are Democrats. Exactly one year before the president was to face the American people in the 2004 election, the White House announced, as the *Washington Post* put it, that it was "irritated by pesky questions from congressional Democrats about how the administration is using taxpayer money" and that it had developed "an efficient solution; it will not entertain any more questions from opposition lawmakers."

The White House might not be receiving many e-mails, but it can still send them. It e-mailed the House and Senate Appropriations committees to say that, in future, the administration would accept only questions originating with the committee chairs—Republicans all. This, the White House opined, would eliminate "duplicate requests." It also eliminated, for the first time in American history, the oversight function of the opposition party and totally excluded almost half of the sitting members of Congress from access to government information.

The administration's zeal in limiting public participation recalls the example of the early Federalist and Whig parties, which believed that only the economic elite possessed the necessary wisdom and virtue to make decisions for the nation. A new elite in Washington is asserting its privilege, and the sunshine that illuminated the workings of government is fading fast.

"I think man is always in danger of letting his whole system of life, the whole system of rules which in a grown-up world we call law . . . slip altogether. The change can happen almost overnight. Seems as though one day you have a country which is civilized, and the next day you can have a country which has fallen flat on its face and is tearing itself to pieces."

—William Golding, Nobel Prize–winning author of *Lord of the Flies*

"Obedience to the law is demanded as a right, not asked as a favor."

—Theodore Roosevelt; cited by Eric Schaeffer, director of the EPA Office of Regulatory Enforcement, in his resignation letter, February 27, 2002

"There's no law north of the Klamath."

—California saying about the lawless attitudes of the timber industry on California's redwood coast

12

Be Sued and Settle
The Law as a Partisan Tool

Lt might have been more fitting if John Blair had been tarred and feathered, or ridden out of town on a rail. Instead he spent two days in jail for standing outside a Republican fund-raiser in Indiana holding a sign that read, "Dick Cheney, 19th Century Energy Man." The vice president was inside; hence, Blair was a security threat. When he refused an order from a plainclothes policeman to move away on the grounds that protesters "were not allowed" on the open sidewalk where he was standing, he was arrested.

The Bush administration's approach to law enforcement is substantially different with regard to wrongdoers better connected and better heeled than John Blair. The radical right, particularly its corporatist wing, is highly selective in its view of the law. George W. Bush has always favored "voluntary" environmental standards—not that they ever did much good for Texas, which under his governorship led the nation in the number of polluters in violation of Clean Air standards. As senator, John Ashcroft had consistently voted against adequate funding for Environmental Protection Agency (EPA) enforcement activities; once he became attorney general, environmental enforcement joined civil liberties at the bottom of his to-do list. And both House Majority Leader Tom DeLay (R-Tex.) and Senate Environment Committee Chair James Inhofe (R-Okla.) have compared EPA enforcement agents to Hitler's Gestapo.

Bush made his priorities clear from the outset when he suspended a Clinton-era regulation barring flagrant violators of federal environmental laws (among others) from getting new federal contracts. And a lucky thing, too. Otherwise Cheney's Halliburton might not have been eligible for its sole-source, multibillion-dollar deal to rebuild Iraq, given the federal laws it had broken—most spectacularly the law prohibiting dealings with Saddam Hussein's regime.

The EPA enforcement operation that Bush and Ashcroft took over was hardly an environmental pit bull. A quarter of the nation's largest industrial plants and water treatment facilities were routinely violating their clean water permits, half of them releasing more than double the allowable levels of toxic chemicals into rivers, lakes, and streams. The EPA was taking enforcement action against only one in four violators, fining fewer than one in eight, and levying average fines of only $6,000. Doing so was simply "easier," the agency said, than seriously enforcing the law with an overburdened staff.

Bush found even this relaxed-fit enforcement level of the laws of the land too heavy-handed. His first budget cut 223 staff positions from the EPA and cut its national regulatory budgets by $158 million—with $11 million coming out of the enforcement budget. Bush justified the cut by pointing to an increase of $25 million in grants to state enforcement programs, in effect taking the federal cop off the beat in states like Texas, notoriously lax on enforcement. The EPA insisted that these cuts would not affect its efforts, but a year later enforcement chief Eric Schaeffer submitted a blistering letter of resignation, saying that enforcement was being crippled by "endless delays" and a lack of resources. Even the Republican-controlled House of Representatives found Bush's proposed cuts to environmental enforcement too much to stomach and rejected them by an overwhelming voice vote. Even so, within two years criminal prosecutions for violating environmental laws had dropped by a third, and assessed fines dropped by two-thirds.

The New Federalism:
States' Rights When It Suits

A major tenet of the modern conservative movement is a new version of federalism, which holds that power should be retained as much as possible at the state and local levels and, if necessary, wrested from an overweening federal government. The major training ground for right-wing legal minds is a think tank known as the Federalist Society. Its members and alumni in the administration include Ashcroft, Solicitor General Theodore Olson, Interior Secretary Gale Norton, Energy Secretary Spencer Abraham, and Assistant Attorney General for Environment and Natural Resources Thomas Sansonetti. Conservative politicians pay almost as much deference to the worship of federalism as they do to saluting the flag.

Except, that is, when local jurisdictions take a tougher line on polluters than the feds do.

Even when he was a senator, Ashcroft's commitment to federalism and states' rights was tempered by the even more important priority of avoiding vigorous enforcement of environmental laws. Ashcroft had voted, for example, to allow real-estate developers to take challenges to local planning and zoning ordinances directly to federal court as potential violations of the Constitution. As attorney general, his devotion to local control became more fickle yet.

When California established tough new auto emission standards, including the nation's first limit on carbon dioxide from tailpipes, Ashcroft and Bush joined the auto industry (including White House Chief of Staff Andrew Card's former employer, General Motors) in suing to block California's long-established right to set independent standards under the Clean Air Act—a principle that even Ronald Reagan had strongly upheld. (When California also moved to regulate highly polluting small and mid-sized engines, like those used in lawnmowers and leaf blowers, Republican Senator Kit Bond from Ashcroft's home state of Missouri got the Senate Appropriations Committee to adopt language prohibiting the states from such action. Bond led the effort at the behest of Briggs & Stratton, a Missouri manufacturer that did not want to be bothered making its small engines less polluting. The rider was weakened only when California's new Republican governor, Arnold Schwarzenegger, started working the phones—California kept the right to regulate the polluting lawnmowers. Other states were stuck with the dirty models.)

When the federal courts ruled that the states, not the federal government, had the power to control plans by oil companies to drill on old offshore oil leases, Bush and Ashcroft quietly put aside their federalism and proposed rules that would shift control to the federal government—all the while denying that doing so would limit states' rights. How could this be? The logic apparently was that the states should not have been given these rights by the courts in the first place, so that as soon as the power was shifted back to the feds, the states would no longer have any rights to limit!

Bush also found federalism flawed in the pursuit of one of his administration's major legal initiatives, the limiting of class-action lawsuits. Such suits are increasingly used both by investors to sue corporate management and by citizens addressing public health hazards (tobacco), environmental risks (PCBs and dioxin), and violations of civil rights (employment discrimination). Since juries in some states tended to be more generous to injured plaintiffs than were the federal courts, Bush sought to take away from state courts the ability to hear such class actions.

Buried deep inside the class-action bill was this bomb: any case where citizens sued in state court on behalf of the public at large—not just themselves—

would be treated as a class action, even if it was not, and would be removed to federal court. It sounds like a minor change, but it could have far-reaching effects for states that permit citizens to bring civil suits to enforce environmental laws. Under California's Proposition 65, for example, citizens can sue to prevent the release of toxic chemicals into drinking water. This provision has ensured that even during periods of lax enforcement by elected officials, citizens and public interest groups could fill the gap.

Now Bush proposed to snuff out these laws. Since federal courts cannot consider cases in which citizens sue to enforce state laws on the public's behalf, the effect was to completely eliminate citizens' rights—even when all involved in the case lived within the state and that state wanted to grant its residents this opportunity. (The Foundation for Taxpayer and Consumer Rights noted that thirteen of the sixteen members of Bush's cabinet had "been employed by, served on the board of, have significant financial interest in" corporations that have been the targets of class-action suits.) Ashcroft could only hope that none of his colleagues in the Federalist Society noticed. (Senate Democrats narrowly succeeded in blocking the bill.)

Bush and his allies accomplish such feats of intellectual legerdemain by appealing to the same anti-government sentiments they work so hard to promote. As 2000 popular-vote-winning presidential candidate Al Gore put it in an August 2003 speech, "The administration has developed a highly effective propaganda machine to embed in the public mind mythologies that grow out of the one central doctrine that all of the special interests agree on, which—in its purest form—is that government is very bad and should be done away with as much as possible—except the parts of it that redirect money through big contracts to industries that have won their way into the inner circle."

Non-highways to Nowhere

In 1995, a desert cloudburst washed out 1.5 miles of the South Canyon Road, which dead-ends in a wilderness near Jarbridge, Nevada. Since the Jarbridge River, which runs alongside the road, sustains a population of the endangered bull trout, the Forest Service opted to simply close this road to nowhere rather than rebuild it and threaten the trout. The only practical consequence was that backpackers had to begin their hike 1.5 miles earlier. Elko County officials, however, decided to make a stand against the concept that national concerns—like protecting the bull trout—should govern the management of federal land. Hundreds of local citizens calling themselves the Jarbridge Shovel Brigade were led to the trailhead by local officials, where they broke the law by trying to rebuild the road and faced down federal officials. The district attorney publicly called on merchants to stop selling groceries to Forest Service employees, and the national forest supervisor resigned over Washington's failure to confront this atmosphere of intimidation.

The moment Bush took office, an olive branch was extended to the Elko County lawbreakers. Within months, an out-of-court settlement granting the county ownership of the road was agreed upon—sparing the administration the inconvenience of convincing a federal judge that it had the right to give up this small but symbolically important piece of America's national heritage.

This giveaway presaged what became the classic Bush approach to his obligation to uphold federal law: when faced with disputes in which they are expected to protect the public interest, federal agencies simply abandon the field. Why go through the motions of defending environmental laws and regulations when you can just roll over and negotiate sweetheart settlements that favor your friends, allies, and former employers?

Another example was Interior Secretary Norton's unnecessary capitulation to a non-adversarial legal challenge from Utah Governor (and future EPA Administrator) Mike Leavitt over an antique law intended to give Civil War–era miners access to their claims on federal land. For decades, Utah and Alaska have tried to use the obscure 1866 statute known as RS-2477 to claim that jeep trails and mining tracks are in fact highways. If recognized, the effect would be to foil future wilderness claims, because a wilderness area with a road running through it is, by definition, no longer a wilderness.

Utah had barely announced its intention to sue when the Justice Department promptly sat down in secret and negotiated a settlement of the lawsuit, which had yet to be filed. This odd sequence had a method to it: had Bush allowed Utah to actually file the lawsuit before sitting down to settle, pesky environmental organizations might have intervened and insisted that a federal judge look at the settlement before it was finalized. In this case, when Earthjustice sued to find out what was being discussed, Governor Leavitt refused to make public his plans to construct highways on such public lands as Zion National Park—even though he claimed that these rights-of-way had existed for a century.

Norton and Leavitt's deal encouraged the anti-wilderness counties of southern Utah to send their bulldozers to blade gashes in the desert in hopes of creating "facts on the ground." Although the Jarbridge road led nowhere, at least it was a road; some of the RS-2477 claims are "rights of way" running up narrow slot canyons replete with ten-foot waterfalls—quite a leap even for an SUV. Now Norton had granted the state its fictional creations—and in doing so given away the very real wilderness they crossed.

Shortly after Norton's sweetheart deal, the Tenth Circuit Court of Appeals spoiled the party by endorsing a lower-court decision that the only possible valid claims under RS-2477 were roads that were clearly constructed (not simply created by the repeated passage of off-road vehicles) and that had an identifiable destination—thus wiping out the scores of claims by Utah counties to tracks that simply petered out in the desert. As a result of the Tenth Circuit's decision, said Heidi McIntosh, conservation director of Southern Utah Wilderness Alliance, "the law of the land in Utah is that faint hiking trails, two-tracks, and abandoned prospecting trails cannot be raised from the dead as a weapon against wilderness protection for Utah's spectacular canyon country." But not for Gale Norton's lack of trying.

(Leavitt and Bush were undeterred. In another Leavitt-Norton partnership, Utah intervened to claim that citizens had no right to insist that the federal government enforce federal laws protecting wilderness-quality areas, because many of these places had rights-of-way across them that only the state could define or regulate—unmapped non-highways to nowhere!)

The strategy described above—dubbed "be sued and settle"—has become standard for Bush administration agencies hoping to reach industry-friendly conclusions without even the minor trouble of clearing their aims with a compliant Republican Congress. To carry it out, federal agencies adhere to the fiction that they are protecting the public and the law of the land, even pro-environmental legislation passed under previous administrations. But when it comes to defending the law in court, the agencies purport to be so awestruck by industry's superior arguments that they throw in the towel and surrender completely in an out-of-court settlement. The most sweeping application of this cynical process has been to dissolve the landmark Clinton-era protections against construction of new logging and mining roads in wild, unroaded sections of national forests. The policy was developed after the largest public input process in U.S. history (see chapter 7) and protected 58.5 million acres of public land in 39 states. And during his confirmation hearings, Ashcroft had sworn under oath to defend it:

> *Senator Dianne Feinstein (D-Calif.):* There are court cases already now being filed in challenge to the roadless area policy that has now been implemented by the Administrative Procedures Act. So even if the president-elect is opposed to that policy, will you, as the enforcement agency underneath your office, enforce and uphold that law and defend those cases?
>
> *Ashcroft:* I will, regardless of whether or not I supported something as a senator, defend the rule. And if it is a rule with the force and effect of law, I will defend those cases.

Ashcroft's promise was echoed by Agriculture Secretary Ann Veneman. As a private attorney, Veneman had represented anti-environmental, "wise use" groups, but like Ashcroft she professed a change of heart. "We're here today," she proclaimed on May 4, 2001, "to announce the department's decision to uphold the Roadless Area Conservation Rule. Through this action, we are reaffirming the Department of Agriculture's commitment to the important challenge of protecting roadless values." The Forest Service, she said, would implement the plan—albeit with minor changes.

Despite these assurances, the administration caved at the first opportunity. When the Roadless Rule came under legal attack from Boise Cascade, the American Forest and Paper Association, and the state of Idaho, Ashcroft and Veneman issued only a skimpy twelve-page brief in the rule's defense. Judge Edward Lodge of the U.S. district court in Idaho invited Veneman to present her proposed supplemental arguments, but they never appeared. So lame was the administration's case that when Judge Lodge issued a preliminary injunction to halt implementation of the rule, he used the administration's own arguments against it to buttress his ruling.

(As much as Ashcroft might wish it, his broken promise did not disappear down the memory hole. "Mr. Ashcroft's lawyers have since done almost nothing to defend the [roadless] rule against court challenges from industry," the *New York Times* editorialized, "a failure that has encouraged the timber lobbyists who now run the Forest Service to proceed with their parallel campaign to destroy the roadless policy by administrative means.")

Since Ashcroft and Veneman were not appealing the ruling, various environmental groups did instead. On December 12, 2002, the Ninth Circuit Court of Appeals overturned Lodge's injunction and, in a strongly worded decision, reaffirmed the Roadless Rule as the law of the land.

For a few months. In a separate suit in Wyoming, U.S. District Court Judge Clarence Brimmer struck down the rule again, saying that it was an attempt to establish de facto wilderness. (It was later revealed that more than a third of Brimmer's reportable income was invested in energy development companies that stood to make a killing if the Roadless Rule were struck down.) Again, the Justice Department declined to appeal—and this time it argued that environmentalists should not have the right of appeal, either: "Private persons should not be permitted to use the judiciary to interfere with this core function of the United States," Justice argued.

The cock crowed a third time when, in response to yet another suit by the state of Alaska and the timber industry, the Bush administration capitulated yet again, this time exempting all of the Chugach and Tongass national forests—which contain one-fourth of all inventoried roadless land in the country—from the Roadless Rule. It further allowed state governors to request "waivers" of the rule for "reducing hazardous fuels," a condition that could easily be decreed to exist in nearly every forest, opening up millions of acres to logging roads and clearcuts. Thus, Ashcroft snatched defeat from the arms of victory, just as his old friends and allies in the timber industry would have wished.

What's That Smell? Sweet Deal for Big Pig

The easiest way to stack the legal deck for your friends is to redefine the law, even when it is as explicit as the Clean Water Act. That landmark law has produced tremendous results by cleaning up our rivers and streams, but it now faces a new monstrosity on the American landscape: the enormous factory farms known as "combined animal feeding operations," or CAFOs. Although they are classified as farms in most states, some produce as much sewage as a city of 500,000—but with no sewage treatment controls at all. Instead, billions of gallons of stinking muck is sprayed on farm fields, where it releases ammonia, hydrogen sulfide, methane, and dust into the air and drains as raw sewage into waterways. Thirty-five thousand miles of rivers and streams in 22 states have already been polluted, while small-scale ranches and farms are driven out of business and rural communities destroyed by the stench and filth. A billion fish died in 1991 in North Carolina's Neuse River alone from polluted runoff. Polluted runoff from hog farms may be giving rise to *Pfiesteria piscidia,* a toxic microbe known as "the cell from hell" because it morphs into 24 different forms, many of which kill fish and cause neurological damage in humans.

Well-connected campaign contributors like Tyson and Purdue were able to hold off regulation for years, claiming that CAFOs were more like farms than industries. But slowly, nudged by lawsuits from outraged citizens and environmental groups, the EPA moved toward requiring factory feedlots to control their pollution. North Carolina, which by 1999 had more hogs than people, did not act against the hog farms until Hurricane Floyd drowned 30,000 hogs and spread millions of gallons of untreated sewage across a third of the state. In Floyd's aftermath, North Carolina began a buyout of hog farms in the floodplain. Some states banned the facilities altogether. And, nationally, the EPA began to close in. Cleanup was about to happen.

Once Bush was elected, however, Big Pig realized it did not have to clean up. Instead, the industry hired a well-connected lobbying firm and went to Washington to cut a deal. The lobbying firm, in secret, proposed to the EPA an amnesty agreement that would provide CAFOs protection from prosecution. Under the proposed agreement, the entire CAFO industry would be granted immunity from prosecution for Clean Air Act, Superfund law, and Clean Water Act violations in exchange for a commitment from a small percentage of operations to engage in voluntary monitoring. CAFOs would not be required to reduce emissions or even apply for a permit. Instead, the agreement would perpetuate the status quo and allow CAFOs essentially to operate outside the law without any fear of prosecution. If not blocked, the rule will be a get-out-of-jail-free card for America's most obnoxious industry.

Once compromised by Big Pig, the Clean Water Act was subjected to indignity upon indignity. Based on a limited Supreme Court opinion, the Bush administration decided that the EPA and the Army Corps of Engineers were no longer to enforce the Clean Water Act with regard to what it called "isolated wetlands" and "intermittent streams." Bush simply declared that such waterways were no longer "waters of the United States" and thus outside the jurisdiction of the Clean Water Act. The administration acknowledged that 20 million acres—one-fifth of the nation's wetlands—would no longer be protected. (Other observers put the figure at 60 percent.) This wholesale abdication of protection led the House of Representatives, including an unusual number of Republicans, to protest. In December, the administration announced that it would not promulgate a new rule exempting the areas, even though its final "guidance document" to the agencies advised the EPA and Army Corps not to protect these vital wetlands.

Superficial redefinition has a hoary tradition in Washington. After the nation's last major energy crisis back in the 1970s, for example, Congress allotted tax credits to so-called synfuels. Real synthetic fuels proved uneconomical even with the tax credits, but clever lawyers discovered that it was just barely possible to pretend that, if you sprayed coal with kerosene or diesel oil, the resulting product could be called a synthetic fuel. Companies adopted the practice and raked in billions of dollars in bogus tax credits. When the Internal Revenue Service finally cracked down on the transparent dodge in 2003, Bush's new Treasury secretary, John Snow, was heavily lobbied by the coal industry. The IRS backed down, leading Bill Henck, one of the IRS lawyers involved in the crackdown, to charge that political pressure had been brought to bear by the Bush White House. The *Wall Street Journal* reported that, after Henck made this charge, the IRS shifted its focus. Instead of auditing companies raking in billions in tax credits for diesel-laced coal, it audited Henck.

When simply changing a definition would not work, regulations that implemented the law could always be tweaked by changing the word "shall" to "may." Just making a legal requirement optional instead of mandatory was often enough to undermine what Congress had provided. The Healthy Forests bill signed by Bush permitted wide-open logging on fire-prone areas of the national forests, but the extent of land that could be cut under its authority was capped at 20 million acres. The administration then created a variety of exemptions for logging outside that 20 million acres, again using the excuse of fire prevention. But 41 million acres of national forest was not at any risk from fire and was still protected by environmental statutes—particularly the Endangered Species Act—so could not be opened for logging with that excuse. In December 2003, however, Bush got around this simply by dropping the requirement that the Forest Service consult with the Fish and Wildlife Service or the National Marine Fisheries Service about endangered species.

Exit Whitman, Stage Right

In the Bush administration, the revolving door between government and business has whirred so rapidly that it has become invisible. Vice President Cheney gets annual checks from Halliburton, and J. Steven Griles, the number two official at the Interior Department, receives ongoing payments of $284,000 a year from his former lobbying firm, which represented the coal industry, coal-bed methane and offshore drilling companies, and industries involved in clean air disputes. Griles had sworn, however, to the Senate Energy and Natural Resources Committee that "I will do my utmost . . . to prevent the appearance of any improprieties or conflicts in terms of my prior associations." Yet there he was at sixteen meetings with administration or industry officials talking about air pollution issues, as well as making decisions about coal-bed methane development in Wyoming's Powder River basin and oil and gas leasing on the Outer Continental Shelf. Environmental groups asked for a special prosecutor to investigate; as of this writing, Ashcroft had yet to appoint one.

Conflict accusations even dogged EPA head Christie Whitman, the white sheep of the administration. Her agency had agreed to reduce from $100 million to $7.2 million the share of the controversial Shattuck Superfund nuclear cleanup to be paid for by Citigroup, the huge financial services firm in which Whitman's husband was a major investor. When Robert J. Martin, the EPA ombudsman, objected to the deal, Whitman dissolved his position and transferred him. Whitman seemed quite blasé about the frequency with which federal judges found that she had violated the law. When asked how she felt about the fact that, on her watch, the EPA lost an extraordinary number of cases filed against it by citizens, she laughed it off, saying, "We get sued all the time. It doesn't make any difference in what we do." A subsequent investigation absolved Whitman of conflict of interest, but the Senate did pointedly vote to reinstate the ombudsman's office.

On the same day it did so, May 21, 2003, Whitman finally resigned. Ever the good soldier, she never even hinted at displeasure with Bush's hard-right approach but said she was stepping down to spend more time with her family. From the very start of Bush's tenure, Whitman had found herself on the losing side of White House debates; by the time she left, Bush no longer felt much need for a moderate face to show the nation. The Competitive Enterprise Institute crowed that her departure created "an opportunity for revolution" if Bush were able to find a replacement even less friendly to regulation.

He did just that with his choice of Utah Governor Mike Leavitt. The National Environmental Trust commented that Leavitt would be a "better partner in crime" for Bush than Whitman. In 1996, then Governor Leavitt had fired a Division of Wildlife Resources enforcement official who had fined his family's fish farm for violations that brought the devastating whirling disease to Utah wild fish stocks. In addition, numerous wildlife scientists were reassigned or demoted by Leavitt for recommending needed protections for endangered species in the state. Under Leavitt, Utah joined George Bush's Texas as one of the states with the worst water pollution control record in the country. And the new EPA chief shares the Bush team's apparent fondness for heavy metals: in a 1999 *Deseret Morning News* article, Leavitt described toxic releases reported by the mining industry, including mercury, by saying "in reality it is not pollution."

Thumb on the Scales of Justice

The perfect complement to weak regulations and lackadaisical enforcers is an ideological judiciary. It seems like only yesterday that conservatives were complaining about the "judicial activism" of liberal jurists, but when it comes to ideologically driven decisions, disregard of legislative intent, and creative reading of the Constitution, it is hard to match the current crop of right-wing federal judges. These judicial Samsons are seeking to pull down the legal pillars that support much of our environmental law, replacing them with "states' rights" and "property rights."

Tilting the courts was an old Karl Rove specialty. Before he hooked up with the Bushes, Rove had targeted the Texas Supreme Court. Rove figured, and subsequently demonstrated, that if he put together enough money from the business community toward the goal of electing judges who would make it harder for citizens to recover damages in lawsuits, he could change the law in Texas. (One of his recruits was Priscilla Owen. When she went to the state's business community for support in her run for the Texas Supreme Court, she was told to look up Rove. He signed up to run her campaign and raised a record $1.1 million for her successful run.) Rove's strategy succeeded. "The cases all started getting decided anti-consumer, on the side of big business," said Phil Hardberger, a retired Texas appellate judge. Defendants, mainly corporations, started winning 89 percent of the cases before the new, Rove-designed supreme court.

The hostility of some sitting judges to environmental protection is quite overt. For example, in a dissenting opinion in *National Association of Home Builders v. Babbitt,* D.C. Circuit Judge David Sentelle ridiculed the Endangered Species Act for "prevent[ing] counties and their citizens from building hospitals or from driving to those hospitals by routes in which the bugs smashed upon their windshields might turn out to include the Delhi Sands Flower-Loving Fly." (In the case before him, the ESA did no such thing.) Another federal judge forbade New York's Bedford High School to celebrate Earth Day, asserting that "[t]he worship of the Earth is a recognized religion."

The nominees President Bush has made to the federal bench are of a piece with the most reactionary of the current court. One is Rove's old client, Priscilla Owen. William Pryor, nominated to the Eleventh Circuit Court of Appeals, has been particularly outspoken regarding environmental policy. As attorney general of Alabama, Pryor argued that the federal government lacks the authority to prevent the destruction of wetlands that serve as stopovers for migratory birds. He complained about federal enforcement of the Clean Air Act (calling it "the blunt tool of enforcement instead of a collaborative rulemaking process") and asked the U.S. Supreme Court to reverse a decision banning the killing of endangered red wolves on private land.

Janice Rogers Brown, the California Supreme Court justice nominated to a lifetime seat on the D.C. Circuit Court, sees government as a "leviathan" that is "crushing everything in its path." Her speeches betray a yearning for the pre–New Deal era, before what she calls "the triumph of our own socialist revolution." A series of solo dissents in "takings" cases betrays a very broad view of the takings clause—one that could, for example, require government to compensate landowners for losses they might incur due to ordinary zoning or environmental regulations.

Some are ominous ciphers, like Miguel Estrada, the mystery nominee to the D.C. Circuit Court of Appeals. Estrada simply refused to express any opinions on the issues of the day. (Asked, for example, about the Supreme Court case that upheld requirements that motor vehicles eliminate soot and smog, Estrada declined to state a position.) Rather than explain his philosophy, Estrada finally withdrew his name from consideration.

Estrada's "omerta" strategy, as *Slate* columnist Michael Kinsley dubbed it, becomes more understandable given the volubility of candidates like Victor Wolski, nominated to the U.S. Court of Federal Claims. The bulk of Wolski's legal career has been spent challenging environmental and other regulations on behalf of the industry-funded Pacific Legal Foundation. In an amicus brief arguing against Clean Water Act protection for migratory birds, he had ridiculed seasonal ponds as "puddles," asking, "Will one fewer puddle for the birds to bathe in have some impact on the market for these birds?"

Wolski bragged to the *National Journal* in 1999 that "every single job I've taken since college has been ideologically oriented, trying to further my principles." These he helpfully described: "I'm essentially a libertarian. I believe in limited government, individual liberty, and property rights." Given that the claims court has jurisdiction over most "takings" claims (resulting, for example, from the application of environmental protections), Wolski would appear to have his mind made up in advance on most issues that might come before him.

Expanding the takings clause in the Constitution's Fifth Amendment is a key goal of anti-environmental judges. This narrow provision requires the government to compensate landowners when it seizes their private property—for example, when a house is condemned to build a railroad. But anti-environmental judicial activists are now claiming that compensation is required for just about any government regulation of private property. In 1992, Justice Antonin Scalia led a U.S. Supreme Court majority in ruling for a would-be South Carolina beachfront developer who argued that his property had been "taken" by regulations that limited building in sensitive tidal areas. In *Tulare Lake Basin Water Storage District v. The United States,* the U.S. Court of Federal Claims ruled in favor of farmers who asserted that federal protections for salmon and delta smelt resulted in a "physical seizure" of the federally subsidized water that the farmers claim as a property right. "The federal government is certainly free to preserve fish," the claims court held. "It must simply pay for the water to do so."

Also targeted for reinterpretation is the commerce clause, which gives Congress the power to regulate matters that affect interstate business. Since pollution from one state can harm the economic welfare of another, and animals that provide tourism and hunting income migrate from state to state, this clause provides federal authority for many environmental laws. But the commerce clause's traditional protection of migratory birds could not stop the U.S. Supreme Court from ruling in 2001 that Cook County, Illinois, could dump its trash on the birds' wetland home. And in a dissent in a case challenging federal protection for red wolves in North Carolina and Tennessee, Appeals Court Judge J. Michael Luttig rejected the idea that the presence of wolves might encourage tourism (amply demonstrated in Montana and elsewhere) and urged that the wolf protection be struck down.

Luttig's dissent might not be so alarming were he not on the short list of possible Bush appointments to the U.S. Supreme Court. Already Bush has declared his favorite justices to be Scalia and Clarence Thomas, the foremost anti-environmental judicial activists on the high court. With one more like-minded justice, the court would have a solid anti-environmental majority that could set back environmental law by half a century.

"Superfund has never worked. The law, based on misunderstanding and distortion, was zipped through a lame-duck Congress in 1980 in a spirit of vengeance against 'the polluters.' It has been amended and operated on the same principle and stands as a sad reminder that revenge mixed with hypochondria is a poor basis for public policy."

—James V. DeLong, Competitive Enterprise Institute, 1995

"You did everything you could to elect a Republican president. You are already seeing in his actions the payback."

—William D. Raney, president, West Virginia Coal Association,
at the association's annual meeting, May 2002

"While this nation's citizens were stranded and sweltering in darkened subway tunnels in New York and without drinking water in Cleveland and Detroit, more rewards were being handed out. . . . While our electricity system was in a shambles, the Administration was eagerly handing out hundreds of millions of dollars in sole source contracts to Halliburton and Bechtel to rebuild Iraq's water and electricity infrastructure."

—Senator Robert Byrd (D-W.Va.)

"This country will not be a permanently good place for any of us to live in unless we make it a reasonably good place for all of us to live in."

—Theodore Roosevelt

13

Uncle Sam Turns Scrooge
No More Help from Washington

Seeptember 30, 2003, was the day Superfund died. The deceased left behind some 1,000 toxic waste sites—many of them "orphans," whose original owners had fled or gone out of business. George Bush's plan is that henceforth any clean-ups of these orphan sites will be paid for not by the industries that created the problem but by the taxpayers and victimized communities themselves.

The White House did not even put out one of its tepid Friday-afternoon press releases announcing the demise. Nor did the president—who has often proclaimed that he was elected to solve problems, not leave them to future generations—call on Congress for additional funds to keep Superfund going. But in the hard-right think tanks and K Street lobbyist suites, the champagne corks should have been popping. For the program's death was the culmination of a decade-long dream, not only saving their patrons and clients a lot of money but also undermining the historical partnership between the federal government and local communities. For the radical right, government is the problem, not the solution. It is not supposed to be cleaning up intractable problems that no one else wanted to deal with, especially if that involves forcing industry to clean up its mess.

The problem is that Superfund is a popular program. "No matter how many experts know that Superfund law or the Clean Water Act or Clean Air rules don't work as they should," pollster Frank Luntz had warned GOP politicians in his leaked memo, "the public doesn't perceive them as broken. There is not a public outcry to fix them." According to both Republican and Democratic pollsters, among the Bush policies rousing Americans to the greatest fury was letting companies that had dumped toxic wastes off the hook.

To the radical right, Superfund's very popularity made it all the more dangerous. By showing Americans that the national government (and, in fact, only the national government) could be counted on to protect their communities, it encouraged them to think of protection as a legitimate governmental function. To the right, that was reason enough to put a stop to this coddling.

Requiem for Superfund

Superfund (officially known as the Comprehensive Environmental Response, Compensation, and Liability Act, or CERCLA) had been signed into law by President Jimmy Carter in the wake of the Love Canal scandal. During the course of ten years in the 1940s and 1950s, the Hooker Chemical and Plastics Corporation had dumped 352 million pounds of highly toxic wastes in the abandoned upstate New York canal, shoveled some dirt on top, and sold the land, which eventually became the site of a school and housing development. Eventually, the chemical poisons started leaching up through the soil and seeping into basements, and Love Canal citizens organized to demand that something be done. The eventual response was Superfund, launched to clean up not only Love Canal but the thousands of toxic dump sites, abandoned factories, and played-out mines that littered the country, endangering the health of nearby residents.

Superfund is—or, rather, was—based on the "polluter pays" principle. If the company responsible for a toxic site was identifiable and still in business, it was ordered to clean up its mess. If the company did not act, then the Environmental

Protection Agency would do the cleanup and send the bill. Cleanups of "orphan" sites, where the owners had fled or gone bankrupt, were paid for with a tax on the oil and chemical raw materials that had been the original source of the mess. The EPA set the standards and ensured that the job got done. For the thousands of smaller, less contaminated sites, the states would take responsibility.

Superfund was not established until 1980, so for its first eight years it was implemented by the fundamentally hostile administration of President Ronald Reagan. Racked by scandal during the Reagan administration and under corporate attack since its inception (by many of the same figures who went on to staff the George W. Bush White House), the program was reorganized in the 1990s under Clinton. In its first 20 years, some 2,000 sites were listed by the EPA, of which 840 have been cleaned up. Although new sites are identified each year, real progress was being made toward eliminating the backlog; as Bush came into office, it appeared that, all things being equal, in another fifteen years America would have cleared up its toxic legacy.

But all things were not equal. Superfund was one of the first major pollution cleanup programs to draw the full wrath of corporate conservatives, who

loathed the idea that operating a business entailed responsibilities to the future. When General Electric dumped millions of gallons of PCBs in the Hudson River in the 1950s and 1960s, it was arguably legal. "Why, then, should GE have to clean up the mess now?" ran the corporatist argument. If you break your neighbor's window, even doing something innocent and legal, you fix it. But to the radical right, corporations were different. If people did not want to be exposed to chemical emissions, they should not live near factories or power plants. Superfund was especially offensive because it reached back in time and held corporations responsible for past deeds, whether doing so fell within the letter of the law or not.

To the oil and chemical industries, Superfund was also expensive; detractors routinely complained about its enormous legal costs (most of which, however, were due to litigation among companies, or between companies and their insurers, over how to allocate responsibility). They also argued that the cleanup standards were too stringent. Terry Anderson's Political Economy Research Center complained, for example, that Superfund "led to tough, costly standards for cleaning up these places—such as the requirement that soil be clean enough for children to eat daily, even if children are never going to be near the place." (Never is a long time. Hooker Chemical probably did not imagine that anyone would build a grade school on top of its waste dump.)

The administration even made toxic waste cleanups dirtier, by exempting them from the Clean Air Act. This meant that organic solvents in a dump could be vaporized in an incinerator, converting soil pollutants to air pollutants— which Bush's EPA decided not to regulate.

In addition to the legal, ideological, and financial objections to Superfund, it became a political football. In 1993, almost everyone involved—environmentalists, small businesses, the chemical industry, the Chamber of Commerce, the states, and the EPA—agreed on a proposal to streamline the program. But Senate Republicans, egged on by the insurance industry and corporatist ideologues and eager to deny the Democrats a legislative success on the eve of the 1994 midterm election, filibustered the bill to death. After that, the Republican congressional leadership refused to take up any Superfund legislation. They even allowed the tax on the oil and chemical industries to expire, in spite of Clinton's efforts to renew it. The fund steadily declined from its 1996 level of $3.8 billion, demanding ever heavier infusions of taxpayer dollars.

Given its composition, the Bush administration was only too happy to see Superfund waste away. Prior to 2001, James Connaughton, the head of Bush's Council on Environmental Quality, had earned his living lobbying against Superfund. While a senator, Vice President Dick Cheney had voted against allowing citizens to sue when they were damaged by toxic waste dumping. Cheney's company, Halliburton, was itself responsible for the Tri-State Mining District Superfund site in southwestern Missouri. And risk maven John Graham had made his career at Harvard deriding toxic waste cleanups.

During the 1990s, Superfund had been cleaning up about 86 sites a year. By 2002, that number had dwindled to 40, and taxpayers—the victims of the pollution—were footing half the bill. The inspector general found that, in 2002, the EPA had failed to fund a single dollar for toxic waste cleanups at 32 high-priority Superfund sites, including those where toxic waste was still polluting water and risking families' health. In 2003 there was funding for only 10 new sites. Ten others originally proposed by the EPA were delayed yet again.

One of these was the Mohawk Tannery, which sat on the floodplain of New Hampshire's Nashua River. When it shut down in the 1980s, its owners left behind puddles of chromium, zinc, and phenol leaching into the ground from unlined lagoons and washing over into the river in heavy rains. Trichloroethylene has already leaked into local drinking-water supplies, and a major storm could unleash a torrent of poisons into the river. The EPA estimated that, once work began, the site could be cleaned up within a year. But despite being listed by the EPA, and even though New Hampshire is a politically critical state, the stranglehold on funding means that nothing will be done. The chain-link fence surrounding the property has rusted away, and children use the toxic spoils as a bike track. Nashua Alderman Mark Plamondon is afraid that the toxic site "will be brushed under the carpet . . . with the mentality that, 'Nashua has put up with this for 20 or 30 years, what's another 10, or 12, or longer?'" What Plamondon fears is what the radical right hopes for. If people in Nashua are worried, they can pay for the cleanup themselves or just move elsewhere and sell their homes to those too poor to have an option.

(Superfund was not the only program to become an example of private recklessness being turned into a public obligation. Cleanups of leaking underground storage tanks were financed through a national trust account administered by the EPA and supported by gasoline taxes; now the Bush administration proposes that the federal government be barred from seeking repayment from tank owners for those costs. As a result, the public may wind up paying the bill to clean up the messes irresponsible polluters have left behind.)

By 2004, progress in reducing the nation's backlog of hazardous waste sites had come to an end. New sites were being added to the list as fast as old ones were being cleaned up with the anemic levels of funding. We now have a seemingly permanent backlog of 1,000 toxic dumps, and a problem that had been on the verge of being solved has become a permanent economic and public health nightmare for millions of Americans.

Rivers Shouldn't Catch Fire

Superfund was just a small part of the safety net created since the New Deal ("our own socialist revolution," as Bush's circuit court nominee Janice Rogers Brown called it). Actually, the national government's role in helping to provide vital infrastructure goes all the way back to Henry Clay and the Whigs, with their "American system" of federally supported roads and canals, which eventually led to the interstate highway system. With the Cold War and Sputnik came a national commitment to federal support for new technology, showcased in the space program and the massive public health investment in the National Institutes of Health. And with Earth Day came a new federal partnership devoted to cleaning up our sadly abused environment.

The national partnership in environmental restoration has taken many different forms. During the Depression, Franklin D. Roosevelt created the Civilian Conservation Corps, the Tennessee Valley Authority, and the Works Progress Administration as federal agencies—primarily to create jobs and jumpstart the economy but also to address the health of our natural commons. In the 1960s and 1970s, the New Frontier/Great Society model emerged: the federal government would establish national standards for health care, education, and poverty and then provide funds to help local governments meet them. The final piece in this model was the forging of a national commitment to repair and restore communities and natural resources that had been devastated by the intense industrial advances of the previous century.

By 1965 Lake Erie was dying; tourists in New York City routinely changed their shirts—the collars filthy by noon—twice a day; and most American water-fronts were stench-ridden wastelands to be avoided. The mighty Potomac flow-ing through our nation's capital was no exception: while Carl Pope was growing up outside Washington, unfortunate canoeists who fell into the river were taken to the emergency room—not as drowning victims but to get inoculated against tetanus and hepatitis.

When the Cuyahoga River in Cleveland caught on fire; when an offshore oil spill at Santa Barbara, California, captured the public's attention with images of volunteers trying to rescue oil-soaked waterfowl; and when millions of Amer-icans turned out for demonstrations, protests, and cleanups around an envi-ronmental teach-in that became the first Earth Day, politicians of both parties embraced environmental cleanup as a new national cause. The underlying prem-ise—that the federal government would guarantee every American air that was fit to breathe, water that was safe to drink, and swimmable and fishable rivers and shores—was rapidly embodied in the Clean Air and Clean Water acts. In 1973 Congress dealt with solid and hazardous waste, in 1974 the nation's food supply was guaranteed against contamination by pesticides, and in 1976 Con-gress adopted the premise that new industrial chemicals should be tested for safety before they were put into commercial production.

Progress came quickly. In 1972, for example, cities and industries rou-tinely dumped untreated sewage and industrial waste into our waters, and two-thirds of America's lakes, rivers, and beaches were too polluted for swimming or fishing. Under the Clean Water Act, industry had to install pollution con-trol equipment, and sewage treatment plants were paid for with a mixture of federal and state funding. Under President Reagan, the program was converted from a straight grant to the states to a revolving loan fund, which required repay-ment. The pace of new investment slowed, but still, by the time George W. Bush took office, only 40 percent of the nation's waterways remained contaminated.

Addressing that last 40 percent requires taking on the two most difficult issues. One is contaminated runoff: pesticides from agriculture, manure from feedlots, eroded soils from logging operations, and heavy metals and oil washed by rain from city streets, parking lots, and highways. As we saw in chapter 12, lobbyists for the enormous animal feeding operations drafted a proposal by which, in exchange for a few farms reducing their pollution, the rest would be given amnesty. Unsurprisingly, the EPA's final proposal in June 2003 was, both conceptually and in its details, modeled closely on the one submitted by industry. So the most rapidly growing source of toxic runoff was exempted from the Clean Water Act.

The other unaddressed clean water problem is that, in older cities, the drains carrying waste to sewage treatment plants are combined with storm sewers. During heavy storms the systems become overloaded, causing raw sewage to flow past sewage treatment plants and into rivers, lakes, and beaches.

Suburban sprawl exacerbates the problem of combined sanitary and storm-water systems. For example, in Hamilton County, Ohio, outside Cincinnati, sprawl had drastically overloaded the area's combined storm-water and sanitary sewers. When it rained, thousands of homeowners found their backyards and basements flooded with raw sewage. An investigative report concluded that some 10,000 homeowners "have a dirty little secret many are too afraid to tell because no one would want to buy their homes if they knew: their basements, sometimes yards, flood with sewage. And so far, they haven't been able to get anyone to do anything about it." Resident Rhonda Nunlist told reporters that sewage in her yard has caused her staph infections, and she no longer let her kids play in their backyard. Hamilton County was not alone. Lake St. Claire, east of Detroit, was regularly fouled with raw sewage. Nationally there were a near-record 12,000 beach closings due to sewage spills in 2002.

The original plan was that cities would use the revolving loan fund to separate their storm-water and sanitary-sewage systems. But once again Bush brought progress to a halt. A September 2002 EPA report found that, unless the federal government provided additional resources, there would be a $535 billion gap between the need for new water pollution control facilities and available funding—a figure EPA Administrator Christie Whitman admitted was "clearly beyond the ability of any one entity to address." The Senate suggested increasing funding by $5.2 billion, $3 billion over the previous year's funding. The Republican leadership in the House, instead, *cut* funding by $500 million. And the administration suggested a miserly $1.7 billion for the programs, 32 percent less than in the previous year.

Under continued pressure to help cities fund the cleanup of overflowing sewers, Bush took his usual tack. Rather than help cities comply with environmental standards, he weakened the standards. On November 3, 2003, the EPA announced a draft policy that would allow operators of sewage treatment plants to "blend" (like a fine scotch) partially treated sewage with rainwater and then release it into the nation's waterways. In Fernald, Ohio, they went further. Not only sewage but also radioactive wastewater was now to be dumped, untreated, into the Great Miami River. It was simply too expensive, the Department of Energy decided, for the federal government to clean up the mess it had left behind at its nuclear weapons facility at Fernald.

The combination of regulations written by Big Pig and pervasive fiscal neglect means that not only will America's waters never be cleaner than they are now, but they have already begun to get dirtier. For the first time since the passage of the Clean Water Act, the EPA reported in 2003 that national water pollution levels were rising.

It is a risky proposition for Bush—should word get out. As Luntz warned his readers, *"The* number one *hot button to most voters is* water quality—*including both infrastructure and pollution protection.* People don't understand the technicalities of environmental law—but they do understand the benefits of conservation of water, land, and open spaces." People might, but to the radical right, the cure for the water pollution problem—an effective national/local partnership—was worse than the disease.

Poisoning America to Defend It

Another principle enunciated by Luntz was that "local problems require local solutions." Given the costs of cleaning up enormous toxic waste sites or building new sewage systems, this often translates as "no solution." But when the pollution is at a military base, the local entity is a branch of the national government. In these cases, Bush's approach has simply been to exempt the military from the law.

By 1980, U.S. military installations, together with the nuclear facilities operated by the Department of Energy, had become some of the nation's biggest polluters. A prevalence of high-tech and highly toxic technologies, combined with a "get the job done, this is war" mentality, made these facilities very bad neighbors indeed. For example, in the late 1990s the prosperous Washington, D.C., neighborhood of Spring Valley found itself to be a toxic waste site due to the mustard gas and other military munitions that had been abandoned there 80 years earlier during World War I, when the area was still woodland.

In an interesting twist, however, by century's end the armed services also ranked among the nation's most creative environmental innovators. In Hawaii, some of the finest work to protect endangered species on federal lands is being done by the military. At Fort Stewart, Georgia, a thriving population of red-cockaded woodpeckers—5 percent of the world's total—coexists happily with the Third Infantry Division. "The same landscape that supports our training needs also supports the ecosystem," says Lieutenant Colonel Michael Case. "These seemingly opposing activities are inherently compatible."

Complying with environmental laws, the military pioneered cleaning aircraft by blasting them with plastic pellets instead of toxic solvents. And the Defense Department (with a little prodding from the Sierra Club) learned how to destroy chemical weapons without burning them in dangerous incinerators.

How did the White House and the Pentagon celebrate this progress? By seeking, in March 2003, blanket waivers for the military from the nation's landmark environmental regulations, claiming that they compromised readiness. EPA Administrator Whitman told Congress that she did not know of any cases where they had, and the armed forces had never even asked for the temporary waivers they are already allowed under existing regulations. Even so, Donald Rumsfeld demanded that Congress create a permanent legislative exemption from all major environmental laws for his Defense Department. A Pentagon "fact sheet" argued that having to train in landscapes like Fort Stewart, dotted with environmentally and historically sensitive sites, reduced "training realism." The army documents the Pentagon used in preparing its fact sheet, however, made a point that was exactly the opposite: that "maintaining a landscape that supports wildlife also enhances training realism." Only a few weeks later, the army was in a real war in which it had to fight around mosques, oil wells, and enough other sensitive sites to make Fort Stewart look like a free-fire zone. The Third Infantry fought very well.

Base commanders were ordered to make compliance look difficult. Navy Secretary Gordon England warned his commanders that signing cooperative agreements with local communities on habitat protection—which was ostensibly what the Bush administration favored—could undermine the real goal, which was to rewrite the Endangered Species Act. "It is important that well intentioned personnel in the field not make local accommodations to introduce new species, habitats, etc. . . . because concessions could run counter to legislative relief we are continuing to pursue with Congress."

Why this abrupt retreat on multiple fronts? It could be that Rumsfeld simply saw an opportunity, with U.S. forces in the field, to make life simpler for the military. But it also fits with this administration's broad assault on environmental regulations. If the work of the military can be judged important enough to elevate it above environmental standards, why not that of other federal agencies, or even private corporations? The idea is already being bandied about in right-wing venues. Referring to the Endangered Species Act, David Horowitz's neoconservative *FrontPage* magazine editorialized, "Why should this siege against science and good sense be lifted only when and where it impacts the military? The armed forces could burnish their credentials as freedom's defenders if they fought this battle on a broader front."

The Defense Department is even making an about-face on the issue of chemical weapons disposal. In recent years the department has safely destroyed its own chemical-weapons stock using water and microbes—and continues to do so in Colorado, Indiana, Maryland, and Kentucky. The Pentagon, however, refuses to apply these methods to facilities in Arkansas, Oregon, and Alabama, where an army depot at Anniston houses 2,254 tons of rockets, shells, and mines loaded with outmoded nerve gas, mustard gas, and other chemical weapons. Anniston is a poor, predominantly African American community, and many residents wonder if this is why its weapons of mass destruction are simply going to be incinerated.

The army's trust problem in Anniston was compounded by the fact that local residents are already suffering from its carelessness. On August 3, 1995, 55-year-old schoolteacher Arametta Porter was hauling her recycling to the curb when a sudden gust of wind almost blew her over. A few minutes later she had a seizure—her first, but not her last. Today Porter suffers from severe chemical sensitivity and repeated facial spasms, and she has been advised by her doctor never to return to Anniston. Porter's doctors describe her symptoms as a classic case of exposure to nerve gas. The Army admitted that in the first three days of August 1995, as it was shifting chemical weapons at the depot, a powerful nerve gas called GB did leak. But, says the military, Porter cannot prove that her illness was the result of the leaked nerve gas—there being no test available to detect past exposure.

When Anniston residents protested the incineration plans, the military bluntly declared that neutralization with water-based technologies was feasible but not part of the battle plan. "We've invested more than $500 million to get to where we are. We're within days of beginning our work. It's a matter of what's been spent and a matter of what would have to be spent," said Pentagon spokesperson Mike Abrams (ignoring the fact that, all through the decade the army was spending that $500 million, local residents and environmentalists had been urging the army to use a safer technology).

The army acknowledged that things might go wrong. It designated a "pink zone" around the incinerator, issued gas masks and protective hoods to local residents living inside the zone, and recommended that local schools and churches be equipped with pressurized rooms to serve as emergency evacuation shelters. (But it began burning even before the pressurized rooms were finished, saying it would burn only "slowly" and only from 6 P.M. to 6 A.M.—so that children would be "safe" in their beds asleep during the burning, rather than being in school.)

"If this were Westchester or Nassau County, this would not be happening," said Craig Williams of the Chemical Weapons Working Group, one of the strongest incineration opponents. "We didn't break the back of segregation only to die together from toxic chemicals," said Reverend Fred Shuttlesworth, vice president of the Southern Christian Leadership Conference. "We must fight for freedom from this toxic oppression, from a government who cares more about filling the pockets of contractors than it does protecting this community from harm."

Although the Sierra Club and other organizations sued to block the incineration, the Bush administration refused to back down. While American soldiers fruitlessly searched Iraq for weapons like VX, mustard, and GB, American contractors in Anniston began burning the same poisons in an incinerator whose strongest justification was: "We've already built it, so we have to use it."

People in Anniston can be pardoned for wondering whether, in the eyes of the Bush administration, they were an enemy population. They had, after all, voted for Al Gore. But, in fact, they were merely victims of one of the administration's deep-seated beliefs—taxpayer dollars spent to protect taxpayers would only make them less self-reliant.

Cop-out in the Coal Belt

The coal belt—western Pennsylvania, West Virginia, southwestern Virginia, eastern Kentucky, and southern Ohio—had been turned by Karl Rove into the Republican column in 2000, thanks partly to Al Gore's alleged environmental extremism. Bush's solicitude for the region, however, did not include extending the helping hand of the federal government.

On the eve of the 2000 election, on October 11, a 2.2-billion-gallon coal-slurry pond near Inez, Kentucky, leaked into an abandoned underground coal mine, spilling 250 million gallons of sludge into two creeks, obliterating all aquatic life, and blackening 50 miles of the Big Sandy River. Walls of sludge eight to ten feet deep piled up in the beds of Coldwater and Wolf creeks, threatening residents. EPA officials called it "the worst-ever environmental disaster in the Southeastern United States"—20 times the size of the *Exxon Valdez* spill.

Kentucky Governor Paul Patton declared a state of emergency for ten counties. Many residents developed red splotches on their bodies, which local children dubbed "sludge bumps." Federal analyses revealed that the sludge contained copper, vanadium, manganese, barium, arsenic, and cobalt in toxic quantities. Martin County Coal initially agreed to restore the community and "get things back to normal," admitting that "we've messed up a bunch of times."

But after the results of the November election came in, the company changed its tune, calling the slurry spill "the direct, sole and proximate result of an act of God, the occurrence of which was not within the control of Martin County Coal." The company further claimed that any negligence had occurred more than five years earlier and was therefore covered by the statute of limitations.

Why did Martin Coal conclude that Bush's election was going to let it off the hook? Perhaps because of how the new Bush team reacted to an official investigation of the incident and its treatment of one of the investigators. Jack Spadaro, superintendent of the National Mine Health and Safety Institute in Beckley, West Virginia, was a member of the federal team looking into the Martin disaster. He and other members of the team wanted to issue eight notices of violation against Massey Energy, which owned Martin County Coal. They favored heavy fines and wanted to hold accountable the federal regulators who had allowed the company to expand its slurry ponds without completing safety measures. The administration overturned their recommendations. When Spadaro protested, he was fired, despite 26 years of stellar performance.

Martin County Coal had correctly identified where the harsh wind from the White House was blowing; there was to be no relief for mining communities but lots of support for mining companies. Pennsylvania, for example, had been under federal court order to reform its coal-mining regulatory program— in particular, to ensure that mining companies posted bonds to cover the cost of cleanup after they shut down. But Pennsylvania's bonding program was so inadequate that it had accumulated an enormous deficit, with the result that mine sites were not being properly reclaimed, and abandoned mines were discharging toxics and heavy metals into Pennsylvania's lakes and streams.

The Pennsylvania Sportsmen's Federation, along with the Sierra Club, sued; the state settled by agreeing that the bonds posted by companies would provide adequate funding. The Bush administration stepped in, however, and authorized the state to collect far lower levels of bonds. It also moved to rewrite national rules so that coal mine–bonding programs no longer needed to demonstrate "solvency." The message: the Pennsylvania coal industry could do nothing, and states like West Virginia that had fully funded bonding programs could backslide. It was the proverbial license to pollute.

Shell Game with Park Funds

Although Bush was determined to stamp out environmental restoration partnerships between the national government and the states and communities, such partnerships remained very popular. Americans liked the idea of their tax dollars being spent on parks, sewers, toxic cleanups, and stream restoration. Conventional public works like highways and dams were often controversial, but everyone liked more open space. ("Becoming a champion of national parks and forests," advised Luntz, "is the best way to show our citizens that Republicans can be FOR something positive on the environment.")

So the White House slashed federal funding for environmental restoration but concealed its cuts with the fiscal sleight of hand Bush had derided as "fuzzy math" during his campaign. While running for president, Bush had promised to fully fund the Land and Water Conservation Fund, which receives a portion of federal revenues from leasing oil and gas off the coasts to purchase critically needed parklands. The fund was so popular that more than 300 members of the House voted in 2000 to expand and guarantee its funding, with Alaska's Representative Don Young, virulently right-wing on most issues, working in partnership with the liberal George Miller of California. Bush also promised to eliminate a $4.9 billion backlog in maintenance funds for facilities and infrastructure in the parks.

Once in power, however, Bush found that his most ardent supporters on the radical right abhorred the idea of one more square foot of public land. When the administration suggested additional tax incentives for landowners to protect open space through conservation easements, the right went crazy. Texas Senator Phil Gramm called it a "dangerous concept" that "favors conservationists over churches, schools and orphanages. . . . It's one thing to encourage charitable giving; it's another thing to distort the marketplace." Carol LaGrasse of the Property Rights Foundation called the proposal "a land grab program," even though it was entirely voluntary.

As Bush had shown in Texas, he really did not care about parks. So he took a number of existing programs that funded park acquisition, wildlife protection, and open space preservation, and he lumped them all into the Land and Water Conservation Fund—without transferring the funds to support them. So the "full funding" of $900 million for the LWCF that the administration asked for actually meant less money for its core purpose of park acquisition. And when the administration asked the Park Service to deploy rangers at locations like Fort Point underneath the Golden Gate Bridge as part of its war on terrorism, $4.6 million to pay for this initiative was cannibalized from repair budgets at places like Yosemite.

Security was not the only ploy Bush used to drain funds intended for the parks. Another was to divert funds Congress had intended for park maintenance to pay for the costs of privatizing 1,700 National Park Service jobs. Privatization was supposed to save money, so there was a certain irony in needing extra funds to accomplish it. But the program was as close as Bush was going to get (at least in a first term) to Terry Anderson's vision of privatizing the parks themselves, so the economics were less important than the principle.

Interior Secretary Norton's part of an overall plan to privatize 850,000 federal workers was to make more than a quarter of the Park Service's 20,000 employees private contractors. Heading the administration's overall privatization effort was Jack Kalavritinos, formerly the chief lobbyist for a group of engineering firms that were major Bush campaign donors and were deeply interested in getting contracts for work in the national parks.

The retired supervisor of Yellowstone National Park, Bob Barbee, points out that the whole idea seems driven by ideology. "We need a strong cadre of professionals steeped in Park Service traditions, and with a commitment to its goals," he protested. "That shouldn't be bartered away. It's like turning over the Army to a bunch of mercenaries." Other park advocates worried that privately employed scientists might not be able to stand up to their employers: a firm that was going to profit by building a new road might easily pressure its ecologists to ignore possible damage to the park's wildlife. Scientists under contract to the owner of a dam were less likely to come down on the side of removing the dam to restore fisheries. Park Service Director Fran Mainella warned that the plan would have "serious consequences for visitor services." But the hard right kept pushing Bush, and the administration overruled Mainella's objections.

The National Parks Conservation Association had praised Bush for his campaign promises on the parks—among the few kudos his campaign received from the environmental community. But in 2003 the association issued a report card on Bush's park stewardship and gave him a D-minus. "The administration is not doing the job they need to do to fully protect, to fully fund, to fully improve our national parks," said association president Tom Kiernan. The report card caustically noted that "the administration has fallen far short of its pledge to eliminate the backlog of maintenance projects in our national parks and yet persists in touting the pledge without allocating significant new funds." It pointed out that, of a billion dollars Bush claimed to be spending on eliminating the infrastructure backlog, all but $174 million was accounting legerdemain. Bush's operating budgets for the parks actually fell by a third—$600 million short of what was needed—resulting in the loss of one-third of the visitor education activities at Death Valley and in Yellowstone turning away 60 percent of the school groups that sought to use the park's educational facilities.

One of Bush's most influential right-wing supporters has been Grover Norquist, the head of a group called Americans for Tax Reform and influential convener of regular strategy sessions—known simply as "the Wednesday Meeting"—of right-wing activists to ensure that all are marching to the same talking points. He's been called "the most powerful man in Washington you never heard of" and is known for his amazing bluntness. "I don't want to abolish government," he told National Public Radio in March 2001. "I simply want to reduce it to the size where I can drag it into the bathroom and drown it in the bathtub."

This approach is obviously incompatible with fully funding a program for parkland acquisition, let alone cleaning up toxic waste dumps, or building new sewers, or disposing of nerve gas in a safe way. A government vigorous enough to do those things for its citizens would be a government strong and vigorous enough to resist the murderous ministrations of Grover Norquist and the hard right.

"Such blatant disregard for the law weakens governments, encourages corruption, [and] undermines democracy."

—Secretary of State Colin Powell, announcing a new U.S. campaign to help developing countries fight unlawful deforestation, even as the Bush administration evades international treaties

"Today, the United States remains the preeminent economic, military, diplomatic, and cultural power on a scale not seen since the fall of the Roman Empire. . . . At the dawn of the 21st century, the task of the new administration is to develop a military and foreign policy appropriate to our position of overwhelming dominance . . . that recognize[s] the new unipolarity and the unilateralism necessary to maintain it."

—Charles Krauthammer, "The Bush Doctrine"

"Oderint, dum metuant." ("Let them hate us, so long as they fear.")

—Caligula, third emperor of Rome (A.D. 37–41), cited in American diplomat John Brady Kiesling's letter of resignation in protest over Bush's unilateralism

Alone in the World
America as Global Outlaw

As the United States prepared to lead a rather small "coalition of the willing" into Iraq, a senior *Wall Street Journal* editor made a candid assessment: "We're paying a very high price for walking away from Kyoto." The bill came later: $87 billion to be paid by U.S. taxpayers, with the promise of more to come. After politely listening to entreaties that it help finance the rebuilding of Iraq, the international community ponied up $13 billion in pledges, all but $3 to $4 billion in the form of loans. In November 2003, Bush's state visit to our closest international ally, Great Britain, was met by tens of thousands of demonstrators. Earlier in the year, in a British poll asking who was the greatest threat to world peace, George Bush and Saddam Hussein tied at 45 percent each.

Bush's decision to isolate the United States from the world has been very conscious and scripted—and celebrated by his right-wing backers. "The alacrity and almost casualness with which Bush withdrew from Kyoto," wrote hardright columnist Charles Krauthammer, "sent a message that the United States would no longer acquiesce in multilateral nonsense just because it had pages of signatories and bore the sheen of international comity." Bush, like most of the Republicans in the Congress (as well as many Democrats), opposed the ratification of Kyoto because of its failure to bind Third World nations to join the industrial world in limiting their emissions of carbon dioxide. This supposed favoritism, critics concluded, would cause a hemorrhage of jobs to countries like China and India. (Ironically, in November 2003, China announced that it was adopting auto fuel-efficiency standards significantly tougher than those in the United States. In 1999, U.S. emissions of carbon dioxide averaged about 5.6 tons of carbon per person—20 times the per capita figure for India, and more than 10 times that of China.)

During the 2000 campaign, Bush had heartened some environmental leaders when he met with prominent experts on global warming, declared that he believed the phenomenon was real and required action, and embraced the principle that older coal-fired power plants should be retrofitted to reduce their emissions not only of sulfur, nitrogen, and mercury (the so-called three pollutants) but also of the fourth pollutant—carbon dioxide. Bush's commitment to this "four-pollutant" solution was presented as balancing his rejection of Kyoto: if elected he would not ratify Kyoto, but he would take action to begin reducing carbon dioxide pollution in his own way. As elsewhere in the campaign rhetoric carefully crafted by Karl Rove, the hard-edged rejection of Kyoto was softened and blunted by the "compassionate" pledge (albeit unquantified) to do something to limit carbon dioxide.

It all ended in early 2001, after Environmental Protection Agency Administrator Christie Whitman attended a meeting of environmental ministers of the G8 nations in Italy. Once home, she wrote a letter to Bush: "Mr. President, this [global warming] is a credibility issue for the U.S. in the international community. It is also an issue that is resonating here at home. We need to appear engaged and shift the discussion from the focus on the 'K' word [Kyoto] to action, but we have to build some bona fides first."

As we saw in chapter 10, the hard right successfully mobilized in the run-up to Bush's first State of the Union message to get him to abandon his carbon dioxide pledge. (Subsequent events demonstrated the hollowness of the pledge to deal with the other three pollutants.) Having forsaken Kyoto and put nothing in its place, the United States under Bush began its full-scale retreat from the broader world community.

It was not until February 2002 that the Bush administration finally announced its alternative to Kyoto—a plan the Sierra Club called a "Valentine's Day present" for the carbon lobby. Instead of agreeing to reduce or even stabilize absolute carbon dioxide emissions, Bush proposed a plan to reduce the amount of carbon dioxide pollution per dollar of gross national product. The major tool for doing this was a series of voluntary agreements with industry. Under the plan, greenhouse gas intensity would be cut by 18 percent over a decade. But because the economy will continue to grow, by 2012 the United States would still emit more carbon dioxide than it does now. Combined with a program to "research" aspects of the greenhouse problem that scientists concluded had already been amply studied and the billions of dollars in new subsidies for the production of oil, coal, and natural gas, the Bush plan constituted a thumb in the eye of the international community.

Mad as Hatters: No Promises on Mercury

The new Bush unilateralism is reflected in the U.S. approach to mercury pollution. For years, a major international effort had been under way to develop a global protocol to reduce and eventually eliminate emissions of toxic mercury. According to the United Nations Environment Program (UNEP), mercury concentrations in the air have tripled since pre-industrial times. One of the largest sources is burning coal; when mercury settles out of the atmosphere into oceans, rivers, and lakes, it rapidly accumulates in the food chain. Marine species like tuna, swordfish, and shark, which live at the top of that food chain and are among the most popular menu items for health-conscious seafood eaters, now carry potentially dangerous levels of mercury in their flesh.

The hazards of mercury have been recognized since the eighteenth century, when its use in making felt hats caused serious neurological damage to felters (whence the expression, "mad as a hatter"). Today, the most dangerous consequences of mercury exposure are developmental and nervous system problems in infants exposed in utero, although high exposures can damage the brain, kidneys, and liver in those of any age. The Food and Drug Administration and all but nine states warn against consumption of certain fish because of mercury contamination; in April 2003, California Attorney General William Lockyer brought suit against grocery stores and major restaurant chains to require them to warn consumers that tuna, swordfish, shark, and other top predators should not be eaten at all by pregnant women, and eaten only infrequently by children and women of childbearing age.

When UNEP met in Nairobi in February 2003 to draft a global mercury convention, the unilateralists in the administration were prepared. An internal document leaked in advance of the conference revealed the obstructionist U.S. position: "We believe that negotiating a binding convention on mercury is not the most effective way to approach this issue at this time, and we should block any attempts to move forward on one at this meeting." This led to widespread anger by supporters of strong action on mercury poisoning. According to Michael Bender of the Mercury Policy Project, "The U.S. is proposing just enough to say that it didn't do nothing, but it's barely more than doing nothing." Representative Henry Waxman (D-Calif.) and Senator Patrick Leahy (D-Vt.) sent a blistering letter to the White House: "Under previous administrations, the United States had a well deserved reputation as a world leader on the environment," the letter said. "The series of decisions you are making diminishes that reputation."

True to the playbook, at Nairobi the United States blocked any binding restrictions on mercury use, pushing in its place a non-mandatory program paid for by voluntary contributions. Instead of keeping mercury out of the environment, the Bush administration had the State Department suggest, world governments should be content with simply informing people that fish in their oceans and rivers were no longer safe to eat.

Pandering on Population

Back in 1969, the United States helped to found the United Nations Family Planning Agency (UNFPA), which works in 160 countries to make sure that women have access to the things that have been shown to work to reduce unwanted births: voluntary family planning as well as economic opportunities and education for women.

In 2002, however, Bush bowed to his anti-abortion constituency and eliminated all U.S. funding for the UNFPA's vital international family planning services. Against the advice of Secretary of State Colin Powell, the White House yanked $34 million in previously appropriated funds—enough money, according to the UNFPA, to prevent the deaths of 4,700 mothers, 77,000 children under age five, and 800,000 abortions by providing access to safe family planning. Ironically, the reason Bush eliminated funding was the allegation that the UNFPA approves forced abortion and sterilization in China. The UNFPA insists that it only funds voluntary programs in China, a position supported by a State Department fact-finding mission, which found no evidence that the agency "knowingly supported or participated in the management of a program of coercive abortion or involuntary sterilization." Powell himself had praised the agency in his confirmation hearings, referring to its "invaluable work," but he was overruled by the White House's need to placate its right-wing base. As the *New York Times* reported, the decision to withdraw funding "underscored long-running tensions within the administration between Mr. Bush's conservative advisers, like his political mastermind, Karl Rove, and more moderate officials, like Secretary Powell, as the White House heads into midterm elections eager to energize its political base."

The $34 million that was to go to the UNFPA was distributed instead by the U.S. Agency for International Development, which operates in some 60 fewer countries than the U.N. body. Programs supported by USAID are also subject to the "global gag rule," a measure imposed by Bush on January 22, 2001, as one of his very first acts upon taking office. The "gag rule" prohibits U.S. support for any population program that provides abortion services, lobbies for legalization of abortion, or even provides accurate medical information concerning the procedure. Thus, family planning organizations abroad must choose between speaking freely or giving up U.S. assistance.

"How can we export a policy that denies free speech and still say we support democracy?" asked California Senator Barbara Boxer (D). According to the BBC, the rule has resulted in the closing of thousands of family planning clinics around the world, to the satisfaction of Bush's supporters. It quoted Wendy Wright of the right-wing group Concerned Women of America, who spoke in support of the gag rule: "It's not that I know what is right for other women," she said. "It's that I know what is right."

Stop the World, We Want to Get Off

While Washington retreated into a cocoon, the rest of the world continued to look for cooperative international solutions to pressing environmental problems. The focus of these discussions was the fourth U.N. Conference on the Environment, scheduled for Johannesburg, South Africa, in August 2002. Seizing control of the internal planning process within the Bush administration, the unilateralists blocked efforts by mainstream voices within the State Department and Environmental Protection Agency bureaucracies to position the United States as a willing partner at the meeting. Instead, the administration adopted the stance that any usual form of binding international environmental agreement—anything that contained environmental goals, standards, or timetables—was equally reprehensible and unacceptable. Instead of agreements among nations, the Bush administration began a drumbeat for what it called "public-private partnerships"—in effect surrendering the future of the global environmental commons to whatever deals multilateral corporations would offer individual nations, particularly those in the Third World, where governmental institutions for environmental protection are least developed.

In order to ensure that Johannesburg failed to develop any concrete environmental objectives, the U.S. delegation at the final preparatory meeting in Bali, Indonesia, simply refused to allow any concrete commitments or pledges to be placed on the agenda for the upcoming Earth Summit. While U.N. Environment Program head Klaus Toepfer begged the meeting for "a concrete action plan... concrete projects... and above all a clear political declaration," the U.S. delegates refused even to schedule a discussion of the Kyoto Protocol. Long before delegates even arrived in South Africa, the Bush administration had decided to use the summit to end the era of international environmental treaty making.

"What are we going to do about the USA?" asked conference chair Emil Salim of Indonesia. In the end, the Bali meeting failed, for the first time in U.N. history, to complete agreement on a draft text for the summit, setting the Johannesburg meeting up for failure. Global environmental scientists were dismayed. "It is really very depressing. It doesn't look like there will be any science at Johannesburg. Everything is stuck in politics," said Professor Georgina Mace, director of science at the Zoological Society of London.

President Bush declined to attend the shipwreck of his making at Johannesburg. (Many delegates sported buttons saying, "Where is W?") Secretary of State Powell was dispatched to rescue what he could of America's reputation from the wreckage—and was booed by delegates from all over the world on the final day. U.N. Secretary General Kofi Annan, who specializes in not giving up, could only sum up the conference with an understated, "Obviously, this is not Rio" (referring to the previous Earth Summit). So little had been accomplished that the next summit, normally announced as part of the ending communiqué, remained in limbo.

The New Unilateralism: Fearing to Negotiate

The kindest interpretation of the new American approach is that the administration wanted to avoid the post-Rio embarrassment of signing environmental commitments it knew it would not keep. (The United States is, for example, in default on its 1992 pledge at Rio to stabilize greenhouse gases at 1999 levels.) This is in keeping with Bush's unilateralism: if we are alone on top of the world, why make commitments to the international community? And Bush's philosophy of corporate voluntarism can be seen as a global extension of the philosophy he first enunciated as a presidential candidate: that you can neither legislate nor litigate clean air and clean water. The Clean Air and Clean Water acts, however, prove otherwise. They have been spectacularly successful in accomplishing their aims. The idea that vague corporate partnerships will prove more effective than mandatory agreements not only is incorrect but is so demonstrably false that it is almost certainly insincere as well.

Among the casualties at Johannesburg was an international effort to restore fisheries. The decline of the world's fish stocks is, next to global warming, probably the greatest problem afflicting our environmental commons. The Food and Agriculture Organization of the United Nations estimates that nearly 30 percent of the world's marine fisheries are either overharvested or in actual collapse.

The exception to this dismal trend is the phenomenal recovery of the world's whales. Blue whales, once thought doomed to extinction by overhunting, have rebounded. What yielded this amazing success? A corporate partnership? No, an international treaty, one with teeth and one that has been vigorously championed by the United States. The International Whaling Commission remains controversial, but the issue is not its lack of effectiveness; no one questions that it has succeeded beyond its founders' wildest dreams. Having restored whale populations, the commission is now being attacked for continuing to protect them from commercial harvest for ethical and moral reasons. The international body, as far as Japan, Norway, and Iceland are concerned, has been *too* effective.

Bush killed Johannesburg for a similar reason: not because treaties do not work but because they work too well. Shortly after the summit concluded, Australian scientists confirmed that chlorofluorocarbons in the atmosphere had begun to decline and that the hole in the ozone layer over the Antarctic should close by 2050. At its most extensive, the 11-million-square-mile hole sent skin cancer risks soaring in Australia and threatened the entire oceanic food chain. In the fourteen years since the Montreal Protocol banned most ozone depleters, a catastrophic global menace has begun to recede. Now Bush is trying to undermine even that triumph of international cooperation. The United States is demanding that the phaseout of ozone-destroying methyl bromide be halted so the chemical can continue to be used for, among other things, growing strawberries and maintaining putting greens on golf courses. "The U.S. is reneging on the agreement, and working very, very hard to get other countries to agree," David Doniger, a former senior U.S. government official dealing with ozone issues, told the London *Independent*. The paper went on to quote Joe Farman, the British scientist who first identified the ozone hole over Antarctica: "This is madness," he said. "We do not need this chemical. We do need the ozone layer. How stupid can people be?"

Merely stopping multilateral environmental initiatives like the mercury convention and abandoning the legacies of the Clinton and Bush Senior administrations on global warming was not enough for Bush Junior's unilateralists. They wanted to root out each and every enforceable international environmental treaty, so they went after the granddaddy of them all, the venerable Convention on the International Trade in Endangered Species (CITES).

For decades this country and every major international wildlife organization have tried to eliminate the market for endangered creatures and plants as well as the products that are made by killing them: elephant ivory, rhinoceros horn, bear gallbladders, tiger penises. CITES left specific enforcement measures to the discretion of the signatory countries; the United States simply prohibited any form of trade in endangered species. The premise was that if endangered wildlife products could not be exported to America and other industrial nations, the market for them would dry up and poaching could be more easily controlled.

The Bush administration turned this policy on its head. It objected to the fact that conservation programs were paid for by the public, through taxes. Along with the ocean and the atmosphere, the world's biological inheritance is the third great global commons—and the radical right believed that it, too, needed to be privatized. So Bush now proposes to permit trade in endangered species and products, on the theory that if countries can make money from the vanishing creatures they will value and protect them, and apply the profits to conservation. If a legitimate market in rhinoceros horn is established, however, it will only feed the demand for poached rhinoceros horn. And how likely is it that a kleptocrat like Liberia's Charles Taylor would actually use profits from exporting chimpanzees as pets to preserve rain forest habitat?

Wildlife biologists were shocked. Famed primatologist Jane Goodall charged that the change was "terrifying" and that "her beloved apes and other species face a threat from the Bush administration that could undo decades of conservation efforts." But, given an opportunity to both reinforce U.S. unilateralism and privatize a global commons, the administration marched ahead.

Tellingly, the United States has always taken a much different approach to world trade—the one global engagement that the administration's business allies take most seriously. The international trade agreements that Bush claims to champion have rules, penalties, and adjudication processes—there is nothing voluntary about them. If we need a rule-based international trade order, why do we oppose a rule-based international environmental order? (Bush's negotiators are adamant, however, that international trade agreements are not to be loaded up with labor rights and environmental protections—issues better dealt with in other forums, they say. But when it comes to those other forums, like Kyoto or Nairobi or Johannesburg, it turns out that there is no room for international agreements on the environment, either.)

John F. Kennedy once said, "Let us never negotiate out of fear. But let us never fear to negotiate." The Bush administration appears to have turned that admonition on its head: it refuses to negotiate on environmental matters not from fear of its adversary but from fear that the negotiations might succeed.

"The only thing I can tell you is evidently the word 'tomorrow' no longer exists in the vocabulary of otherwise responsible members of Congress. They are acting as if there is no tomorrow."

—Warren Rudman, former New Hampshire Republican senator

"What is the use of a house if you haven't got a tolerable planet to put it on?"

— Henry David Thoreau

"The wrongs done to trees, wrongs of every sort, are done in the darkness of ignorance and unbelief, for when the light comes, the heart of the people is always right."

—John Muir, 1920

Progress Is the Best Revenge
Challenging Strategic Ignorance and Reclaiming America's Future

Biologists have a term for species whose habitat or gene pools are so diminished that extinction is only a matter of time: "the living dead." The Bush administration has banished many of our most important environmental protections to this limbo. The Clean Air Act is still on the books but is not being enforced. The national forests that Teddy Roosevelt mapped out on the White House floor with Gifford Pinchot still show in green on the map, but on the ground chainsaws are converting them into clearcuts and tree farms. Superfund, bankrupt, is a shadow of itself; polluters no longer fear it. The Clean Water Act still boldly calls for swimmable streams and fishable rivers, but its jurisdiction no longer includes the huge factory feedlots or 60 percent of the nation's wetland habitat. (You can still fish in most places, but you might think twice about eating what you catch.) In only three years of Bush oversight, one-tenth of our nation's surface area—234 million acres—has been stripped of environmental designations that protected these lands from exploitation and destruction.

The comforting belief of most Americans that we are gradually but surely protecting our land, air, water, and wildlife is no longer justified. The environmental safety net that took a century to weave has been shredded. The hope that our children and grandchildren will have a life better and richer than ours in a clean and thriving natural world is no longer grounded in our framework of laws.

We will not regain what we have lost until we recognize that it has been stolen. Nor will we regain it if we despair at our loss. Despair breeds weakness and passivity: qualities the Bush administration and its cohorts can exploit. What we have not lost is love for the land—the same love that nourished the "nester" settlers of the West and runs in a powerful undercurrent throughout American history. It propelled us twice before, once in the time of Teddy Roosevelt and John Muir, and again after Earth Day 1970, to rise up in the face of blind, corrosive, shortsighted devastation, to insist that America redeem its better self.

If we are going to tap into that deep wellspring of love and hope a third time, we need to understand why we have lost so much in the past three years, and what we must do to win back our heritage and our future. Here the Bush administration has something to teach us about the value of a clear tactical and strategic plan.

Bush and his radical supporters do not express their goals on the environment explicitly. In fact, as we have seen, they do everything they can to conceal those goals from the general public: they shut down scientific research, close off public information, make up numbers, give their programs misleading titles, defy the courts, and calmly, resolutely stick to their line. But even while they are concealing their objectives and deceiving the public about their policies, they stick to their strategy. The radicals, the True Believers who share the social Darwinist vision of a brutal world in which fierce competition lets ever fewer winners take all, understand what Bush is doing. The hard right follows Bush's plays, not his announced photo ops. They read his budget, not the press release about the budget.

The unity of Bush's allies pays off. When a coal company gets a tax break, its executives do not care if it is labeled part of a "hydrogen fuel cell initiative." Timber companies have shifted effortlessly from bidding on timber sales to public-spiritedly offering to cut the same old growth under "fuels-reduction contracts." The Southern Company was glad to be creating "clear skies" by forgoing pollution scrubbers on Plant Scherer. Interior Secretary Gale Norton was able to tell the property-rights extremists and leftover boomers that, while the administration might be "fully funding" the Land and Water Conservation Fund, there was less and less money to buy parkland. The Competitive Enterprise Institute may have lost its battle to allow more arsenic in drinking water, but it won a bigger war when Superfund cleanups ground to a halt.

As we have seen, Bush has a clear game plan. It is not publicly transparent, but it is clear enough to anyone who wants to understand. The administration models it, the think tanks refine it, the pollsters give them language to fire up their followers. Their plan is founded on a few simple steps or principles, and we can learn from them.

What We Can Learn from Bush

Step one for Bush was to stop moving forward. Bush acted most assertively wherever Clinton had been boldest—wild forests and clean air were the prime examples. Bush called his predecessor's late-term actions "midnight regulations" promulgated "as Clinton walked out the door." In reality, they were the cutting edge of American environmental and social change. Bush stopped them cold.

Step one for us, then, is to start walking forward again, to resume our path to the future instead of retreating into the past. We can do this by picking our fights. We should demand that Congress put back in place just one of the public health protections Bush has dumped—but make clear that it is just the first step on a new path for America. Given people's anger when they learn that Bush has shifted the burden of cleaning up toxic waste dumps from the polluters to the taxpayers, restoring the Superfund tax might be a good start. But then we need to keep our promise to ourselves and our kids: to get rid of our toxic inheritance once and for all, to finish the job we started in 1980.

Bush & Co. also have done their best to lower our expectations and dash our dreams. Since 1970 it had been firmly understood that every American refinery, chemical factory, and power plant would be modernized and cleaned up. But Bush took 16,000 of them off the cleanup list and called it "Clear Skies." Since 1973 all of America's waterways had been subject to the Clean Water Act. Bush simply redefined 60 percent of our wetlands as not being "waterways" and thus not deserving protection.

So it is up to us to restore those dreams. We must recall the promise of the early 1970s: every power plant cleaned up, every waterway fishable and swimmable, every chemical plant made secure, every water faucet safe to drink from. It was this universal principle that made environmentalism America's great civic endeavor. We are one nation, and we were all going to be protected, kept healthy, allowed to enjoy our great natural heritage.

With progress blocked and dreams dashed, Bush finally defied even commonsense solutions. Military base commanders were ordered not to protect wildlife even when they knew how; district rangers in the Forest Service had funding yanked away as they were on the verge of protecting rural homeowners from wildfire; government scientists had research contracts canceled if they might show how to restore endangered salmon runs.

The response is obvious: restore common sense to the public agenda. We know what needs to be done and how to do it. Let's get started.

Ten Commonsense Solutions for the Next Twenty Years

Poll after poll has shown that what the American people want and expect from their leaders is progress. They believe that a combination of common sense, commitment, and American ingenuity will enable the country to solve its environmental dilemmas, and that their children should be able to look forward to a better and brighter, not a grimmer and harsher, world.

Here are ten eminently practicable steps that could, in the next twenty years, transform the nation. They will not solve all of our problems; the next generation will have its own challenges, but we owe them a nation that is moving forward on the old ones.

1. Require automakers to make cars, SUVs, and light trucks that go farther on a gallon of gas.

Simply improving the technology of the cars, trucks, and SUVs we drive will reduce our dependence on Middle East oil, shrink our disproportionate 25 percent contribution to the global warming problem, and reduce our trade deficit, while enabling us to save money at the gas pump, clean up air pollution, and reinvigorate the Big Three automakers.

We do not need to wait for an all-hybrid auto fleet, much less the hydrogen fuel cells of the future, because the "freedom package"—a combination of already available technologies including more efficient engines, smarter transmissions, and sleeker aerodynamics—would enable a Ford Explorer, for example, to get 35 mpg instead of 19, with no loss of roominess or acceleration. Ford, General Motors, and Chrysler could all offer the option tomorrow. The most efficient cars on the road already use these technologies to achieve 45 to 60 mpg. In twenty years our vehicle fleet could be averaging 40 mpg, reducing the amount of oil we need to drive a mile by 50 percent from current levels, saving 4 million barrels of oil daily and cutting global warming emissions from autos in half.

Another advantage to doing this would be to preserve the American auto industry by getting the Big Three off their duffs. At present they are trying to compete as technological laggards, and failing. General Motors, which used to sell 50 percent of the cars purchased in the United States, has sunk to almost half that level (28 percent). Toyota is threatening to overtake DaimlerChrysler as the number three automaker. New government standards are needed to make Detroit start modernizing, just as the original fuel economy standards did in the 1970s.

But Detroit cannot do it alone. At present, car buyers do not pay enough attention to fuel efficiency, even though they may regret their decision later when emptying their wallets at the pump. Those who buy gas guzzlers do not pay the full costs of their decision—costs that range from more forest fires in Colorado as the climate dries due to global warming, to American soldiers killed in Iraq because of our continued dependence on Mideast oil. It is up to us to promote efficiency and economy.

We should also put a serious tax on fuel inefficiency. The proceeds from an expanded gas-guzzler tax could be used for two purposes: to subsidize the purchase of hybrids or other efficient vehicles, and to help the auto industry build new assembly lines and fabricating plants to replace the outmoded ones on which Detroit can build only inefficient, badly designed SUVs and pickups. Thus we could protect the jobs and economic base of Michigan, Wisconsin, Ohio, and Missouri while encouraging a future in which cars are still made in the United States. The alternative—our current trajectory—is to have the entire industry flee to low-wage Third World nations with low environmental standards.

2. Reindustrialize America by creating a twenty-first-century energy industry.

America's energy policy is a problem desperately scrambling to escape its solutions. Policy is stuck in the 1920s, when the rapidly industrializing United States was the world's largest exporter of oil. Two generations later, our highest energy priorities are still cheap gasoline and big domestic coal and oil industries. That might make sense for Venezuela, but it is a silly energy policy for a post-industrial society that burns 25 percent of the world's oil but has only 5 percent of its population and 3 percent of its oil reserves.

We do not have space to list all of the available solutions. The amount of electricity we could generate in 20 years from solar, wind, and other renewables is limited largely by the investments we are willing to devote to the project now. One of the most intriguing proposals comes from a group of labor unions led by the Steelworkers, the Machinists, and the Electrical Workers, called the Apollo Project. It calls for investing $300 billion over ten years into a new energy economy based on innovation and efficiency and envisions major investments in high-performance buildings, efficient factories, energy-efficient appliances, and better mass transit as well as efficient hybrid vehicles. It should be noted that $300 billion is only a fraction of what America spends in a single year on imported oil, and economic modeling shows that these programs could create 3 million new manufacturing jobs.

The Apollo Project sets the right goals and provides industry with financial assistance to achieve them. But if the public is paying the bill, we should also make clear that modernization is not optional. The Apollo Project's investment strategies need to be backed by enforceable standards and mandatory requirements. By investing in the industries of tomorrow and rebuilding the infrastructure of our cities today, we can turn the Rust Belt into a global hub for hybrid cars and the hydrogen future.

3. Install modern air pollution control equipment in old power plants, refineries, and factories.

Many states have already done this. California has retired all its "grandfathered plants," and Florida makes coal-fired boilers scrub their emissions. Why should citizens of Arizona and Georgia breathe unnecessary and avoidable soot and smog?

The owners of these dirty old plants have had 30 years to clean them up. Now it is time to pull the plug. Legislation proposed by Senator Jim Jeffords (I-Vt.) would require all power plants to be cleaned up by the time they are 40 years old, or by 2014 at the latest. Cleaning up pollution from just the 51 power plants that the Clinton administration had already sued would save between 4,300 and 7,000 lives a year and prevent between 80,000 and 120,000 asthma attacks.

Anthony Dorsey's mother will not be able to start cooking up the bass he catches just yet—but his future wife will. Only a decade after Florida cleaned up its mercury emissions, mercury levels in fish from the Everglades had fallen 60 to 70 percent.

4. Restore the Superfund tax.
Getting the program back up and running—with the polluters rather than their victims paying for it—is the first step. There are 1,000 facilities sitting on the list today, and probably another 600 that ought to be added over time. If Congress restores the Superfund tax, we can get back to cleaning up 80 sites a year. This means that in another 20 years we would be free of the curse of toxic waste dumps, and Alderman Mark Plamondon and the citizens of Nashua, New Hampshire, could stop worrying that their children were biking through one of them.

5. Reinstate the environmental protections enjoyed by our national forests, rivers, wetlands, wildlife habitat, and public lands as recently as January 21, 2001.
This one would not even take 20 years—it can be accomplished within six months of a president listening to the people. Restoring these safeguards will leave us with a core of wild country that can act as a repository and nursery for endangered and threatened species fighting for survival, and as a sanctuary where future Americans can find renewal and inspiration. Our solution is Aldo Leopold's dictum, "To keep every cog and wheel is the first precaution of intelligent tinkering." Freed of the strictures of politicized science, biologist Michael Kelley could retire from whistle-blowing and get back to saving endangered species. And Tweeti Blancett would be able to focus on cattle ranching instead of fighting oil companies.

6. Restore rural America.

Right now we are spending $18 billion a year on agricultural subsidies, 70 percent of which go the largest agribusinesses—giants like Cargill and J. G. Boswell. These huge corporate conglomerates leverage their subsidies, drive family farmers out of business, bid up the price of land, and bankrupt small, integrated farms that combine grain and livestock production. They destroy rural communities and environments with hellish factory feedlots, virtually exempt from environmental laws. The subsidies even affect other nations: subsidized U.S. corn, for example, drives Mexican farmers into urban slums. At one blow, American taxpayers finance environmental devastation and the destruction of rural communities, health, culture, and property values.

We could get back on the path we started down with the 1995 Farm Bill. We could take the $18 billion in wasteful subsidies in the current Farm Bill and use it to help small farmers, restore wildlife habitat, clean up rural waterways, and reduce erosion and pesticide use. Rural America would have more jobs, rural families would have better health and more economic security, the quality of our food supply would be enhanced, and the country's air and water would be cleaner and healthier.

Actually, we could do all these things for a lot less money if we helped farmers in places like Texas, Kansas, and the Dakotas grow a new crop: windmills. We need the electricity a lot more than we need surplus wheat, and the more the wind blows in North Dakota, the better it would be for business.

7. Retire Smokey Bear. Prevent fire in endangered communities, restore it to forest landscapes.

If we refocus the Forest Service on protecting communities from fire and invest $2 billion a year to thin trees in Community Protection Zones—the half-mile perimeters around homes or towns that firefighters need to stop wildfires from destroying structures—we should be able to safeguard most communities from fire danger within five years. (See chapter 5.) (This would also require shifting resources from backcountry ranger stations to areas around communities.) We need to prioritize community protection over timber preservation. We can embark on a program of controlled burns and—combined with careful testing—judicious thinning to reverse the damage of 50 years of misguided total fire suppression.

8. Restore our national patrimony of public lands.

As we make progress on protecting communities from fire, we should shift to the next challenge: beginning to restore the 75 percent of our national forests that have been logged or roaded. We should phase out the Forest Service's commercial timber program and begin managing our national forest system exclusively for public benefits like wildlife, recreation, and watershed protection. Most of America's best commercial timberland is already in private hands. We do not need to log our national forests to meet our need for timber—they only provide 4 percent today. Since we waste about half the timber we consume, just reducing that waste by a small percentage would replace the timber from the national forests. (In addition, private timber lands are not optimally managed and could produce more wood if they were not competing with subsidized timber sales on the national forests.)

We also need to start keeping the promise Congress made to use royalties from oil and gas drilling to fund the federal Land and Water Conservation Fund. America is not done preserving wild places forever as public lands. The public wants them, royalties from oil on public lands can pay for them, and then they will be ours.

9. Solve the sewage problem.

Finish the job of preventing urban storm-water pollution by restoring watershed quality and, where necessary, separating storm-water and sewage systems. Deal with the problem of runoff from farms, feedlots, and logging and development sites. Thousands of beaches are still closed every year because of inadequately treated sewage, and 40 percent of our waterways are still not safe to swim in. It is time to finish the job the Clean Water Act started. Rhonda Nunlist and her neighbors around Cincinnati deserve backyards and basements their kids can play in.

10. Rejoin the world.

The rest of the planet is waiting for the United States to join the coalition of the environmentally willing. Our agreement alone could put the Kyoto Protocol into effect. Then we need to move ahead and propose a more fundamental system to stabilize the global climate. (If the United States adopted the first two solutions in this section, we would achieve far more than Kyoto demands.)

In addition, we need to rejoin such international initiatives as the proposed convention to reduce emissions of mercury, to protect rain forests, to stop over-fishing, to end discrimination against women, and to preserve biodiversity.

On trade policy, we need to start by fixing the North American Free Trade Agreement (NAFTA), not by signing new agreements that embody all of NAFTA's flaws. But we will have to fix our own farm subsidy programs as well, since our artificially cheap meats and grains, flooding Mexico under NAFTA, are forcing hundreds of thousands of Mexican families off the land, into cities where there are no jobs or into the United States as illegal immigrants.

Once we have stopped destroying Mexican peasants' lives with our huge subsidies to agribusiness, we can get rid of NAFTA's language on investment rights, which allows foreign companies to sue state and local governments in the United States and Mexico whenever they enforce their environmental laws against a foreign polluter. We can require U.S. companies located in Mexico to meet the same environmental standards they would have to meet in the United States. General Motors might still decide to locate a new plant in Guadalajara—but it could no longer do so to reduce its environmental compliance costs. (The rights of workers to speak out in the workplace and organize unions should be protected as well. U.S. companies should not be able to escape their obligations to meet basic human rights by skipping across the Rio Grande. These companies demand their right to speak out under our Constitution; they should respect those rights for their workers wherever they locate their plants.)

Finally, if we simply began to fulfill our commitment to the world's families under the Amsterdam Declaration on a Better Life for Future Generations (adopted at the International Forum on Population in the Twenty-first Century in 1989), developing countries could reduce their childbearing rate by a third. We could save the lives of more than half a million women who die from pregnancy-related problems each year and also prevent 80 million unintended pregnancies and 45 million abortions each year.

Goals for the Grandchildren

The Bush administration and its cohorts have a long-range vision, one they have used to unite and motivate their hard-right supporters. Just as the twentieth century saw the pace of environmental progress gradually swell and increase, they intend for the first decade of the twenty-first century to reverse 100 years of progress. It is a breathtakingly bold enterprise: not only to change environmental law but to do so as part of remaking the American character and returning American society to a no-holds-barred, winner-take-all jungle.

If they have that much courage, why should we have less?

We were making progress up to November 2000. We should be proud of that progress. But even the pace at which we were going was not sufficient to reach our goal. The ten commonsense solutions outlined above are only a short-term agenda. Just as Bush's team did, we need to lay out our long-range vision for the twenty-first century.

We will climb these peaks step by step. But we need to be clear that we plan to get all the way to the top of the mountain. That visionary path will require a good deal of collective dreaming; here are some goals that might make our grandchildren proud of the path we chose:

First, leave behind the carbon economy of oil, gas, corrupt Saudi princes, and Dick Cheney, not only here in the United States but globally. Have the patience to stay the course in the necessary transition to renewable energy sources while the global climate teeters and eventually stabilizes. It is probably already too late to avoid some climate shifts from carbon dioxide loading in the atmosphere, but a shift of two degrees will be far less damaging than one of ten degrees. The climate will recover more rapidly from a low fever than a high one.

Moving toward a climatic recovery will require reducing our emissions of greenhouse pollutants, principally carbon dioxide, not by the 22 percent envisaged in Kyoto but by 60 percent or more. Doing so will require shifting energy production in a fundamentally new direction. The short-range investments of the Apollo Project will only start the process. We need to tax excessive producers of carbon dioxide and, with the payments, ensure that as villages in China and India electrify they are able to go directly to solar and wind without passing through a nineteenth-century dependence on coal. The planet cannot afford a second carbon-based industrial revolution in Asia, Africa, and Latin America—but the nations that reaped the benefits of the first industrial revolution will need to pay to avoid it.

Second, substitute sustainable agriculture for the industrial model based on pesticides, herbicides, and poorly tested genetically engineered foods. Getting rid of outrageous subsidies and restoring family farms is only a first, relatively easy step. Next comes making serious public investments in agricultural research, to put the world's cumulative, sophisticated knowledge of plant ecology to work. Home gardens, for example, have provided families in Java with a huge part of their fruits and vegetables for centuries, growing hundreds of species in small courtyard gardens with neither pesticides nor artificial fertilizers. We need to develop agricultural systems of comparable sophistication, productivity, and diversity for other climates and continents—and then invest in helping farmers shift from chemical-based industrial monoculture to these new patterns. (Genetic engineering may have a place in this future—but not the place agribusiness currently imagines, where it is an excuse for driving out small farmers and expanding herbicide-dependent monocultures of quasi-corn and doctored soybeans.)

All this almost certainly means that we will have more farmers, and that some of the billions of people who have been driven off the land by agribusiness will be able to return. More of the food dollar will flow to the farmer and less to the pesticide manufacturer. This shift does not mean that food will cost the average consumer more; in fact, nutritious, affordable, and varied diets for six billion humans can be sustained only by agriculture on the model of gardening rather than industry.

Third, abandon both the metaphor and the practice of unifying human communities with networks of roads, railroads, and sprawling strip cities, and instead focus on reconnecting fragmented natural communities with green belts, reserves, corridors, floodways, and wild rivers. Human communities need to nest within a connected and naturally functioning landscape, but wilderness cannot survive in isolated pockets within an urbanized wasteland. Nature needs elbow room. It needs connection. Our current parks and wilderness areas are largely disconnected, and in too many places we have left far too little space for natural processes to function.

We need to combine our love of special places with greater respect for our entire landscape—what Aldo Leopold called "the land ethic." We are lucky in this way, for, try as we might, all our technology cannot prevent the natural processes needed to sustain wildness—flooding, fire, migration, predation, alluvial deposition, eutrophication, speciation, hybridization, and succession. Nature's ecological processes are robust, functioning quite effectively around us and our works. We need to get out of the way and let restoration happen.

The promise of wilderness is everywhere, not just on the public lands of the West. Much of the wild East that sustained the Huron and Iroquois remains. Inside the blue line of the Adirondacks lies the Great Oswegatchie Wilderness. Across central Maine, northern forests abandoned by the timber industry offer the hope and scope for a new park, bigger than Yellowstone. The Everglades need only space and water to anchor a great southern wild area. Up and down the Mississippi lie wetlands, floodplains, and riparian forests waiting to turn back to the rhythms of the river. In Utah we have found far more wilderness than we imagined possible, and the northern Rockies still provide enough wildlands to stitch a living habitat for the mighty grizzly. On the West Coast we could bring back a salmon fishery—or a hundred.

Fourth, amortize and retire our 200-year investment in toxic technologies based on heat and pressure applied to metals and hydrocarbons. We have the new technologies but do not want to write off the capital invested in the old ones. A green economy is now a technological reality and an economic practicality. It is penetrating the market very slowly, however, because it must compete with older, polluting technologies in which enormous capital has been invested and which enjoy tremendous subsidies from government in the form of inadequate enforcement of environmental standards. Throwaway batteries, for example, constitute 75 percent of the cadmium going into U.S. landfills. Rechargeable batteries would reduce that figure to a tiny fraction, but consumers do not pay for the toxic results of the slightly cheaper, one-time variety, so they keep buying them.

Similarly, a huge part of the value of any chemical company is rooted in the fact that the company and its customers are allowed to dump the waste from producing and consuming those chemicals into the oceans, rivers, and atmosphere that belong to all of us. Their bottom lines would look very different if they had to account for the true cost of their activities. But these companies do not want to write off their investment in old technologies, so they fight for and keep their subsidies. New technologies are prevented from competing on a level playing field. We need to stop the hidden subsidies for technologies that are poisoning the planet.

Finally—and this may seem the most preposterous suggestion yet—we need to create and measure wealth, not waste. We then should distribute it fairly enough that excess consumption is no longer the measure of either security or dignity. The connection of this principle to the environment may seem tenuous, but in cultural terms it is profound. Can we really imagine a society that would ensure the survival of obscure but important families of beetles while remaining oblivious to the welfare of members of our own species who are ethnically different, geographically distant, or educationally disadvantaged? Can we care for migratory birds while ignoring children? Can we be stewards of the earth while neglecting humanity?

Our Vision Thing: America the Beautiful

Unlike the ten short-range solutions outlined earlier in this chapter, this long-range agenda is speculative. People of good will can disagree over the particulars and methods; some will require new science, others new laws, and all demand new thinking. This is a sketch of a vision, not a blueprint.

Realizing this dream will call on the same fundamental social and political traits we need to stop the Bush administration from shredding our environmental safety net. Protecting our health, our land, our children, and our heritage is a fundamental moral test of our time and must be a common endeavor. It requires us to be as bold, tough, and realistic as those who would trade away that heritage for short-term gain. Here is how we can prepare for a brighter twenty-first century:

Hold on to our dreams. We need to raise our sights, opt for hope over despair, and trust in our human capacity to do better.

Demand leadership. We need to make our political leaders accountable. They are supposed to be the stewards of our dreams and aspirations as a society; they work for us, however it may sometimes seem. Supervising someone who works for you is hard work, and we are often lazy about it. (The radical right is temperamentally much more diligent about such oversight.) "Eternal vigilance is the price of liberty," said Thomas Jefferson; it is also the price of a tolerable, living planet. As the 2004 election approaches, the administration, the Congress, and other public officials will be listening more closely than usual to demands from the American people. Public comments on forest plans may no longer be counted individually, but votes still are.

Finally, we need to unite. De Tocqueville called it "the single greatest skill of democracy." After all, we are in this together. It is not a question of rich and poor, or brown and black and white, or urban and rural, or Republican and Democrat. We all breathe the air, we all drink the water, we all care about children. People should not suffer unnecessary risk because of the color of their skin, the size of their wallet, or whether their neighborhood is downwind or downstream. We are all Americans.

America the Beautiful is at a fork in the road—one path leads backward toward the nineteenth century, the other forward into the twenty-first. The Bush administration has been intent on taking us backward, through strategic ignorance and the other radical strategies laid out in this book. But this crabbed, Hobbesian spirit of social Darwinism has been bested before, and our union of air breathers and water drinkers and parents and neighbors can overcome it again. After that, the future will be ours to make.

Appendix
The Bush Record on the Environment

Compiled by the National Resources Defense Council and used with permission in abridged form; for full details and links to each item, see http://www.nrdc.org/ bushrecord/default.asp.

2001

January
White House announces regulatory freeze (01/20/01)
New raw-sewage rules delayed by Bush regulatory freeze (01/20/01)
Bush seeks to open Arctic National Wildlife Refuge to oil development (01/20/01)

February
Bush administration seeks to weaken efficiency standards for air conditioners (02/12/01)
EPA delays, then upholds, new rule protecting wetlands (02/15/01)
Bush administration to try to adjust the boundaries of 19 new national monuments (02/20/01)
EPA upholds Clinton decision to clean up diesel pollution (02/28/01)

March
Bush appoints industry apologist John Graham as regulatory gatekeeper (03/06/01)
Fish and Wildlife Service withdraws call for protection of endangered salmon and trout (03/07/01)
President nominates J. Steven Griles as deputy secretary of Interior (03/09/01)
Bush retreats from campaign promise to reduce carbon pollution (03/13/01)
Bush administration seeks to roll back Roadless Area Conservation Plan (03/16/01)

Bush administration settles pesticides lawsuit brought by NRDC against EPA (03/19/01)
Bush withdraws new arsenic-in-drinking-water standard (03/20/01)
Bush administration delays hard-rock mining regulations that protect watersheds (03/21/01)
Bush administration rejects Kyoto Protocol on global warming (03/28/01)
Bush administration suspends the "contractor responsibility rule" (03/30/01)

April

Bush supports U.N. treaty on Persistent Organic Pollutants (04/09/01)
Bush seeks to relax requirements of Endangered Species Act (04/09/01)
Yellowstone snowmobile ban goes into effect, but perhaps not for long (04/23/01)
Gale Norton nominates William G. Myers III as solicitor for Department of the
    Interior (04/24/01)
Interior will not reintroduce grizzly bears into Idaho, Montana wildlands (04/25/01)
EPA drops objections to Florida rule that undermines Clean Water Act protections (04/26/01)
Cheney sketches out a misguided energy policy (04/30/01)

May

Bush launches a "sneak attack" on the Roadless Area Conservation Plan (05/04/01)
Bush administration won't release information on industry participants in Cheney energy task
    force (05/10/01)
BLM fails to comply with agreement to protect threatened desert tortoises (05/12/01)
Agriculture secretary undercuts forest management process (05/17/01)
Bush releases his energy plan (05/17/01)
Bush administration formally suspends arsenic-in-drinking-water protections (05/22/01)
EPA moves ahead with Clinton-era rule that will reduce haze over wildlands (05/29/01)
Bush pledges improvements to maintenance of national parks (05/31/01)

June

California's ocean waters off-limits to fishing (06/04/01)
Boundaries of some protected public lands may be "redrawn" to allow drilling and min-
    ing (06/05/01)
EPA announces final radiation standards for Yucca Mountain waste repository (06/06/01)
BLM upholds "non-controversial" portion of hard-rock mining rules (06/15/01)
Bush will not change fuel efficiency standards (06/19/01)
U.S. Department of Energy sued over final rule on air conditioners (06/19/01)

July

Energy Secretary Abraham lauds coal-burning power plant (07/02/01)
Bush will open Gulf tract to offshore drilling; NRDC says drilling would threaten waters and
    beaches (07/02/01)
Largest U.S. marine reserve becomes official (07/10/01)
Bush nominates "timber beast" Mark Rey to oversee national forests (07/10/01)
Bush budget cuts for international global warming programs more significant than
    reported (07/12/01)
Bush outlines an "all talk, no action" approach to global warming (07/13/01)
White House favors limiting president's authority to protect federal lands (07/17/01)
Bush seeking to weaken federal environmental enforcement (07/23/01)
Norton balks at defending wildlife in the face of local opposition (07/23/01)
Bush unlikely to offer alternative global warming plan (07/26/01)
EPA wants to scrap air pollution regulations for power plants (07/26/01)

August

Army Corps of Engineers abandons plan to save Missouri River wildlife (08/02/01)
Corps to weaken wetlands protections (08/08/01)
Tongass and other forests open to road building, logging (08/12/01)
EPA postpones action on power plants, expected to favor limited approach (08/14/01)
Bush administration appeals federal judge's decision to ban drilling off California's coast (08/17/01)
Forest Service stalls roadless protection, allows logging to continue (08/22/01)
Norton reneges on agreement to protect endangered desert tortoise (08/27/01)
Bush administration seeks to fast-track missile defense program, but coalition sues to force drafting of environmental impact statements (08/28/01)
Bush administration considers disposing of radioactive waste in consumer products (08/28/01)

September

Bush backing away from pledge to clean up federal facilities (09/07/01)
Bush administration wants farm policy overhaul (09/19/01)
DOE to fund biomass research (09/19/01)
USFS to reduce public participation (09/20/01)
Corps official uses terrorist attacks as excuse to weaken environmental protection (09/21/01)
White House rule change could inflict "paralysis by analysis" on regulatory process (09/24/01)

October

GAO slams Forest Service for poor fiscal management (10/01/01)
Forest chief asks Norton to end Oregon mining ban (10/02/01)
EPA considers standards that could slow cleanup of PCBs in the Hudson River (10/04/01)
Norton guts tough mining protections (10/25/01)
EPA issues an arsenic-in-tap-water standard higher than that recommended by public health advocates (10/31/01)

November

Corps of Engineers ignores "no net loss" wetlands policy (11/02/01)
Bush signs Interior bill that boosts spending but includes harmful riders (11/05/01)
Bush administration shutting down Everglades restoration office (11/06/01)
Forest Service makes hasty salvage logging decision, forces court battle (11/27/01)
White House plans deep cuts in environmental spending (11/28/01)
EPA may lift ban on human testing of pesticides (11/28/01)
Voyageurs National Park reopening areas to snowmobiles (11/29/01)

December

Corps keeps Snake River dams (12/03/01)
Environmentalists launch first legal challenge to Bush administration's national energy plan (12/06/01)
Snowmobile ban unlikely to be implemented in Yellowstone and Grand Teton (12/10/01)
Interior calls for fiscal reform of mining law (12/10/01)
NRDC sues Department of Energy to expose Cheney energy task force secrets (12/11/01)
DOE weakens standards for Yucca nuclear storage (12/14/01)
USFS guts protections for undeveloped forest lands (12/14/01)
EPA enlists National Academy of Sciences on issue of human pesticide studies (12/15/01)
Forest Service won't allow drilling in New York's Finger Lakes (12/18/01)
Sierra Nevada plan limits logging, grazing activities in California national forests (12/27/01)

2002

January

New Corps study backs Columbia River dredging (01/03/02)
Bush administration bends rules for favored coal company (01/03/02)
Bush administration plans to get ready to resume nuclear weapons testing (01/08/02)
Bush administration backs pollution-free automobile initiative (01/09/02)
Bush administration plans to double "Brownfields" cleanup funds (01/10/02)
Environmental enforcement suffers under Bush (01/10/02)
Bush administration nuclear weapon cuts less than advertised (01/10/02)
Bush administration fighting for new oil drilling off California coast (01/10/02)
Norton withholds government critique of proposal to relax wetlands rules (01/14/02)
Corps relaxes wetlands protections, White House approves (01/14/02)
Park Service okays drilling expansion in Florida preserve (01/14/02)
Justice Department finally justifies air pollution lawsuits (01/15/02)
Bush administration changes science on polar bear impacts to suit Arctic drilling (01/17/02)
Interior proposes spending boost for refuges (01/21/02)
BLM backs gas drilling in national monument (01/21/02)
Forest Service appeals salvage logging legal decision (01/22/02)
New NRDC report documents sweeping rollback of environmental protections by federal agencies (01/23/02)
BLM pushes oil exploration near Utah park (01/24/02)
Bush administration refusing to release energy task force records (01/28/02)
Court asked to force immediate release of secret energy task force details (01/30/02)

February

EPA initially criticized Bush-Cheney energy plan (02/02/02)
Bush budget cuts student research (02/03/02)
Bush slashes environmental education spending (02/04/02)
Bush unveils "slash and burn" budget for 2003 (02/04/02)
Bush to boost logging in national forests (02/04/02)
Former Energy Department official blasts Yucca storage plan (02/05/02)
Park snowmobile phase-out delayed (02/05/02)
Bush proposes "charter" forests (02/06/02)
Bush using Everglades plan to target endangered species (02/07/02)
Forest Service compromises on Bitterroot salvage logging plan (02/07/02)
Park Service wants motorized access in Georgia wilderness (02/11/02)
Bush administration's secret plan for strengthening U.S. nuclear forces (02/13/02)
Bush announces rollback of power plant pollution rules (02/14/02)
White House global warming plan "cooks the books" (02/14/02)
Bush backs Yucca Mountain for nuclear waste dump (02/15/02)
National forest in Missouri opened to drilling (02/15/02)
Bush administration seeks to weaken endangered species protection in California (02/16/02)
Snowmobile ban dealt another blow (02/19/02)
Corps doesn't give a dam for Snake River salmon (02/21/02)
BLM rule could block federal land protection (02/22/02)
Bush administration intends to shift Superfund cleanup from polluters to taxpayers (02/23/02)
EPA official admits that Bush clean air plan is weak (02/26/02)
Bureau of Reclamation Klamath plan endangers fish (02/27/02)
Top EPA official resigns in protest of Bush's pro-polluter policies (02/27/02)
Energy Dept. ordered to release task force records to NRDC (02/27/02)

March

Whitman remarks undermine government's Clean Air Act lawsuits (03/03/02)
BLM Idaho director forced to resign (03/06/02)
U.S. Fish and Wildlife Service employees silenced on Arctic Refuge (03/06/02)
"Drill first, ask questions later" energy policy threatens wild lands (03/07/02)
Forest Service proposes oil and gas leasing in Los Padres National Forest (03/11/02)
Bush administration scraps plans for new wildlife refuge (03/12/02)
Desert tortoise finally protected (03/12/02)
EPA sends industry lobbyist to testify before Congress on proposed cuts to enforcement
    budgets (03/12/02)
Gas drilling returns to Padre Island National Seashore (03/15/02)
BLM plans to open more lands to drilling (03/18/02)
Hawaiian marine reserve protections preserved (03/18/02)
Department of Defense agrees to complete new environmental impact analyses on missile
    defense testing (03/18/02)
EPA will weaken federal clean air rules (03/18/02)
White House touts aggressive regulatory review (03/19/02)
Endangered species habitat under attack (03/19/02)
White House misuses clean energy funds to print dirty energy plan (03/25/02)
Energy Department papers show industry is the real author of administration's energy
    policy (03/27/02)
BLM sets sights on drilling Powder River basin (03/27/02)
Bush administration revisiting Rocky Mountain Front protections (03/28/02)
Pentagon seeks exemption from environmental laws (03/29/02)
Forest Service reverses mine approval (03/29/02)
BLM proposal could doom California dunes (03/29/02)

April

Bush administration fails to boost automobile efficiency (04/01/02)
White House ends environmental research funding (04/02/02)
Bush administration trying to dump global warming scientist (04/02/02)
Bush administration promotes coal-bed methane development (04/04/02)
Bush administration scales back habitat protection for endangered butterfly (04/05/02)
Alaska oil drilling would harm environment, despite Bush claims (04/07/02)
Bush administration to ax Northwest Forest Plan (04/08/02)
White House moves one step forward, two steps back on chemical treaty (04/11/02)
Corps of Engineers approves Everglades mining (04/11/02)
Forest Service wants to circumvent environmental laws (04/12/02)
Bush administration fails to protect manatees (04/16/02)
Administration's plan allows overfishing in New England (04/16/02)
Administration may weaken lead testing for kids (04/16/02)
Administration bans jet skis in a few parks, may allow them in others (04/16/02)
Bush clean air plan would boost coal use (04/17/02)
Bush administration speeding up drilling in Rockies (04/18/02)
Bush administration ousts top global warming scientist (04/19/02)
EPA watchdog resigns in protest over Bush policies (04/22/02)
Norton vows to limit Florida oil drilling (04/23/02)
Administration establishes habitat protections for endangered kangaroo rat (04/23/02)
Bush administration debates management of monuments (04/24/02)
White House rejected more stringent EPA air-pollution proposal before issuing so-called
    "Clear Skies" plan (04/28/02)

NRDC issues subpoena to former head of White House energy task force (04/29/02)
Huge win in the battle over snowmobiles in national parks (04/30/02)
Powder River drilling leases ruled illegal (04/30/02)

May

EPA charged with understating impact of Yucca Mountain nuclear dump on Nevada drinking water supplies (05/03/02)
EPA to let mining industry dump waste in water ways (05/03/02)
Corps of Engineers' plan threatens to pollute Florida Everglades (05/03/02)
Salmon protection temporarily rescinded (05/07/02)
Bush budget cuts billions from natural resources spending (05/08/02)
Bush administration blocks testimony of key energy official (05/09/02)
Bush administration agency secretly fights mine reforms (05/10/02)
Bush asks judge to suspend mountaintop mining decision (05/13/02)
EPA proposes water pollution trading scheme (05/14/02)
White House backtracks on plan to ease lead testing regulations (05/14/02)
Bush signs disastrous farm bill (05/14/02)
Forest Service advises against protecting wilderness in Alaska's Tongass (05/16/02)
Energy Secretary admits Yucca Mountain won't hold all nuclear waste (05/16/02)
Alabama nuclear plant to be reactivated (05/16/02)
EPA gives failing grade to Powder River drilling projects (05/16/02)
Public criticism forces EPA to get tough on polluters (05/16/02)
Federal scientists say Columbia dredging won't hurt salmon (05/20/02)
Bush administration lifts ban on mining in Oregon national forest (05/21/02)
Bush administration sends conflicting signal on Clean Air Act enforcement (05/21/02)
Army Corps of Engineers' flip-flops on project reviews further damage its credibility (05/23/02)
Bush administration rolls back air conditioner energy efficiency standards (05/23/02)
Bush-Putin summit produces deeply flawed nuclear arms treaty (05/24/02)
Bush administration lets construction companies off the hook for protecting environment (05/24/02)
Bush blocks Florida Gulf, Everglades drilling (05/29/02)

June

Bureau of Reclamation balks at Klamath water plans (06/03/02)
Bush administration finally admits big trouble from global warming (06/03/02)
Bush administration refuses to crack down on diesel pollution (06/07/02)
On offshore drilling, Bush administration won't give Californians the same relief it gave Floridians (06/07/02)
BLM officials address conflict-of-interest charges (06/10/02)
EPA signs off on safety of all but two of 30 pesticides (06/10/02)
Bush administration pushes oil drilling in Alaska reserve (06/10/02)
U.S. signs off on endangered salmon harvest (06/12/02)
Bush and Whitman distance themselves from EPA global warming report (06/12/02)
Missouri River restoration put on hold (06/13/02)
EPA rolls back clean air protections for power plants (06/13/02)
Judge rules against Bush administration on endangered species protection (06/13/02)
Judge rejects Corps request to lift ban on mining pollution (06/17/02)
Bush administration backtracks on land preservation (06/19/02)
EPA backs off mandatory plan to clean up stormwater pollution (06/24/02)
Bush administration blames wildfires on environmentalists (06/25/02)

Snowmobiles to be restricted, not banned, in parks (06/25/02)
EPA stymied investigation of Yucca Mountain radiation standards (06/25/02)
FWS flip-flops on trout protection (06/26/02)
Bush slashing EPA funding for toxic cleanups (06/30/02)

July

Bush administration revokes habitat protection for California frog (07/04/02)
Wildlife officials block Corps plan to move endangered birds (07/05/02)
EPA may allow the use of Carbofuran, a formerly banned toxic pesticide (07/08/02)
Bush administration stalls on global warming solution (07/10/02)
Bush administration forced to protect endangered whipsnake (07/10/02)
White House backs delay in river changes (07/14/02)
Navy's sonar threatens whales (07/16/02)
Bush cleanup plan could leave behind more nuclear waste (07/19/02)
EPA's scientific review on pesticides questioned (07/19/02)
Bush administration opposes renewable-energy requirement (07/19/02)
EPA restores some Superfund monies (07/21/02)
Bush's revised Everglades plan falls short of restoration goals (07/23/02)
Fish and Wildlife Service reneges on manatee protection plan (07/24/02)
Bush administration plans to give away oil and coal holdings in Utah (07/25/02)
Another EPA official resigns in protest over Bush policies (07/25/02)
Bush uses national security to gain corporate secrecy and immunity (07/26/02)
EPA seeks cleaner motorbikes, boats (07/29/02)
Bush administration supports protecting endangered foreign fish (07/31/02)

August

EPA fails to meet pesticides review deadline (08/03/02)
EPA rolls back Clean Water Act's water cleanup program (08/07/02)
White House looks to sink environmental law (08/10/02)
Bush administration allows energy development in national monument (08/12/02)
EPA cedes Idaho cleanup authority to state (08/13/02)
Bush skipping U.N. Earth Summit (08/15/02)
Fish and Wildlife Service ordered to develop list of manatee protection zones (08/16/02)
Bush administration backing away from California coastal protection (08/19/02)
EPA forced to withdraw new penalty calculations scheme (08/19/02)
EPA cracking down on North Dakota air polluters (08/19/02)
Bush administration employs stonewall strategy at World Summit (08/21/02)
Bush administration weakens whale protections that hindered oil and gas industry (08/22/02)
Interior Department allows more air pollution at national park (08/22/02)
Bush calls for increased logging in the name of fire prevention (08/22/02)
Bush administration abandons California water plan (08/23/02)
White House Utah drilling plans under fire from local businesses (08/26/02)
U.S. undermines renewable energy proposal at World Summit (08/27/02)
Interior Dept. approves water storage under Mojave Desert (08/29/02)
Bush's new wildfire expert no friend of forests (08/30/02)

September

White House seeks unprecedented exemption from public disclosure rules (09/02/02)
Federal officials reject call to add white marlin to endangered list (09/04/02)
Park Service temporarily bans personal watercraft on Nevada lakes (09/06/02)
U.S. EPA air-quality enforcement sinks to new lows (09/07/02)

EPA seeks to boost recycling (09/09/02)
Norton rules out citizens panel for Trans-Alaska Pipeline (09/10/02)
Army Corps of Engineers dawdling on Missouri River plan (09/10/02)
EPA backs off issuing strong antipollution standards for off-road vehicles (09/13/02)
BLM's plans for California desert favor commerce over conservation (09/13/02)
EPA omits global warming section from pollution report (09/15/02)
National Park Service removes controversial ranger (09/17/02)
Bush replacing health scientists who don't favor industry views (09/17/02)
U.S. EPA misses deadlines on air toxics standards (09/17/02)
Bush orders agencies to streamline environmental review of transportation projects (09/18/02)
Forest Service smoothing the rails for Bush's logging proposals (09/19/02)
Bush administration to reconsider Clean Water Act protections (09/19/02)
Bush administration plans to lift federal protection on wolves (09/25/02)
Bush administration revives controversial California gold mine (09/27/02)
Bush administration relinquishing federal water rights (09/30/02)
Bush administration rewriting rules to boost logging in Northwest (09/30/02)
New EPA water quality report shows U.S. waters are getting dirtier (09/30/02)

October

Army Corps rejects order to increase Missouri River flow (10/02/02)
White House blocking conservation funding for farms (10/03/02)
Judge considers contempt of court for Interior Secretary Norton over manatees (10/03/02)
BLM approves oil and gas drilling in Utah (10/04/02)
EPA admits clean water takes back seat to war on terrorism (10/08/02)
Bush stacks panel on lead poisoning with industry experts (10/08/02)
EPA memo improperly encourages employees to support Bush (10/08/02)
Forest Service may exempt environmental protection from forest management plans (10/09/02)
Bush administration sides with auto industry against lower emissions (10/09/02)
Bush approves bill to enlarge California recreation area (10/09/02)
Justice Department lax on chemical security (10/10/02)
Interior panel's ruling against coal-bed methane leases upheld (10/15/02)
Former EPA official blasts Bush commitment to enforcement of clean air rules (10/16/02)
Fish and Wildlife Service proposes special wildlife habitat on Guam (10/16/02)
EPA lagging in Superfund cleanups (10/16/02)
Bush administration ordered to release energy documents (10/17/02)
Forest Service in violation of Endangered Species Act (10/20/02)
U.S. EPA fails to meet deadline for handing over air documents to Senate (10/25/02)
Bush administration limiting scope of federal coal mining study (10/28/02)
Agriculture Department offers program to aid Florida farmers, Everglades (10/28/02)
Whistleblower says Bush administration pressure forced inadequate salmon protection (10/28/02)
EPA approves Louisiana's controversial pollution-trading program (10/29/02)
Interior Department to oppose commercial whaling (10/30/02)
Interior Department joining fight for Nevada cat litter mine (10/31/02)
Interior Department finally designates manatee protection zones (10/31/02)
EPA set to launch new study on causes of asthma (10/31/02)
EPA halts funding at several Superfund sites (10/31/02)

November

Bush officials suppress science on Klamath River policy (11/01/02)

EPA no longer making polluters pay (11/05/02)
Bush administration looking for legal loopholes on manatee protection (11/06/02)
Federal courts overturn habitat protections, per Bush request (11/09/02)
Bush officials intervened to silence objections to coal plant near Mammoth Cave National Park (11/09/02)
BLM grants quickie approval of another energy project in Utah (11/11/02)
Bush administration supports renewed elephant ivory trade (11/11/02)
Bush administration reverses snowmobile ban for national parks (11/12/02)
Bush administration outlines steps for nuclear security (11/14/02)
EPA agrees to clean up smog pollution (11/14/02)
Interior plans to limit environmental reviews for grazing (11/18/02)
Bush administration opens Padre Island National Seashore to drilling (11/22/02)
EPA proposes weakening of Clean Air Act (11/22/02)
Bush administration wants to expedite logging at expense of fish in Northwest forests (11/25/02)
Forest Service rewriting rules to increase logging, remove wildlife safeguards (11/26/02)

December

Bush administration loses appeal in California offshore drilling case (12/02/02)
Bush administration fosters policy of delay on global warming (12/04/02)
GAO suit against Cheney energy task force rejected (12/09/02)
Bush administration approves limited river restoration plan for Glen Canyon (12/09/02)
Army Corps of Engineers misses deadline on rules for Everglades restoration project (12/11/02)
White House fire plan would boost logging at expense of environment, public input (12/11/02)
U.S. appeals court upholds Roadless Area Conservation Rule (12/12/02)
White House proposes minor increase in automobile fuel economy (12/12/02)
Judge blocks Snake River dredging plan to evaluate risk to salmon (12/13/02)
EPA factory-farm rule favors polluters (12/15/02)
Government doing big business with lawbreaking companies (12/16/02)
White House discounts human life in cost-benefit analysis (12/18/02)
Bush administration optimistic about Powder River Basin energy supplies (12/18/02)
Bush administration faces tough time tapping oil in the Rockies (12/18/02)
White House begins process of relaxing government regulations for industry (12/19/02)
Judge gives Department of Interior extension on manatee plan (12/19/02)
BLM denies drilling access in Colorado wildlife range (12/20/02)
Judge slaps restraining order on plan to dredge Snake River (12/20/02)
Bush administration weakens federal program for cleaning up dirty waters (12/21/02)
Judge deals setback to Bush oil drilling plans in Utah (12/23/02)
Bush administration backtracking on policy of "no net loss" of wetlands (12/26/02)
EPA exempts oil and gas industry from stormwater pollution rules (12/30/02)

2003

January

Forest Service loosens logging restrictions for small-scale projects (01/03/03)
Bush administration blamed for Klamath River fish kill (01/05/03)
Bush administration pushing to lift grizzly bear protection (01/05/03)
Bush administration paves way for new roads in parks, wilderness (01/06/03)
EPA seeking legislative "fix" to let air polluters off the hook (01/07/03)
Bush administration considers new nukes (01/10/03)

Despite scientific concerns, Interior Department approves power plant near Yellowstone (01/10/03)
Bush administration planning to remove federal protection for America's wetlands and small waterways (01/10/03)
EPA proposes water pollution trading scheme (01/13/03)
Defense Department targets environmental laws (01/13/03)
Bush administration says logging good for wildlife (01/14/03)
Court sides with environment, upholds EPA stormwater rule (01/14/03)
Bush administration to revisit spotted owl protections (01/14/03)
Environmental experts nixed from international development agency (01/16/03)
EPA sticking with unsafe perchlorate standard (01/16/03)
Federal study contradicts Bush claims of curbs on Western energy development (01/17/03)
Bush administration setting its sights on oil in Western Arctic Reserve (01/17/03)
Pentagon again taking aim at environmental laws (01/19/03)
Ignoring health risks, EPA chooses not to ban dangerous weed killer (01/21/03)
Manatees finally get protection (01/24/03)
Interior Department may privatize National Park Service (01/27/03)
California's giant trees threatened by Bush forest plans (01/27/03)
Bush administration wins court victory on mountaintop removal mining (01/29/03)
Sierra Nevada forest protections under fire by Bush administration (01/29/03)
Polluting industries getting off easier under Bush administration (01/29/03)
Bush snowmobile decision defies logic, not to mention scientific findings (01/30/03)
BLM putting grazing restrictions out to pasture (01/30/03)
Bush administration seeks waiver on ozone-destroying pesticide (01/30/03)
GAO faults EPA oversight on factory farms (01/31/03)
New EPA air rules for ocean vessels too weak (01/31/03)

February

OMB pushes for industry-skewed cost-benefit analysis (02/04/03)
EPA failing to protect Louisiana's environment and public health (02/04/03)
White House fuel cell plan ignores today's oil insecurity (02/06/03)
Bush administration wins sweetheart water settlement for wealthy California farmers (02/06/03)
GAO halts lawsuit over Cheney energy files (02/07/03)
Bush administration pushing for pesticide exemptions from international environmental treaty (02/07/03)
Spotted owl denied federal protection despite additional logging threat (02/10/03)
Bush official touts Western coal, weaker mining regulations (02/10/03)
EPA plans to relax toxic air pollution standards (02/11/03)
White House gets industry support for voluntary pollution cuts (02/12/03)
BLM opening sensitive Wyoming lands to drilling (02/18/03)
National Park Service overturns ban on snowmobiles in national parks (02/20/03)
EPA delays report on mercury risk for children (02/20/03)
White House ordered to reveal climate change documents (02/21/03)
Bush administration using guise of security to expand corporate secrecy (02/25/03)
Scientists debunk Bush's global warming plan (02/25/03)
Bush administration sets sights on drilling in Western Arctic Reserve (02/26/03)
Bush administration flunking on salmon recovery (02/26/03)
Bush air pollution plan weakens current law, threatens public health (02/27/03)
U.S. EPA seeks to weaken endangered species protections (02/27/03)
Bush administration to build world's first emission-free power plant (02/27/03)

Department of Transportation to expedite more environmentally harmful road
   projects (02/27/03)
Bush administration rejects wilderness protection in Alaska's Tongass (02/28/03)
Interior officials escalate rhetoric over Arctic Refuge (02/28/03)

March

Bush administration intervened in Nevada mining dispute at request of industry (03/03/03)
New EPA guidelines assess cancer risks for children (03/03/03)
U.S. Fish and Wildlife Service outlines sea otter recovery plan (03/04/03)
Judge orders federal protection for California fish (03/04/03)
National Park Service sends Yellowstone bison to slaughter (03/04/03)
Defense Department seeking exemptions from environmental laws (03/06/03)
Pentagon chiefs ordered to hunt for environmental exemptions (03/07/03)
EPA exempts oil and gas industry from water pollution rules (03/10/03)
EPA withdraws water pollution cleanup rule (03/13/03)
EPA conflicted over Pentagon proposal to exempt the military from environmental
   laws (03/13/03)
EPA halts the use of toxic wood preservative (03/17/03)
Forest Service to double logging in Sierra Nevada forests (03/18/03)
EPA allows sludge dumping in Potomac River to continue for seven more years (03/18/03)
Bush administration proposes stripping protections for endangered wolves (03/18/03)
Interior ordered to continue protecting manatees (03/18/03)
GAO slams Bush administration for stalling on chemical security (03/18/03)
EPA cooks fish data to allow more pollution (03/21/03)
EPA backtracks on pledge to close loophole for California air polluters (03/25/03)
National Park Service officially adopts snowmobile plan (03/25/03)
Interior Department favors boosting offshore drilling by reducing corporate costs (03/26/03)
Whitman changes her tune on Pentagon environmental exemptions (03/26/03)
U.S. Fish and Wildlife Service proposes stream protection in Alabama (03/28/03)

April

Bush administration ends court battle over California off-shore drilling (04/01/03)
Bush administration slightly raises SUV gas mileage requirements (04/01/03)
EPA fines company $34 million for pipeline spills (04/02/03)
Bush administration giving away federal water rights in national park (04/03/03)
Bush administration begins diverting water from Klamath River—where salmon kill
   occurred—to farmers (04/03/03)
Bush administration looking to privatize park service jobs (04/04/03)
New U.S.-Mexico pollution treaty lacks funding to make a difference (04/04/03)
Bush administration attacks world heritage status of Yellowstone (04/07/03)
Bush taps another timber industry insider, Mark Rutzick, for environmental post (04/07/03)
Bush administration short-changing endangered species protection (04/07/03)
Corps keeps oil spill secret, citing national security concerns (04/08/03)
Bush administration abandons protection plan for California coastal treasure (04/08/03)
Interior Department paves way for new roads on federal lands in Utah (04/09/03)
EPA stifles staff objections to Pentagon pollution exemptions (04/09/03)
Interior Department paves way for new roads on federal lands in Utah (04/09/03)
EPA tries to bolster urban cleanup efforts (04/10/03)
U.S. Fish and Wildlife signs off on plan to reopen Imperial Dunes to off-road
   vehicles (04/10/03)
BLM to relax permitting process for oil and gas development (04/14/03)

BLM moves to overturn drilling ban in Alaska's Western Arctic Reserve (04/15/03)
EPA will force mining company to clean up pollution in Montana river (04/15/03)
EPA cracks down on diesel pollution (04/15/03)
EPA cleaning up far fewer toxic waste sites (04/18/03)
Bush administration considers delaying endangered species protection (04/19/03)
White House favors offshore oil drilling in Alaska (04/21/03)
Independent panel challenges Bush administration air pollution policies (04/21/03)
New Missouri River management plan imperils protected birds (04/22/03)
Forest Service permits grazing in violation of federal law, says judge (04/24/03)
White House unveils its pro-industry chemical security bill (04/24/03)
Fish and Wildlife Service holds the line on habitat protection plans for imperiled wildlife in
    California (04/24/03)
EPA Administrator Whitman misusing agency investigators (04/26/03)
White House bans EPA from discussing perchlorate pollution (04/28/03)
BLM approves Powder River Basin development (04/30/03)
EPA reports record drop in fuel economy (04/30/03)

May

Fish and Wildlife Service drops controversial manatee rules (05/05/03)
Energy Department illegally approved Mexican power plants, says judge (05/05/03)
EPA secretly considering amnesty for livestock farm polluters (05/05/03)
EPA drops "senior death discount" calculation (05/07/03)
Navy's illegal use of sonar blasts dolphins, whales in Puget Sound (05/08/03)
Bush chills on subsidizing Alaskan gas pipeline (05/09/03)
Fish and Wildlife Service signs off on mining in Montana wilderness (05/13/03)
Park Service pushes for personal watercraft on Lake Powell (05/13/03)
Department of Interior official under ethics investigation (05/13/03)
FWS designates critical habitat in Hawaii (05/14/03)
White House transportation plan steamrolls environmental protections (05/14/03)
EPA proposes easing, delaying smog control rules (05/14/03)
GAO report on forest fires a blow to Bush administration policies (05/15/03)
Pentagon accused of covering up perchlorate pollution (05/16/03)
National security, privatization put chokehold on funding for parks (05/18/03)
Christie Whitman, embattled EPA chief, resigns (05/21/03)
GAO chides Department of Agriculture for lax enforcement of wetlands protec-
    tions (05/22/03)
BLM vows to fix flawed land exchange program (05/23/03)
BLM opens fragile dunes ecosystem to off-road recreation (05/23/03)
Bush administration cuts wildlife protection, boosts logging in Northwest forests (05/27/03)
EPA failing to keep track of water quality (05/27/03)
Interior giving up on endangered species protection (05/29/03)
Park Service opens Maryland seashore to Jet Skis (05/30/03)
White House forest-fire plan axes environmental protections (05/30/03)
White House buries mountaintop mining regulation (05/30/03)

June

DOE moving ahead with new nukes (06/02/03)
DOE snow job helps oil drilling in Alaska (06/03/03)
Forest Service plan would triple logging limits in Sierra Nevada (06/05/03)
Department of Agriculture encouraging farmers to cut greenhouse gas (06/06/03)
EPA letting polluters off the hook (06/06/03)

Bush administration moves to roll back the Roadless Rule (06/09/03)
United States and European Union teaming up on hydrogen fuel cells (06/16/03)
Bush administration undermines critical habitat designations (06/18/03)
BLM vows to fix maligned land appraisal process (06/19/03)
DOD reneges on plan to test for perchlorate pollution at U.S. bases (06/20/03)
EPA concerned about Yellowstone snowmobiles (06/21/03)
Fish and Wildlife Service reduces protected habitat for threatened mouse by half (06/23/03)
White House whitewashes EPA environment report (06/23/03)
Bush administration calls for more gas drilling on public lands (06/24/03)
EPA rejects temporary ozone waiver for power plants (06/26/03)

July

Judge halts Montana timber sale, rules that Forest Service broke its own rules (07/01/03)
Illegal Navy sonar linked to porpoise deaths, environmentalists say (07/01/03)
Fish and Wildlife Service swamped with public comments supporting manatee
   protection (07/07/03)
EPA enforcement program in shambles (07/07/03)
Court rules against Cheney task force secrecy (07/08/03)
Bush administration taps new group to speed up energy development in Rockies (07/08/03)
Bush administration sending mixed signals on energy strategy (07/09/03)
EPA quietly backs off on reducing drinking water pollution (07/12/03)
Interior bumps up funding under ESA for land conservation (07/14/03)
Corps of Engineers rejects judge's ruling on Missouri River management dispute (07/15/03)
Bush pushing to privatize park service (07/15/03)
DOE attempting legislative end-run around court ruling on nuke waste (07/17/03)
Bush asks Supreme Court to overturn roadless protections (07/18/03)
Federal judge forced to intervene in Klamath River water plan (07/18/03)
BLM revs engines of off-road vehicle riders (07/19/03)
Judge holds Corps in contempt in Missouri River dispute (07/22/03)
Inspector General faults Interior officials for faulty land swap (07/23/03)
Bush climate plan all study, no action (07/24/03)
Criticism forces NPS not to raid Mount Rainier repair funds (07/24/03)
EPA reconsidering proposal to weaken Clean Air Act rule (07/25/03)
U.S. Forest Service exempts some logging projects from environmental review (07/29/03)
Bush administration taking on illegal logging abroad (07/29/03)
EPA hides research on Senate clean air plan (07/30/03)

August

Judge holds Corps in contempt in Missouri River dispute (08/04/03)
EPA makes misleading claims about support for Clear Skies plan (08/05/03)
BLM maximizing energy development, minimizing environmental protection (08/07/03)
Bush administration offers to double logging in Northwest (08/08/03)
Bush taps Utah Gov. Leavitt to head EPA (08/11/03)
Third Interior official under ethics investigation (08/14/03)
President making empty promises on parks funding, critics say (08/15/03)
Oily deal on offshore drilling rights (08/21/03)
Park Service spending less than promised (08/21/03)
EPA officially rolls back Clean Air Act protections (08/27/03)
EPA passes the buck on regulating global warming pollution from cars (08/28/03)

September

EPA lifts ban on selling polluted sites for development (09/02/03)
EPA balks at court ruling to protect waterways from pesticide pollution (09/03/03)
EPA offers new water-saving program (09/04/03)
EPA finds nearly 300 mountaintop removal violations (09/04/03)
EPA opposes Bush plan to relax Clean Water Act (09/05/03)
White House instructed EPA to hide potential health risks following 9/11 (09/09/03)
Private contractors to determine endangered species' future (09/12/03)
Interior Department fires worker after land payment scandal (09/15/03)
Bush touts air pollution plan at dirty power plant (09/15/03)
Interior Dept. provides $12.9 million in conservation grants (09/17/03)
Forest Service to sell Tongass timber at a loss (09/23/03)
Corps of Engineers violates judge's ruling, won't lower Missouri River flows for
    wildlife (09/24/03)
GAO finds that energy production pollutes wildlife refuges (09/24/03)
White House recommendations could shut the public out of environmental review (09/24/03)
EPA strikes deal with polluting factory farms (09/25/03)
BLM opens millions of acres of wilderness to energy development (09/29/03)
White House study: benefits of environmental regulation far outweigh costs (09/29/03)
EPA to issue daily air quality alerts (09/30/03)

October

More Superfund sites, but less money (10/01/03)
Privatizing forests doesn't add up (10/05/03)
Interior Department eases mining rules (10/09/03)
New EPA dam proposal threatens salmon (10/10/03)
Bush administration declares open season on endangered species (10/13/03)
EPA dodges Clear Skies comparisons (10/16/03)
EPA will not regulate dioxins from sewage sludge (10/17/03)
EPA may allow continued phosphate dumping in Gulf of Mexico (10/28/03)

November

EPA flushes mandatory sewage treatment rule (11/03/03)
Revised Everglades recovery plan not worth the wait (11/04/03)
Mine safety official fired for whistleblowing (11/08/03)
Forest Service short-changes environmental review on grazing permits (11/10/03)
EPA considers exempting small business from toxic release reporting (11/12/03)
Park Service workers speak out against Bush policies (11/13/03)
Bush administration seeks increase in use of ozone-depleting pesticide (11/14/03)
EPA considers streamlining of toxics release inventory (11/17/03)
Clarke conflicted over role at Interior Department (11/17/03)
EPA moves to fill landfills with radioactive waste (11/18/03)
Judge criticizes White House pro-industry mining rules (11/18/03)
Bush administration finally takes blame for Klamath fish kill (11/18/03)
Alaskan wilderness: Open for business (11/21/03)

Notes

Dedication

Page 5. Theodore Roosevelt, "The Man in the Arena" speech at the Sorbonne, Paris, Apr. 23, 1910.

Chapter 1

Page 15. Dick Cheney on being "a pretty good environmentalist": responding to a question on NBC-TV's *Meet the Press,* as reported in Andrew Clark, "Cheney defends Bush environmental policies," *USA Today,* Apr. 9, 2001.

Page 16, first bullet item. Amount of mercury allowed into the atmosphere: currently, mercury emissions are 48 tons per year. The Clean Air Act (CAA) requires best-available control technology by 2008; according to the EPA, this would get us down to 5 tons of mercury per year from coal-fired power plants, by far our biggest mercury source. (See the EPA's presentation to the Edison Electric Institute in Dec. 2001, http://cta.policy.net/ epamercury.pdf, p. 6.) Bush's "Clear Skies" proposal requires getting down to 26 tons per year by 2010. So it delays imposing any controls for two years more than the CAA, then sets a limit five times higher. In 2018, when the 15-year "Clear Skies" rule would expire, the limit goes down to 15 tons per year, or three times as much as the CAA allows. ("Clear Skies" information is available at http://www.epa.gov/air/clearskies/fact2003.html.) Thus, with the CAA, allowable emissions from 2008 to 2018 are 5 tons per year, or 55 tons over 11 years. With "Clear Skies," assume 48 tons for 2008 and 2009, or 96 tons. Add 26 tons each year for 2010–17 and another 15 tons for 2018, which brings the total to 319 tons. This is nearly six times what the CAA would allow.

Page 16, second bullet item. Number of asthma attacks: from Clean Air Task Force, *Clear the Air, Power to Kill: Death and Disease from Power Plants Charged with Violating the Clean Air Act* (Washington, D.C., July 2001), p. 4. It draws material from an original study by ABT Associates, Inc., *The Particulate-Related Health Benefits of Reducing Power Plant Emissions* (Cambridge, Mass., Oct. 2000).

Page 16, fifth bullet item. The value of a human life: the EPA now uses, for regulatory purposes, a figure of either $3.7 million or $3 million; it used to be $6 million. At $3.7 million, this represents a 38 percent reduction; at $3 million, a 50 percent reduction. Reported in several sources, including Katherine Q. Seelye and John Tierney, "By the Numbers," *New York Times,* May 8, 2003. See chapter 4 for details on the cost-benefit calculus of regulation as manipulated by John Graham, Bush's director of the Office of Information and Regulatory Assessment (OIRA).

Page 16, sixth bullet item. Opening wildlands to logging et al.: Timothy Egan, "The Nation; Bah, Wilderness! Reopening a Frontier to Development," *New York Times,* May 4, 2003 (Sunday edition, Week in Review)

Page 17. Theodore Roosevelt as "patron saint of land grabs": from the Competitive Enterprise Institute's April 2000 "Update." Brian Doherty, attacking Clinton's environmental agenda, says, "He [Clinton] began the brief environmental portion of the speech by summoning Theodore Roosevelt, the patron saint of federal land grabs."

Page 17. Roosevelt quote on "The conservation of our natural resources . . .": from a speech he gave in Jamestown, Virginia, June 10, 1907, as cited on the Web site "T.R.: Man of the Century" (http://users.metro2000.net/~stabbott/trquotes.htm).

Page 19. E. J. Dionne on Bush: from Dionne, "Conservatism Recast: Why This President's Reach Could Be Monumental," *Washington Post,* Jan. 27, 2002.

Page 20. Russell Kirk: quoted in Dionne, ibid.

Page 20. Jerry Taylor: quoted in "Why Did the Greens Win? A Symposium with Fred Smith, Jerry Taylor, Richard Belzer, Victor Porlier, and Kenneth Green," *PERC Reports* (Bozeman, Montana: The Political Economy Research Center, June 2002), http://www.perc.org/publications/percreports/june2002/greens.php?s=2. PERC bills itself as "the center for free market environmentalism."

Page 20. Edward Luttwak on conservatives: from Edward N. Luttwak, "Will Success Spoil America? Why the Pols Don't Get Our Real Crisis of Values," *Washington Post,* Nov. 27, 1994, p. c1; and in Clifford Cobb, Ted Halstead, and Jonathan Rowe, "If the GDP Is Up, Why Is America Down?" *The Atlantic Monthly,* Oct. 1995, www.theatlantic.com/politics/ecbig/gdp.htm.

Page 20. George Lakoff on the right and morality: from his "Framing a Democratic Agenda," *The American Prospect,* Sept. 24, 2003.

Page 22. Lakoff on worldly success: ibid.

Page 22. Rep. John Mica on welfare recipients: when the Republican welfare bill was being debated in Congress in 1995, Mica—holding up a sign that read "Do Not Feed the Alligators"—stated: "We post these warnings because unnatural feeding and artificial care creates dependency" (141 Cong. Rec. H3766, found in "The Right's Cornering of the Debate," The Public Eye, online journal of Political Research Associates, www.publiceye.org/welfare/Decades-of-Distortion-10.htm). Rep. Barbara Cubin on welfare recipients: ibid. Rep. Sonny Bono on endangered species: quoted in "Congressional Chainsaw Massacre," *Time,* Feb. 27, 1995.

Page 23. John Graham on the Precautionary Principle: Samuel Loewenberg, "Precaution Is for Europeans," *New York Times,* May 18, 2003.

Page 25. Frank Luntz advising the administration on framing environmental policy: in a memo from the Luntz Research Companies entitled "The Environment: A Cleaner, Safer, Healthier America" (original date unknown, but first leaked in Feb. 2003), pp. 131–46.

Page 25. Bush on litigating clean air and clean water: quoted in Joel Connelly, "Bush in Seattle to Compete," *Seattle Post-Intelligencer,* Aug. 12, 2000, final edition.

Page 25. Mike Smith on spending tax dollars: quoted in Kelly Regan, "Fossil Fuels Official Gives Oil, Gas Support," *Charleston News,* Jan. 31, 2002.

Page 26. Half of critical habitat opened to development: in Kieran Suckling, "A Review of the Bush Critical Habitat Record," report published by the Center for Biological Diversity, Oct. 8, 2003, p. 1.

Page 30. Senator James Jeffords on the president's environmental policies: in a speech to the National Press Club on the second anniversary of his decision to leave the Republican Party and become the Senate's only Independent, June 5, 2003.

Page 31. Twenty-five percent of Americans live within bicycling distance of a Superfund site: "Superfund Program: Current Status and Future Fiscal Challenges" (Washington, D.C.: United States General Accounting Office, Report no. GAO-03-850, July 2003), p. 1. Refers to an EPA study which says that one in four Americans lives within four miles of a site.

Chapter 2

Page 32. Theodore Roosevelt epigraph: *The Outlook,* Apr. 20, 1912.

Page 32. Ron Arnold epigraph: in Robert F. Kennedy, Jr., "Crimes Against Nature," *Rolling Stone,* no. 937 (Dec. 11, 2003).

Page 32. Bill Clinton epigraph: Bill Clinton, *Between Hope and History* (New York: Random House, 1996), pp. 103–5.

Page 33. John Smith on Chesapeake Bay: *The Proceedings of the English Colonie in Virginia* (1612). Though the book was Smith's, it attributed this account to two members of his party of fifteen, Walter Russell and Anas Todkill.

Page 35. Turner on the frontier: Frederick Jackson Turner, "The Significance of the Frontier in American History," a paper first read at the American Historical Association, Chicago (July 12, 1893) and reprinted widely.

Page 35. Roosevelt on the power of big business: Kathleen Dalton, *Theodore Roosevelt: A Strenuous Life* (New York: Alfred A. Knopf, 2002), p. 204.

Page 35. "We look upon these resources as a heritage": in Charles Richard Van Hise, *Roosevelt's Conservation Conference: The Conservation of Natural Resources in the United States* (1910), www.strom.clemson.edu/policystudies/post852/vanhise1.pdf.

Page 36. "What has posterity ever done for me?": in Dalton, *Theodore Roosevelt,* p. 244.

Page 36. "A million women for conservation" had written letters: ibid., p. 259.

Page 36. Roosevelt and the DAR: ibid.

Page 38. Earth Day 1970, 20 million people took part in thousands of events: from Senator Gaylord Nelson, "How the First Earth Day Came About," http://earthday.envirolink.org/history.html.

Page 38. The Roosevelts' emphasis on "the comfort, prosperity, and happiness of the American People": Van Hise, *Roosevelt's Conservation Conference.*

Page 41. Bush calls Gore "Ozone Man": in Ann Devroy, "Upbeat Bush Steps Up Rhetoric," *Washington Post,* Oct. 29, 1992.

Page 41. Gore on the "biggest mistake": in an interview on PBS with David Frost, Sept. 27, 1996.

Page 41. Clinton "not prepared to discuss ... the ravaging of our environment": in Jeff Shear, "The Big Deal," *National Journal,* Dec. 2, 1995.

Page 42. The Roadless Rule's 600 public hearings and more than a million public comments: from Heritage Forests Campaign, www.ourforests.org.

Page 43. Los Angeles air quality: L.A. air quality trends back through 1976 are available at http://www.aqmd.gov/smog/o3trend.html. The South Coast Air Quality Management District issues a public health warning when there is a "stage 1" air quality episode, meaning that ozone levels exceed .20 ppm. The worst year was 1977, when warnings were issued on 121 days. There were no warnings at all between 1999 and 2002. There was only one in the first three-quarters of 2003.

Page 43. Number of acres contaminated by toxic industrial wastes appeared to be going down each year: no one actually measures this. The Resources Conservation and Recovery Act stopped businesses from contaminating new acres, and the Superfund and other laws got them to begin cleaning up what they had contaminated—but no one measures the areas being decontaminated.

Page 43. Concentrations of lead in the bloodstream of urban children: from *Greenwire,* Feb. 25, 2003. In the "good news" category, the EPA noted that the number of children with elevated levels of lead in their blood has dropped dramatically, from 4.7 million in 1978 to about 300,000 in 2000. EPA officials said the success comes mostly from the phaseout of lead in gasoline between 1973 and 1995 as well as the reduction in the number of homes with lead-based paint, from 64 million in 1990 to 38 million in 2000.

Page 43. Total emissions of toxic chemicals declined: EPA report, "1996 Public Data Release—Ten Years of Right-to-Know." The first chapter, available at http://www.epa.gov/tri/tridata/tri96/pdr/2chapt01.pdf, reports that, between 1988 and 1996, total on- and off-site toxic releases declined by 45.6 percent, a reduction of over 1.529 billion pounds.

Page 43. Sixty percent of waterways were again safe to swim in: the EPA's most recent report, "Quality of the Nation's Rivers and Streams" (2000), estimates that 61 percent of rivers, 55 percent of lakes, and 49 percent of estuaries are safe for fishing and swimming. See http://www.epa.gov/owow/monitoring/nationswaters/quality.htm.

Chapter 3

Page 44. Vanity Fair photo session: Graydon Carter, "Editor's letter," *Vanity Fair,* Sept. 2003.

Page 44. Epigraph on Cheney: Mark Hosenball, Michael Isikoff, and Evan Thomas, "Cheney's Long Path to War," *Newsweek,* Nov. 17, 2003.

Page 44. Tom DeLay epigraph: in Toby Harnden, "Senate Faces Gridlock Unless Republicans Show Restraint," *London Telegraph,* Dec. 14, 2000.

Page 46. Mitch Daniels on ill-conceived or ill-intentioned actions: in Amy Goldstein, "'Last-Minute' Spin on Regulatory Rite: Bush Review of Clinton Initiatives Is Bid to Reshape Rules," *Washington Post,* June 9, 2001.

Page 46. Clinton's supposed "environmental extremism": after much turmoil, the administration had to bow to the overwhelming scientific evidence and approve the Clinton standard, after having suffered a very public black eye in the press. Clinton's 22 new national monuments survived a court challenge and remain to this day, albeit underfunded and underprotected. The Department of Energy overturned the efficiency regulations for air conditioners but, oddly, left in place those for washing machines and water heaters.

Page 46. The list went on and on: for an exhaustive record, see "The Bush Environmental Record" as compiled by the Natural Resources Defense Council in the Appendix.

Page 47. Rove as "Bush's brain": James Moore, *Bush's Brain: How Karl Rove Made George W. Bush Presidential* (New York: John Wiley & Sons, 2002).

Page 47. The bug in Clements's office: "Karl Rove's Greatest Political Hits," *Daily Enron,* Oct. 2, 2003.

Page 47. McCain on Rove: personal report by Margaret Fox, Sierra Club deputy executive director, on a conversation with John McCain at a book-signing party.

Page 47. Bush nicknames for Rove: James Carney and John F. Dickerson, "The Busiest Man in the White House," *Time,* Apr. 22, 2001.

Page 48. Luntz warning GOP leaders: Jim Nichols,"Revisionists Retreat: Republicans Back Off Touted Reform of Environmental Law in Light of Polls Showing Support for Protection of Resources," *Cleveland Plain Dealer,* Oct. 22, 1995.

Page 49. Ashcroft's voting record: see www.lcv.org.

Page 49. Mining permits for Doe Run Co.: editorial, *Columbia (Missouri) Daily Tribune,* Feb. 11, 1998.

Page 49. Ashcroft confirmation hearing promise: press release from Senator Cantwell's office, June 5, 2002, http://cantwell.senate.gov/news/releases/2002_06_05_roadless.html.

Page 49. Andrew Card as Bush's driver: Claire Moore, "Quiet and Loyal Leader? Andy Card, Former Lobbyist and Longtime Bush Family Friend," ABCNews.com, Dec. 20, 2000.

Page 50. Card's farewell party: "Election Overview," www.opensecrets.org/bush/cabinet/cabinet.card.asp.

Page 50. Tom DeLay on DDT: Tom Kenworthy, "A Symbol of Hope: Rising Peregrine Population Prompts Move to End Falcon's Endangered Species Listing," *Washington Post,* July 1, 1995.

Page 50. The EPA as Gestapo: Peter H. Stone, "Taking Care of Business," *National Journal,* Mar. 2, 1996.

Page 51. DeLay's claims on air toxics and science: *Houston Chronicle,* Oct. 28, 1990.

Page 51. DeLay on Nobel Prize: Bob Herbert, "In America; G.O.P. Hit Men," *New York Times,* Apr. 19, 1996.

Page 51. DeLay on climate change: Paul Burka, "Cracking the Whip," *Texas Monthly,* Sept. 1996.

Page 51. DeLay quote, "We have the agenda": in Toby Harnden, "Senate Faces Gridlock Unless Republicans Show Restraint," *London Telegraph,* Dec. 14, 2000.

Page 51. Funding of the Harvard Center for Risk Analysis: see its Web site, www.hcra.harvard.edu/unrestricted.html.

Page 51. Cost-effectiveness of mammograms vs. reducing benzene emissions: Natural Resources Defense Council, "Mr. Bottom Line," *OnEarth* (Spring 2003) 2.

Page 52. John Graham and Philip Morris: ibid.

Page 52. Graham on "flustered hypochondria": in Steve Weinberg, "Mr. Bottomline: John D. Graham," *OnEarth,* NRDC, no. 1, vol. 25, Mar. 22, 2003.

Page 52. Graham on mobile phone productivity: Mary O'Brien, "Natural Resistance," *Eugene Weekly,* Apr. 5, 2001.

Page 52. Graham to Heritage Foundation: Weinberg, "Mr. Bottomline."

Page 52. ALRA lobbying against John Turner: www.off-road.com/fight_back/turner/html.

Page 53. The lucky buyer: testimony of Brent Blackwelder, president of Friends of the Earth, submitted to the Senate Committee on Energy and Natural Resources on the nomination of J. Steven Griles as deputy secretary of the Interior, May 16, 2001; see www.foe.org/camps/eco/interior/brenttest.html.

Page 53. Griles's business arrangements: Michael Shnayerson, "Sale of the Wild," *Vanity Fair,* Sept. 2003.

Page 53. Hansen on Great Basin National Park: *Tribune* staff, "Hansen Suggests Closing Some National Parks," *Salt Lake Tribune,* Nov. 6, 1994.

Page 54. On the funding of right-wing think tanks: see Curtis Moore, "Rethinking the Think Tanks," *Sierra,* July/Aug. 2002.

Page 54. Norton's background with Mountain States Legal Foundation: Ron Arnold, anti-environmental leader and executive director of the Center for the Defense of Free Enterprise, cited in a profile of Mountain States Legal Foundation by CLEAR, the Clearinghouse on Environmental Advocacy and Research, 1998, http://www.clearproject.org/reports_mslf.html.

Page 54. Norton as a lobbyist for a lead company: "Gale Norton, Interior Secretary," profile by CLEAR, Jan. 2001. In 1999, "Norton registered to lobby Congress and the Colorado state legislature in behalf of NL Industries, a Houston company formerly known as National Lead Co. The company has been named as a defendant in suits involving 75 Superfund or other toxic-waste sites, plus a dozen lawsuits involving children allegedly poisoned by lead paint."

Page 54. Norton on the "homesteading right to pollute": in David Helvarg, "Unwise Use: Gale Norton's New Environmentalism; Secretary of the Interior Gale Norton," *The Progressive,* June 1, 2003.

Page 55. Norton and states' rights: "Rediscovering the 10th Amendment," speech by Norton to the Independence Institute in Vail, Colorado, Aug. 24, 1996, http://independenceinstitute.org/Centers/StevinsonCenter/Stevinson/vail96.htm#Norton. (In a letter to Norton, the Environmental Working Group asked the obvious questions: "Who is 'we' in the phrase 'we lost too much,' and what specifically was 'lost' when the Confederacy lost and slavery ended in 1865?")

Page 55. Norton "measure[d] her words": Michael Powell, "The Westerner's Interior Motives: To Gale Norton, Ranchers and Environmentalists Don't Have to Be at Loggerheads," *Washington Post,* Mar. 13, 2001.

Page 55. Norton and "the four C's": Michael Shnayerson, "Sale of the Wild," *Vanity Fair,* Sept. 2003.

Page 55. Mark Rey's background: CLEAR profile, July 2001, www.clearproject.org/reports_rey.html.

Page 55. Rey at wise use convention: cited in CLEAR profile, ibid. "Mark Rey was a featured speaker at the 1992 Grassroots Convention of The Umbrella Group (TUG), an early Washington State 'wise use' umbrella group made up of local timber and development interests." Sourced from Whatcom Environmental Council, "Wise Use in Northern Puget Sound," 1995.

Page 55. Rey on "the radical environmental legal terrorism campaign": American Forest Resources Alliance news release, Sept. 9, 1992, PR Newswire.

Page 55. Rey as "Darth Vader Lite": Katherine Pfleger, "Bush's Timber Czar Loved, Loathed," Associated Press, June 30, 2001.

Page 55. Rey on environmental concerns: American Forest Resource Alliance press release, Mar. 19, 2002.

Page 55. Rey on clearcutting: "Secrets of the Rainforest," *Sunset* magazine, Nov. 1997.

Page 56. Thomas Sansonetti's background: "DOJ Nominee Says Work for Coal Industry Would Not Skew His Work on Environment," BNA, Nov. 7, 2001.

Page 56. Sansonetti on coal leasing: Brian Stempeck, "DOJ nominee's background worries environmentalists," *Greenwire,* Nov. 5, 2001.

Page 56. Sansonetti quote, "The law is the law": Brian Stempeck, "Judiciary Committee Democrats grill DOJ nominee," *Greenwire,* Nov. 7, 2001.

Page 57. Lynn Scarlett's background: CLEAR profile, Apr. 2001.

Page 57. Scarlett on environmentalism: "Back to Basics," *Reason* magazine, Jan. 1997.

Page 57. Scarlett on free recreation: "FAQs About Free-Market Environmentalism," Thoreau Institute, http://www.ti.org/faqs.html.

Page 57. Bergen Record on Whitman: Editorial, "Will Whitman Stand Up? Or Will She Be a Patsy for the Polluters?" *Bergen Record,* Dec. 21, 2000.

Page 58. Colin Powell calls Whitman a "wind dummy": in Gregg Easterbrook, "Hostile Environment," *New York Times,* Aug. 19, 2001.

Chapter 4

Page 60. Spencer epigraph: Herbert Spencer, *Social Statics, or the Conditions Essential to Human Happiness* (1851).

Page 60. Ingersoll epigraph: Robert G. Ingersoll speech, New York, Oct. 29, 1896. Quoted in Roger E. Greeley, ed., *The Best of Robert Ingersoll, Immortal Infidel* (Buffalo, N.Y.: Prometheus Books, 1983), p. 79. Ingersoll, a leading Republican, was tapped to nominate James G. Blaine for president in 1876.

Page 62. Spencer quote on "the natural order of things": Spencer, *Social Statics.*

Page 62. Speaker at the Farm Bureau meeting: quoted in Paul Rauber, "An End to Evolution," *Sierra,* Jan./Feb. 1996.

Page 62. "We want big. We want fast. We want far. We want now": Maureen Dowd, "Drill, Grill, and Chill," *New York Times,* May 20, 2001.

Page 62. The supposed "carnage": Thomas DiLorenzo, "Airbag Murders: Death by Government," Oct. 26, 2003, Ludwig von Mises Institute, http://www.mises.org/fullarticle.asp?record=114&month=3.

Page 63. Attacking the banning of DDT: Angela Logomasini, "Deploy DDT to Fight Malaria," op-ed piece for Competitive Enterprise Institute, Washington, D.C., distributed by Scripps-Howard News Service, June 18, 2002.

Page 63. The "federal nanny state": Mary Sheila Gall, letter to the editor, *USA Today,* Oct. 12, 1999.

Page 63. Gall voted against federal safety standards for baby bath seats: "Statement of the Honorable Mary Sheila Gall on Notice of Proposed Rulemaking for Baby Bath Seats," U.S. Consumer Product Safety Commission, Oct. 16, 2003, http://www.cpsc.gov/cpscpub/prerel/prhtml04/04011.html.

Page 64. Lieberman on Graham: "John D. Graham Nomination, Statement of Senator Joe Lieberman," Committee on Governmental Affairs, U.S. Senate, in Lieberman press release dated May 22, 2001, http://govt-aff.senate.gov/052203_Lieberman-statement2.html.

Page 64. OIRA considered 316 rule changes: Katherine Q. Seelye, "White House Identifies Regulations That May Change," *New York Times,* Dec. 19, 2002. See also "What's Next on the Chopping Block?" by Reece Rushing, policy analyst at OMB Watch, in tompaine.com, Jan. 22, 2003.

Page 65. The 1942 arsenic standard and significant risk of cancer: "Subcommittee on Arsenic in Drinking Water, National Research Council," National Academies Press, 1999 (updated 2001).

Page 66. Millions of Americans drinking water with unsafe levels of arsenic: "Arsenic and Old Laws: A Scientific and Public Health Analysis of Arsenic Occurrence in Drinking Water, Its Health Effects, and EPA's Outdated Arsenic Tap Water Standard," Natural Resources Defense Council, New York, Feb. 2000, www.nrdc.org/water/drinking/arsenic/aolinx.asp.

Page 66. Browner tried to lower the standard to 5 ppb: "EPA to Reduce Arsenic in Drinking Water," EPA press release, May 24, 2000, http://yosemite.epa.gov/opa/admpress.nsf/0/ad1d03867011dc4d852568e900738f40?OpenDocument. During Newt Gingrich's prior assault on environmental regulations, Sierra Club interns surveyed congressional offices and found that 88 percent of the same House Republicans who were proposing to weaken safe drinking water standards for the public used bottled water in their offices. The right may not think the federal government should protect the purity of drinking water—but they were pretty committed to protecting themselves. (Source: Sierra Club, July/Aug. 1995.)

Page 66. Cheney on *Meet the Press:* "Vice President Dick Cheney Discusses Face-off with China, Tax and Budget Plans, and Other Political Topics," *Meet the Press,* Apr. 8, 2001.)

Page 67. Conflict between Rove and Hughes: David Frum, *Right Man: The Surprise Presidency of George W. Bush* (New York: Random House, 2003).

Page 67. Arsenic as "an essential ingredient": Angela Logomasini, "Arsenic and Old Politics," Competitive Enterprise Institute, May 16, 2001, http://www.cei.org/gencon/004,02034.cfm.

Page 67. Browner's science was sound: Edward Walsh, "Arsenic Drinking Water Standard Issued After Seven-Month Scientific Review, EPA Backs Clinton-Established Levels," *Washington Post,* Nov. 1, 2001, p. A31.

Page 67. Ari Fleischer on the president's image: in Carter M. Yang, "The Green Team?" ABCNews.com, Apr. 17, 2001.

Page 68. Jonathan Adler's memo: leaked internal CEI e-mail from Adler to Fred Smith, Wallace Kaufman, et al., Apr. 11, 2001, under the subject line "RE: the costs of writing like Huffington." The message begins: "The issue that Fred raises is perfectly exemplified by the arsenic flap. This should have been a 'gimme' for the administration."

Page 68. The business of preparing regulatory hit lists: all quoted material in this section is from Michael Grunwald, "Business Lobbyists Asked to Discuss Onerous Rules," *Washington Post,* Dec. 4, 2001.

Page 69. Graham sent rules back: Traci Watson, "13 Environmental Rules Up for Review," *USA Today,* Jan. 8, 2002 (final edition), p. A3. See also Natural Resources Defense Council, "Mr. Bottom Line," *OnEarth* (Spring 2003): "At its height, in 1984, OIRA sent fifty-eight rules back to the agencies for rewriting. In the eight years under Clinton, only sixteen were sent back. Graham reversed the trend, sending back nineteen in his first year alone."

Page 70. Result of British test yielding $3.7 million value per life: M. W. Jones-Lee, ed., *The Value of Life and Safety* (Amsterdam: North–Holland, 1982).

Page 71. An elderly person's life was worth only $2.3 million: Katherine Q. Seelye and John Tierney, "By the Numbers," *New York Times,* May 8, 2003.

Page 71. Marilyn Skolnick quote: in Don Hopey, "EPA Gets an Earful on Plan to 'Discount' Seniors' Lives," *Pittsburgh Press Gazette,* Apr. 24, 2003.

Page 72. Alan Krupnick quote: in John Tierney, "Life: The Cost-Benefit Analysis," *New York Times,* May 18, 2003.

Page 72. SUVs and pickup trucks constitute more than half of all vehicles sold in the United States: "Senators Feinstein and Snowe Introduce Legislation to Increase Fuel Efficiency Standards," Jan. 30, 2003, press release, http://feinstein.senate.gov/03Releases/r-cafe03.htm.

Page 72. Fuel-efficiency gains of 33 percent: EPA report, "Light Duty Automotive Technology and Fuel Economy Trends, 1975–2003," reported in Harry Steffer, "Vehicles Gain Power But Not Fuel Economy," *Automotive News,* May 12, 2003, p. 1.

Page 73. A standard mid-sized car could be easily reengineered: "Making the Average Car in America get 42 MPG," report by the Center for Auto Safety and the Sierra Club, http://www.sierraclub.org/globalwarming/cleancars/cafe/taurus.asp.

Page 73. Readily achievable technical innovations: "Freedom Option Package," Sierra Club release, June 2002, http://www.sierraclub.org/freedompackage/.

Page 73. Yates assailed Ford's manhood: Brock Yates, "Pecksmiths Can't Stop the SUV," *Wall Street Journal,* May 17, 2000.

Page 74. A study by the Department of Energy showed that vehicle design is the key safety factor: cited in Marc Ross and Tom Wenzel, "An Analysis of Traffic Deaths by Vehicle Type and Model," March 2002, www.aceee.org/pubs/t021full.pdf.

Page 74. SUVs have the highest rollover rates of all vehicles: "Meeting the Safety Challenge," speech to the Automotive News World Congress in Detroit, Jan. 14, 2003. Cited at http://www.consumeraffairs.com/news03/runge.html.

Page 76. SUVs perfectly symbolize the right's idea of appropriate risk: Hans Eisenbeis, "Four Wheel Drive Fantasies," *Reason,* July 2002, http://reason.com/0207/fe.he.four.shtml.

Page 76. The dangers posed by SUVs made them all the more desirable: David Brooks, "The Scarlett SUV, Who's Against Sport-Utility Vehicles? A Bunch of Geeks," *Wall Street Journal,* Jan. 21, 2003.

Chapter 5

Page 78. Luntz epigraph: Frank Luntz, "The Environment: A Cleaner, Safer, Healthier America," memo (undated but apparently Fall 2002) leaked to the Environmental Working Group, p. 132, http://www.ewg.org/briefings/luntzmemo/pdf/LuntzResearch_environment.pdf.

Page 78. Jim Jeffords epigraph: from a speech to the National Press Club on the second anniversary of his decision to leave the Republican Party and become the Senate's only Independent, June 5, 2003. Found on various Web sites, including www.tompaine.com/feature2.cfm/ID/8028.

Page 79. Luntz on cleaning up the lingo: Frank Luntz, "The Luntz Research Companies— Language of the 21st Century," memo leaked to the Sierra Club in September 1997.

Page 80. Bush's repeated use of the phrase "common sense": in Jennifer 8. Lee, "A Call for Softer, Greener Language," *New York Times,* Mar. 2, 2003.

Page 80. Grover Norquist and Greider quoted: in William Greider, "Rolling Back the 20th Century," *The Nation,* May 12, 2003.

Page 81. Cleaning up today's auto fleets: in chapter 4 we mention the "freedom package," a set of off-the-shelf technologies Detroit could use to make today's vehicles much more efficient. It is unclear whether Rove consciously stole language from the freedom package in dubbing the president's diversionary hydrogen program the "freedom car" six months later, but the coincidence is striking.

Page 81. On "Luntzspeak": see www.luntzspeak.com.

Page 81. U.S. State of the Union Address, 2003, http://www.whitehouse.gov/news/releases/2003/01/20030128-19.html.

Page 82. Sidestepping the legacy of toxic waste: Jennifer Hattam, "Above the Law," *Sierra,* Jan./Feb. 2004. In 2003 the Bush administration took care of 85 million gallons of liquid radioactive waste by changing its classification from "high-level" to "incidental."

Page 82. Anthony Dorsey on fishing in Georgia: testimony heard personally by Carl Pope, Macon, Georgia, May 28, 2002.

Page 82. Georgia Power's Plant Scherer's emissions: Charles Richardson, "Air Pollution Control Is a Regional Problem," Editorial, *Macon Telegraph,* May 9, 2003.

Page 83. Deaths caused by air pollution: "Danger in the Air," Natural Resources Defense Council Report, May 1996, www.nrdc.org/air/pollution/nbreath.asp.

Page 83. Dwight Evans on power plants: Carrie Teegardin, "Electric Utility's Clout Burns Bright in Washington," *Atlanta Journal and Constitution,* Feb. 23, 2003.

Page 84. George H. W. Bush on his overhaul of the CAA: remarks at the Annual Republican Congressional Fundraising Dinner, June 12, 1990. In George Bush Presidential Library, http://bushlibrary.tamu.edu/papers/1990/90061207.html.

Page 85. Philip Perry's work on environmental and natural-resources cases at the Department of Justice: The Lawyer's Column, "Energy Industry's Links to Regulators, Administration Worry Environmentalists," *Washington Post,* Sept. 10, 2001, p. E13

Page 85. Cheney's views on Whitman's legislation: CNN Live Event/Special, "Vice President Cheney Speaks with CNN," aired May 8, 2001.

Page 85. Bush's Clear Skies plan: "President Announces Clear Skies and Global Climate Change Initiatives," White House news release, Feb. 14, 2002, http://www.whitehouse .gov/news/releases/2002/02/20020214-5.html.

Page 86. Clear Skies' toxic mercury allowances: "The Bush Administration's Air Pollution Plan Would Shred Current Clean Air Protections," Clean Air Trust study, www.cleanairtrust .org/release.040803.html.

Page 86. James Inhofe's attempt to raise Clear Skies' mercury pollution allowances: "Inhofe, Voinovich Introduce Revised Clear Skies Legislation," Majority Press Release, U.S. Senate Committee on Environment and Public Works, Nov. 10, 2003, http://epw.senate.gov/ pressitem.cfm?party=rep&id=214908.

Page 86. Mercury levels in women of childbearing age: "America's Children and the Environment," EPA report, Feb. 24, 2003, http://www.epa.gov/envirohealth/children/.

Page 86. Eric Schaeffer's letter of resignation: dated Feb. 27, 2002. See, e.g., http://www .defenders.org/newsroom/letter.html.

Page 86. Leaked memo about Carper plan, and Carper's response: in Guy Gugliotta and Eric Pianin, "EPA Withholds Air Pollution Analysis," *Washington Post,* July 1, 2003.

Page 87. Jeffrey Holmstead on justifying Clear Skies: in Jennifer 8. Lee, "Critics Say E.P.A. Won't Analyze Clean Air Proposals Conflicting with President's Policies," *New York Times,* July 14, 2003.

Page 87. John Graham quoted: in Eric Pianin, "Study Finds Net Gain from Pollution Rules," *Washington Post,* Sept. 27, 2001, p. A1.

Page 87. The EPA drops investigation of power plants: Christopher Drew and Richard A. Oppel, Jr., "Lawyers at E.P.A. Say It Will Drop Pollution Cases," *New York Times,* Nov. 6, 2003.

Page 88. Captain Dorst and fire in Sequoia N.P.: Harvey Meyerson, *Nature's Army: When Soldiers Fought for Yosemite* (Lawrence, Kansas: University Press of Kansas, 2001), pp. 134–35. Pyne on fire suppression as federal policy: Stephen J. Pyne, *Fire in America: A Cultural History of Wildland and Rural Fire* (Princeton, N.J.: Princeton University Press, 1982), p. 228.

Page 88. Sam Farr on management of national forests: Joint Hearing on the Management of the U.S. Forest Service before the Committee on Resources and Committee on the Budget and

Subcommittee on Interior of the Committee on Appropriations, House of Representatives, 105th Congress, 2nd session, Mar. 26, 1998, Serial No. 105-82

Page 89. Pyne on introducing fires deliberately: in Tom Gorman, "17 Blazes Charring the West," *Los Angeles Times,* June 23, 2002.

Page 90. The Rodeo-Chediski forest fire: Brian Stempeck, "Field Hearing to Probe Missteps During Arizona Fire," *Greenwire,* Sept. 23, 2002.

Page 90. Arizona Republic on Governor Jane Hull: E. J. Montini, "Burning Tree Huggers at the Stake," *Arizona Republic,* June 25, 2002.

Page 91. Scott McInnis's alleged "analysis paralysis" and GAO figures: "New GAO Report Shows that 95% of Forest Service Fuel Reduction Projects Get Green Light within Standard 90-day Review Period," Native Forest Network, May 15, 2003, http://www .nativeforest.org/press_room/index.htm. Allegations by Jon Kyl: see Montini, "Burning Tree Huggers at the Stake"; see also Editorial, "Stop the Finger-Pointing and Fix the Forests," *Arizona Sun,* June 25, 2002, and Jon Kyl, "Sensible Environmentalism Has Place in Managing Forests," ArizonaRepublic.com, July 10, 2002.

Page 91. Forest managers' diversion of restoration funds: U.S. Department of Agriculture Office of the Inspector General Western Region Audit Report, Forest Service National Fire Plan Implementation, Report No. 08601-26-SF, Nov. 2001, http://www.usda.gov/oig/ webdocs/08601-26-SF.pdf.

Page 91. Forest Service's "misplacement" of funds: "Forest Service Misplaced $215 Million in Firefighting Funds," Taxpayers for Common Sense press release, Aug. 22, 2002, www.taxpayer.net/TCS/PressReleases/08-22-02fslostmoney.htm.

Page 91. Exposure of the dangers of Healthy Forests legislation: "House Set to Vote on Fire Legislation That Fails to Protect Communities," Wilderness Society press release, May 19, 2003, http://www.wilderness.org/NewsRoom/Release/20030519.cfm.

Page 91. The Community Protection Plan: "Community Fire Protection Plan," American Lands Alliance, www.americanlands.org/community_protection_plan.htm.

Page 92. Vern Vinson's fire protection plan: "Fire Spared Home Where Prevention Measures Were Taken," Associated Press, July 11, 2002.

Page 92. Frank Johnson and the value of prescribed burns: in Bill Redeker, "Prescribed Burns Pay Off: Controlled Fires Thin Forest, Reducing Ability to Spread," http://abcnews.go .com/sections/wnt/DailyNews/prescribed_burns020626.html. All over the West, homeowners and communities were following suit. In the Crescent H Subdivision near Jackson, Wyoming, homeowners began clearing low limbs and brush, installing metal roofs—and begging the Forest Service to do its part to protect their homes. In Summit County, Colorado, 57 volunteers organized by the Sierra Club showed up to demonstrate how clearing brush and slash from around homes could reduce fire risks while preserving the environment. Working along with the Summit County Fire Mitigation office, the volunteers cleared the area around ten homes, removing fourteen tons of slash and filling four dumpsters.

Page 92. Funds for Community Protection Zones: "Fire Facts: Forest Service Studies Show That Logging Increases Fire Risk; Community Protection Is Not Being Prioritized," Fact Sheet, American Lands Alliance, http://www.americanlands.org/new_page_19.htm.

Page 93. Forest managers hope to meet annual logging goals: Michael Milstein, "Forest Managers Optimistic They Will Meet Logging Goals," *Portland Oregonian,* Apr. 17, 2003.

Page 93. Connaughton on thinning projects: in "Press Briefing by Chairman of the Council on Environmental Quality, James L. Connaughton," PR Newswire, Aug. 22, 2002.

Page 93. Testimony of fire ecologists: letter to President Bush, Sept. 9, 2002, by fire ecologists Norman L. Christensen, Thomas Swetnam, et al., available on www .StrategicIgnorance.org.

Page 93. Jeremy Fried on costs of thinning: in Jeff Barnard, "Study Reveals Thinning Forests Costly," Associated Press, Aug. 26, 2002.

Page 93. 2004 budget decreases fire prevention funding: "President Acts to Fund Healthy Forest Initiative," *The Forestry Source,* Mar. 2003. See http://www.safnet.org/archive/ 0303_budget.cfm.

Page 94. Janet Napolitano's fire prevention funds request: Doug Abrahms, "Western States Get Little Aid for Fire Prevention from Feds," *Salt Lake Tribune,* July 13, 2003.

Page 94. California's request for fire prevention funds denied: Gregg Jones and Dan Morain, "U.S. Rejected Davis on Aid to Clear Trees," *Los Angeles Times,* Oct. 31, 2003. As the 2003 fire season began, with no new funds, no priorities for community protection, and a Forest Service determined to turn the national forests back into commercial timber operations, emboldened timber companies abandoned any pretense of corporate good citizenship. When logging crews started two fires on private Plum Creek timberland in the vicinity of Lolo Pass, the firm refused to pay any of the $11 million it cost the Forest Service to fight the fires when they spread to public land. The company said that, since it had hired independent contractors to do the work, it "respectfully declines" to take any responsibility. The contractors, of course, did not have the resources to pay $11 million, but the reality that logging was causing, not preventing, forest fires, seemed lost on the administration.

Chapter 6

Page 96. Mike Smith epigraph: in Kelly Regan, "Fossil Fuels Official Gives Oil, Gas Support," *Charleston Gazette,* Jan. 31, 2002.

Page 96. Dick Cheney epigraph: in Mike Allen and Michael Shear, "Democratic Ads Lambaste Bush Record," *Washington Post,* Oct. 10, 2000.

Page 97. Corporate campaign contributions: www.opensecrets.org.

Page 97. Westar Energy seeks change in regulations: Micah Sifry, "Enough DeLay," June 13, 2003, www.tompaine.com.

Page 97. DeLay on Westar scandal: in R. G. Ratcliffe, "DeLay's Investment Pays Off," *Houston Chronicle,* Oct. 10, 2003, p. 12.

Page 98. DeLay on money and politics: Tom DeLay, "Principles of Real Campaign Reform," *Washington Times,* May 22, 1998.

Page 98. The Farm Bill: see Environmental Working Group analysis, 2002, http://www.ewg .org/farm/region.php?fips=00000&progcode=total&yr=2002.

Page 100. *L.A. Times* automotive critic: Dan Neil, "Toyota's Spark of Genius," *Los Angeles Times,* Oct. 15, 2003.

Page 100. Roger Herrera of Arctic Power: in Tom Hamburger, Laurie McGinley, and David S. Cloud, "Corporate Donors Seek Return on Investment in Bush Campaign," *Wall Street Journal,* Mar. 6, 2001.

Page 100. Ralph Reed letter to Enron: Joe Stevens, "Bush 2000 Adviser Offered to Use Clout to Help Enron," *Washington Post,* Feb. 17, 2002.

Page 101. Halliburton's no-bid contract: "The practice of delegating a vast array of logistics operations to a single contractor dates to the aftermath of the 1991 Persian Gulf War and a study commissioned by Cheney, then defense secretary, on military outsourcing. The Pentagon chose [Halliburton subsidiary] Brown and Root to carry out the study and subsequently selected the company to implement its own plan." Michael Dobbs, "Halliburton's Deals Greater Than Thought," *Washington Post,* Aug. 28, 2003.

Page 101. Halliburton's hydraulic fracturing: Dan Morgan, "Provisions Benefiting Energy Industry Are Folded into Bill: Drilling Technique Pioneered by Halliburton—That Might Pollute Water—Would No Longer Require Special Permit," *Washington Post,* Oct. 12, 2003.

Page 101. Luke Popovich on business practices: in William Gibson, "Oil Industry Sells Bush Energy Plan," *Chicago Tribune,* Aug. 21, 2001.

Page 101. Bush on energy independence: in Ann McFeatters, "Conservation-free Energy Plan Will Put Heat on Cheney," *Pittsburgh Post-Gazette,* May 13, 2001.

Page 101. U.S. laboratories' report: Joseph Kahn, "U.S. Scientists See Big Power Savings from Conservation," *New York Times,* May 6, 2001.

Page 101. Peabody Coal donation of $100,000: see http://www.opensecrets.org/2000elect/other/bush/inaugural.asp.

Page 102. Rob Reiner on the GOP's idea of diversity: in "Democratic National Convention: The Road to L.A.," USNews.com, Aug. 13, 2000, http://www.usnews.com/usnews/news/election/dem/road.htm.

Page 102. Joseph Kelliher's e-mail to Dana Contratto: e-mail obtained by Judicial Watch, Mar. 18, 2001, http://www.judicialwatch.org/1770.shtml.

Page 102. Cheney on the energy problem in California: on NBC's *Meet the Press,* May 20, 2001.

Page 103. Market manipulation by energy company officials: "Final Report on Price Manipulation in Western Markets," FERC, March 26, 2003, http://www.ferc.gov/industries/electric/indus-act/wem/pa02-2/orders.asp#Mar26.

Page 103. Krugman on California power shortages: Paul Krugman, "Delusions of Power," *New York Times,* Mar. 28, 2003.

Page 103. No apologies from the White House: indeed, apologies might have been awkward. In addition to Enron, another energy producer robbing California was the Williams Companies, on the board of which sat one Thomas Cruikshank. By the summer of 2001, Cruikshank knew that his company was colluding with another producer, AES, to keep its power plants offline and drive up prices. Cruikshank could easily have told the vice president that what he was saying about the California energy problem was poppycock. It was Cruikshank, after all, who got Cheney the job as CEO of Halliburton, which made the vice president very, very rich. See David Lazarus, "White House Connections to Energy Giants Under Investigation Emerge," *San Francisco Chronicle,* Nov. 22, 2002.

Page 103. FirstEnergy quotation: in John Funk and John Mangels, "Davis-Besse Workers' Repair Job Hardest Yet," *Cleveland Plain Dealer,* Dec. 29, 2002.

Page 103. Gilinsky on nuclear near-accident: Victor Gilinsky, "Heard About the Near-Accident at the Ohio Nuclear Plant? I'm Not Surprised," *Washington Post,* Apr. 28, 2002.

Page 103. Kucinich on nuclear near-accident: in John Funk and John Mangels, "Report Hits NRC Decisions on Besse," *Cleveland Plain Dealer,* Jan. 3, 2003.

Page 104. The investigative report on Davis-Besse: Funk and Mangels, "Davis-Besse Workers' Repair Job Hardest Yet."

Page 104. Richard Meserve on safety issues: ibid.

Page 104. Nuclear industry on Davis-Besse mishap: ibid.

Page 104. Bush NRC reversal on plant safety procedures: Matthew Wald, "Nuclear Agency Changes Its Stance on a Fire Safety Proposal," *New York Times,* Nov. 19, 2003, p. A11.

Page 105. Distributing potassium iodide pills: "Pills Urged for People Near Nuke Plants," Associated Press, Dec. 4, 2003 (no author cited).

Page 105. Safety of nuclear-waste-storage canisters: "The Good Fight Continues," *Las Vegas Mercury,* Nov. 6, 2003.

Page 105. Public Interest Research Group précis: Alison Cassady, "Polluter Payday," PIRG report, Nov. 2001. See http://newenergyfuture.com/newenergy .asp?id2=4134&id3=energy&.

Page 105. McGrory on "the love letter": Mary McGrory, "Diffident Oilmen?" *Washington Post,* Feb. 24, 2002.

Page 106. Oil and gas would get $47.5 billion: "Oil and Gas Subsidy Giveaways in the Energy Conference Report," Friends of the Earth analysis, Nov. 18, 2003, http://www.foe.org/ energy/oilandgasfact.pdf.

Page 106. Coal and electric utilities would reap $9.3 billion: "Coal Subsidies in H.R.6, the Energy Policy Act of 2003," Friends of the Earth analysis, Nov. 18, 2003, http://www.foe.org/energy/coalfact.pdf.

Page 106. Nuclear industry would pocket $9.2 billion: "Nuclear Power Giveaways in the Energy Conference Report," Friends of the Earth analysis, Nov. 18, 2003, http://www.foe.org/ energy/nukefact.pdf.

Page 107. WSJ on plutonium: Editorial, *Wall Street Journal,* Oct. 2, 2002.

Page 107. Industry advantages in Bush energy policy: "H.R. 4: A Bad Energy Bill," Natural Resources Defense Council analysis, Aug. 1, 2001, http://www.nrdc.org/legislation/ ahr4.asp.

Page 107. Pete Domenici on nuclear subsidies: in "Nuclear Industry Loan Guarantees Kept in Energy Bill," Capitol Update, June 11, 2003, www.asme.org/gric/Update/2003/ 061103.html.

Page 108. Congressional Budget Office on loan default risk: Cost Estimate of Bill S.14, "Energy Policy Act of 2003," May 7, 2003, http://www.cbo.gov/showdoc .cfm?index=4206&sequence=0.

Page 108. The *Chicago Tribune* on "a risky and expensive subsidy": Editorial, "First Aid for the Nuclear Industry," *Chicago Tribune,* June 20, 2003.

Page 108. The *Economist* on "throwing good public money after bad": Editorial, "Fact and Fission," *Economist,* July 17, 2003.

Page 108. McGrory on Cheney and energy policy: McGrory, "Diffident Oilmen?"

Page 109. About 75 energy executives met with Cheney; Don Van Natta, Jr., "A Company's Gain from Energy Reports Recommendation," *New York Times,* Mar. 24, 2002.

Page 109. Pasternak on industry involvement: Judy Pasternak, "Bush's Energy Plan Bares Industry Clout," *Los Angeles Times,* Aug. 26, 2001.

Page 109. Fred Palmer quote: in ibid.

Page 109. Paul O'Neill held his Alcoa stock: Robert F. Kennedy, Jr., "Crimes Against Nature," *Rolling Stone,* Dec. 11, 2003.

Page 109. Sierra Club given 48 hours to respond: "Enviros Given Less Than 48 Hours for Task Force Input," *Greenwire,* Apr. 11, 2002.

Page 110. Letter from the DOE to the GAO: August 2001 memo from Margot Anderson, deputy assistant secretary for policy in the DOE's Office of Policy and International Affairs, to the GAO, cited in "Bush Energy Task Force Consulted Environmentalists: Environmental Groups Given Two Days to Respond to Last Minute Call," Reuters, Apr. 11, 2002.

Page 110. Kenneth Lay's energy policy recommendations: Bill Press, "The Enron Smoking Gun," *San Francisco Chronicle,* Feb. 6, 2002.

Page 110. Cheney meeting with environmentalists: Carl Pope, personal meeting with Vice President Cheney and other White House staff, White House, June 1, 2003.

Page 111. Ann Veneman on the Farm Bill of 2002: "On the Introduction of Farm Bill Legislation by Senator Lugar," USDA Statement No. 0203.01, Oct. 17, 2001.

Page 113. Domenici on his strategy: Carl Hulse, "Consensus on Energy Bill Arose One Project at a Time," *New York Times,* Nov. 19, 2003.

Page 113. MBTE damage to Lake Tahoe: Editorial, "Shifting the Burden," *Washington Post,* Sept. 18, 2003.

Page 113. Domenici on negative reaction to energy bill: Seth Borenstein and Sumana Chatterjee, "Energy Bill Gives Industry Billions," *Philadelphia Inquirer,* Nov. 15, 2003.

Page 113. *WSJ* on GOP leadership: Editorial, "The Grassley Rainforest Act (The Energy Bill)," *Wall Street Journal,* Nov. 18, 2003.

Page 113. *Detroit News* on the bill: Editorial, "ENERGY BILL: House-passed Version Is a Disaster for Environment," *Detroit News,* Nov. 19, 2003.

Chapter 7

Page 114. Nelson epigraph: Robert H. Nelson, "Federal Imperialism," *Forbes,* Feb. 13, 1995, p. 65.

Page 114. Bush epigraph: in Scott Lindlaw, "Working on Range 'Helps Me Put It All in Perspective,'" Associated Press, Aug. 11, 2002.

Page 114. Balzar epigraph: John Balzar, "Ah, Sweet Nature . . . but Only if You Can Afford a Piece of It: Please Save Some for Us, Mr. President," *Los Angeles Times,* Aug. 8, 2002.

Page 115. The Cheneys' attitude toward public land: on one occasion when Carl Pope debated Lynn Cheney on television, she denounced federal protection of wetlands because it was preventing a rancher she knew from blowing up the beavers who were damming his meadow. (Of course, that meadow, like virtually every upland pasture in the Rocky Mountains, had been originally created by beavers. As the ones who created it, they arguably had more right to the meadow than the rancher's cows.)

Page 116. Ring on the new realities of the Mountain West: Ray Ring, "Bad Moon Rising: The Waning of Montana's Once-mighty Progressive Coalition," *High Country News,* Dec. 17, 2002.

Page 117. Bernard DeVoto on the wise users' sentiment: in Wallace Stegner, *The American West as Living Space* (Ann Arbor: University of Michigan Press, 1987).

Page 117. Bush on Gore's "neglect" of national parks: Arshad Mohammed, "Bush Accuses Gore of Neglecting National Parks," Reuters, Sept. 13, 2000.

Page 117. Anderson's proposal to auction public lands: Terry Anderson, Vernon Smith, and Emily Simmons, "How and Why to Privatize Federal Lands," Cato Policy Analysis No. 363, Dec. 9, 1999.

Page 118. Timber management and the Plum Creek Timber Company: Sherry Devlin, "Plum Creek Won't Pay for 2000 Blazes," The Missoulian, Apr. 15, 2003, missoulian.com.

Page 119. Maria Cantwell presses Norton during confirmation hearings: "Gale Norton's Senate Confirmation Hearing," Jan. 18, 2001, The American Presidency Project, www.presidency.ucsb.edu/docs/transition2001/norton_hearing_0118.php.

Page 119. James Hansen's letter to Bush and Cheney: see www.npca.org/magazine/2001_issues/march_april/hansen.asp.

Page 121. Miles of publicly funded roads in national forests: the Forest Service estimates that there are 380,000 miles of roads in the national forests (http://www.fs.fed.us/gpnf/press/2000/pr252.htm). In addition, however, there were (as of 1998) some 60,000 additional miles of illegal "ghost" roads in the forests as well. See Michelle Nijhuis, "'Ghost Roads' Haunt Forests," *Hotline,* Mar. 2, 1998.

Page 121. Sixty million acres of unroaded national forest: see http://www.fs.fed.us/gpnf/press/2000/pr252.htm.

Page 121. Of 2.2 million comments, 95 percent were in favor of wilderness protection: see www.ourforests.org.

Page 121. Rey's testimony: in Lisa Dix, "Fundamental Environmental Protections Jeopardized Under Mark Rey's Leadership," American Lands Campaign, Nov. 9, 2001. See www.fseee.org/fsnews/frey.html.

Page 122. The Justice Department's argument against environmental groups: Bob Egelko, "New Dispute Brewing over Ban on Forest Road-Building," *San Francisco Chronicle,* Nov. 15, 2003.

Page 122. Terry Anderson on the administration's performance: in J. R. Pegg, "Bush Too Soft on Environment, Say Conservatives," Environment News Service, Jan. 21, 2003. See http://www.monitor.net/monitor/0301a/bushperc.html. For the PERC report, see http://www.perc.org/publications/percreports/march2003/perc_march4.php?s=2.

Page 123. Rebecca Watson on the energy development agenda: in Bob Anez, "Bush Team Pushes for Western Development," AP/*San Francisco Chronicle,* Sept. 14, 2003.

Page 124. Typical gas firm spokesman commented: Vincent Schodolski, "West Frets over Energy Policy," *Chicago Tribune,* Mar. 21, 2001.

Page 124. Wells in Powder River basin: ibid.

Page 125. Blancett on natural gas drilling: Tweeti Blancett, "The Coming Gas Explosion in the West," *High Country News,* May 5, 2003.

Page 125. Stoney Burk on drilling in the Rocky Mountains: in Julie Cart, "Critics Fear Energy Plan Will Tame a Wild Land," *Los Angeles Times,* Nov. 9, 2003.

Page 126. Defenders of Wildlife bounty program: see http://www.defenders.org/wildlife/new/facts/faq.html.

Page 126. Popularity of wolf reintroduction program: see http://yellowstone-natl-park.com/sighting.htm.

Page 126. Ecological value of wolf reintroduction: David Stauth, "Scientists: Wolves Helping Rebalance Yellowstone Ecosystem," Press Release, Oregon State University, Oct. 28, 2003.

Page 126. Ed Bangs on wolf recovery: in Scott McMillion, "Wolf Defenders Threaten to Halt Delisting," *Bozeman Daily Chronicle,* Apr. 2, 2003.

Page 127. Brian Vincent on the effects of the Bush plan on wolves: in Joey Bunch, "Wolf Rule Prompts Suit," *Denver Post,* Oct. 2, 2003.

Page 127. Grizzly bear population: Todd Wilkinson, "Grizzly Status Debated as Population Rises," *Christian Science Monitor,* June 24, 2002.

Page 127. Forest Service development in Wyoming: "Wild Wyoming Needs Your Help," action alert from the Wyoming Outdoor Council, http://www.forwolves.org/ralph/wild-wyoming-needs-help.htm.

Page 127. Dirk Kempthorne on reintroducing grizzlies: Kempthorne news release, Nov. 16, 2000, http://www2.state.id.us/gov/pr/2000/November/Pr1116.html.

Page 128. Gale Norton on the recovery of the grizzly population: memo to environmental colleagues from Mark Van Putten, executive director of National Wildlife Federation, and Rodger Schlickeisen, president of Defenders of Wildlife, reporting on a Norton briefing of June 22, 2001.

Page 128. Schlickeisen on the grizzly plan: "Statement of Rodger Schlickeisen, President of Defenders of Wildlife, on Secretary of the Interior's Rejection of Selway-Bitterroot Grizzly Plan," June 21, 2001, http://www.defenders.org/releases/pr2001/pr062101.html.

Page 128. Critical habitat under the Endangered Species Act: "Critical Habitat," Endangered Species Coalition, http://www.stopextinction.org/ESA/ESA.cfm?ID=86&c=21.

Page 128. Bush reduction of critical habitat: Natalie Henry, "Administration Says Critical Habitat Has Little Value Under ESA," *Greenwire,* May 29, 2003.

Page 128. Craig Manson on whether extinction is such a bad thing after all: in Julie Cart, "Species Protection Act 'Broken'; A Top Interior Official Says the Law Should Be Revised to Give Economic and Other Interests Equal Footing with Endangered Animals and Plants," *Los Angeles Times*, Nov. 14, 2003.

Page 129. The northern Great Plains would be better as a "buffalo common": Deborah E. Popper and Frank Popper, "The Great Plains: From Dust to Dust," *Planning* (Dec. 1987), pp. 12–18. Also by the same authors, "The Buffalo Commons: Metaphor as Method," *Geographical Review* (Oct. 1999), pp. 491–95.

Page 129. Destruction of bison: Andrea Barnett, "Political War Continues over Bison Herd," *High Country News*, Jan. 31, 2000, http://www.hcn.org/servlets/hcn.Article?article_id=5523.

Page 129. Charles Clusen on the National Park Service: "Groups Call for Moratorium on Yellowstone Bison Slaughter," U.S. Newswire, Mar. 6, 2003.

Page 129. Gale Norton's restriction of wilderness: "U.S. Plans to Limit Protected Wilderness to 23 Million Acres," *Associated Press*, Apr. 13, 2003.

Page 130. Norton withdraws wilderness protection: ibid.

Page 131. The size of Roosevelt's legacy: Theodore Roosevelt Association, "Conservationist— Life of Theodore Roosevelt," www.theodoreroosevelt.org/life/conservation.htm.

Page 131. 234 million acres stripped of protections: see note for sixth bullet item in chapter 1.

Chapter 8

Page 132. Gale Norton epigraph: in Eryn Gable, "Norton Urges ANWR Drilling in Name of National Security," *Environment and Energy Daily,* Mar. 13, 2003.

Page 132. Tom DeLay epigraph: in Lizette Alvarez and Joseph Kahn, "House Republicans Gather Support for Alaska Drilling," *New York Times,* Aug. 1, 2001.

Page 132. Ted Stevens epigraph: *Washington Post,* Mar. 22, 2002.

Page 135. The administration picked up Frank Murkowski's pitch: Liz Ruskin, "Murkowski Set to Stall Senate," *Anchorage Daily News,* Sept. 28, 2001.

Page 135. Murkowski's denial: in Liz Ruskin, "Murkowski Deflects ANWR Flak," *Anchorage Daily News,* Sept. 21, 2001.

Page 135. James Inhofe on drilling and defense: "Inhofe Seeks Drilling Amendment in Defense Bill," *Greenwire,* Sept. 21, 2001.

Page 135. The "world's largest Chapstick": Amory Lovins and Hunter Lovins, "Fool's Gold in Alaska," *Foreign Affairs,* July/Aug. 2001.

Page 135. Hunter shoots a hole in the pipeline: Bill McKibben, "One Guy, One Rifle, and an Oil Pipeline," *Los Angeles Times,* Oct. 21, 2001.

Page 135. Amory Lovins on creating another Strait of Hormuz: in Lovins and Lovins, "Fool's Gold in Alaska." In the same article, a U.S. Army spokesperson calls the Alyeska Pipeline "indefensible."

Page 135. Cato Institute on the government's oil policy: Jerry Taylor, "Bush's Energy Bobble," Cato Institute Web site, www.cato.org/dailys/09-30-00.html.

Page 136. Norton on Arctic Refuge oil potential: Paul Weyrich, "ANWR: Untapped Resource in Fight for Energy Independence," Mar. 28, 2003, Newsmax.com.

Page 136. Norton's 10.4 billion figure disingenuous: "Arctic National Wildlife Refuge, 1002 Area, Petroleum Assessment, 1998, Including Economic Analysis," USGS, 1998, U.S. Geological Survey Fact Sheet 0028-01, http://pubs.usgs.gov/fs/fs-0028-01/.

Page 136. Krugman on oil production from the Arctic Refuge: Paul Krugman, "At Long Last?" *New York Times,* Apr. 5, 2002.

Page 136 James P. Hoffa's claim that drilling would produce 750,000 jobs: NBC's *Meet the Press,* Sept. 2, 2001. Posted at www.climateark.org/articles/2001/3rd/vowsfill.htm.

Page 136. Drilling foes demolish Hoffa's calculation: Steven Greenhouse, "Study Faults Unions' Math on New Jobs for Drilling," *New York Times,* Sept. 2, 2001.

Page 136. Jerry Hood on drilling foes: in Joe Grossman, "Blue Planet: Hill Faces Key Energy Bills," United Press International, Aug. 29, 2001.

Page 136. Hood's comment to Senate Democratic caucus: personal conversation with Carl Pope, Feb. 27, 2002.

Page 136. Labor leaders hinted at a deal: personal conversations with Carl Pope in the spring and fall of 2002.

Page 137. Tom Daschle on "a desperation move" by the White House: in Dana Bash, "Alaska Drilling Backers Dangle Deals for Votes," Apr. 12, 2002, CNN.com. See www.cnn.com/2002/ALLPOLITICS/04/11/anwr.senate/. Daschle became a particular target for the ire of the thwarted drillers: Republican activists ran ads with his photo side by side with that of Saddam Hussein, claiming that both opposed drilling on the refuge. Asked on *Meet the Press* if that was a little bit over the line, Vice President Dick Cheney did not exactly disavow it: "Well, I'm not responsible for the ad, and you flashed it so fast I didn't have a chance to read the copy. But there is a disagreement with respect to Senator Daschle on energy." "Talking Points Memo" by Joshua Micah Marshall, Dec. 11, 2001.

Page 137. Norton on minimizing environmental concerns: letter from Norton to Senator Frank Murkowski, July 11, 2001. See www.peer.org/alaska/ANWR01.PDF.

Page 138. Prudhoe Bay spills and pollution: see www.defenders.org/wildlife/arctic/subsection.html.

Page 138. Trucker on caribou: in Doug O'Harra, "Semi Crazy: Anything Can Happen to a Winter Trucker on the Perilous and Desolate Dalton Highway," *Anchorage Daily News,* Feb. 27, 2001.

Page 138. Robert Brian's testimony on BP: "Second BP Prudhoe Bay Worker Meets with Senate Staff," *Greenwire,* Mar. 13, 2002.

Page 138. Thomas's statement: Ian Thomas, "I Was Fired for Posting a Map," *Earth Island Journal* 16, no. 3 (Autumn 2001).

Page 138. Norton on caribou calving: in Michael Grunwald, "Departmental Differences Show over ANWR Drilling," *Washington Post,* Oct. 19, 2001.

Page 138. Norton supplied with Fish and Wildlife data: ibid.

Page 139. Public Employees for Environmental Responsibility blast Norton: "Secretary Norton Falsified Arctic Refuge Data," PEER press release, Oct. 19, 2001, http://www.peer.org/press/190.html. A side-by-side comparison of the answers by Fish and Wildlife scientists and Norton to the same questions appears at http://www.peer.org/alaska/Norton_comparison.html.

Page 139. Washington Post quote of a Fish and Wildlife official: in Grunwald, "Departmental Differences Show over ANWR Drilling."

Page 139. Norton's press secretary calls study "science fiction": "U.S. Rejects Study by Its Own Arctic Scientists," *Seattle Post-Intelligencer,* Mar. 30, 2002. The Alaska delegation did its part to abet Norton's distortion of Arctic science. When Murkowski rose on the Senate floor with a picture of three bears walking on an oil pipeline, Ken Whitten, former chief caribou biologist for Alaska's Department of Fish and Game, who had taken the picture, blasted the senator, saying, "I am once again disappointed that Senator Murkowski has misinformed his fellow senators regarding the effects of oil development on the wildlife and wilderness environment of the Arctic National Wildlife Refuge." Whitten pointed out that the bear story "doesn't have a fairy tale ending" because bears that hung around oil camps almost invariably had to be shot "after they became habituated to human food and repeatedly broke into buildings and parked vehicles." Whitten also pointed out that Murkowski had repeatedly attacked California Senator Barbara Boxer (D) for her use of a "fake" picture of caribou herds on the coastal plain, when Whitten himself had taken it. Whitten summed up his anger at his congressman: "Senator Murkowski seems willing to go to any length to convince us that we can improve national security and protect wildlife by drilling the coastal plain, but there is overwhelming evidence to the contrary."

Page 139. Krugman on the impact of oil development: Paul Krugman, "Two Thousand Acres," *New York Times,* Mar. 1, 2002.

Page 139. Booth on the Alpine oil field: William Booth, "Energy Policy's Ground Zero," *Washington Post,* May 15, 2001.

Page 140. Oil executive on Kazakhstan vs. Alaska: personal conversation with Carl Pope in the fall of 2001.

Page 140. Alaska pays millions for oil drilling lobbying: "Special Interest Watch: Arctic Power," Center for Responsive Politics, Apr. 10, 2003. See http://www.opensecrets.org/payback/issue.asp?issueid=EN2&congno=108.

Page 140. "Mad money" for Alaskans: Mary Pemberton, "Alaska Economy Taps into Oil Wealth," Associated Press, Aug. 10, 2003.

Page 141. Frank Hood turned out of office: Dan Joling, "Hood Ousted as Head of Alaska Teamsters," Associated Press, Nov. 4, 2003.

Page 141. Tom DeLay to House Republicans: Cragg Hines, "DeLay to Caribou, Seals, etc: Drop Dead," *Houston Chronicle,* Sept. 26, 2003.

Chapter 9

Page 142. Fred Smith epigraph: Competitive Enterprise Institute Update, Aug. 1995, p. 2.

Page 142. Trofim Lysenko epigraph: in Helena Sheehan, *Marxism and the Philosophy of Science: A Critical History* (Atlantic Highlands, N.J.: Humanities Press International, 1993).

Page 142. George H. W. Bush epigraph: from remarks to the National Academy of Sciences, Apr. 23, 1990.

Page 144. Rewritten EPA statement: Laurie Garrett, "EPA Misled Public on 9/11 Pollution," *New York Newsday,* Aug. 23, 2003.

Page 144. EPA's Office of Inspector General report: for full text of the report, see http://www
.epa.gov/oigearth/.

Page 144. Mitch Daniels accusing New York officials of "money-grubbing games": in Paul
Krugman, "Washington's Poisonous Take on New York's Toxic Dust," *New York Times,*
Aug. 27, 2003.

Page 144. Pat Moore on cleaning up her apartment herself: in Fabrice Rousselot, "Contaminated by the World Trade Center," *La Liberation,* Oct. 21, 2003. See http://www.truthout
.org/docs_03/102203H.shtml.

Page 144. Ground Zero workers suffer from lung ailments: Christine Haughney, "Ground Zero
Workers Afflicted, Study Finds Tests Show Physical, Psychological Ills Persist Nearly a Year
After Rescue Efforts," *Washington Post,* Jan. 28, 2003.

Page 144. Jenna Orkin on respiratory problems at Stuyvesant High School: in Rousselot,
"Contaminated by the World Trade Center."

Page 144. Asbestos levels in Woolworth Building: study conducted by Detail Associates,
Englewood, N.J. Defining "high level": Steve M. Hays and James R. Millette, *Settled
Asbestos Dust Sampling and Analysis* (Boca Raton, Fla.: Lewis Publishers/CRC Press, 1994).

Page 145. Robert Gulack on being rushed back into contaminated areas: in Margaret Ramirez,
"NYers Protest Downtown Air Quality," *New York Newsday,* Sept. 15, 2003.

Page 145. Ronald Reagan said that "facts are stupid things": from an address to the Republican
National Convention, Aug. 15, 1988.

Page 145. Sheehan on Lysenko: Sheehan, *Marxism and the Philosophy of Science.*

Page 147. Sarka Southern on being ordered to withhold her findings: in Christopher Marquis,
"Two Scientists Contend U.S. Suppressed Dolphin Studies," *New York Times,* Jan. 9, 2003.

Page 147. Thelton Henderson on his reasoning behind court decision: in Kenneth R. Weiss,
"Court Blocks Easing of 'Dolphin-Safe' Tuna Labeling," *Los Angeles Times,* Apr. 11, 2003.

Page 147. Federal Advisory Committee Act requirements: see http://www.epic.org/open_gov/
faca.html.

Page 148. Wylie Burke on the Advisory Committee on Genetic Testing: in Rick Weiss, "HHS
Seeks Science Advice to Match Bush Views," *Washington Post,* Sept. 17, 2002.

Page 149. Details of the backgrounds of some of the committee members: in ibid.

Page 149. Exposé of the committee stacking: Jonathan Cohn, "The Lead Industry Gets Its
Turn," *The New Republic* Online, Dec. 23, 2002, http://www.tnr.com.

Page 150. "Any further right-wing incursions": Editorial, *The Lancet* 360, no. 9345 (Nov. 16,
2002).

Page 150. "Scientific advisory committees do not exist to tell the secretary what he wants to
hear": Editorial, *Science* 298, no. 5594 (Oct. 25, 2002).

Page 150. "The present epidemic" and subsequent quotations: *Science* 299, no. 5607 (Jan. 31, 2003).

Page 150. Gale Norton's confirmation hearing pledge: Transcript, Day Two of Senate Energy
and Natural Resources Committee Hearing to Consider Nomination of Gale Norton to Be
Secretary of the Interior, Jan. 19, 2001, S. Hrg 107-33. Available at http://frwebgate.access
.gpo.gov/cgi-bin/getdoc.cgi?dbname=107_senate_hearings&docid=f:72291.wais.

Page 151. Thomas Sansonetti praising Norton: in Editorial, "No Greens Need Apply," *New York Times,* Aug. 19, 2001.

Page 151. "Risks to polar bears": John Heilprin, "Norton Insists Arctic Drilling Safe," Associated Press, Jan. 18, 2002.

Page 151. Charles Clusen on "Out with the old 'good' science": in "Bush Administration Changes Science on Polar Bear Impacts to Suit Arctic Drilling," NRDC, Jan. 17, 2002. See http://www.nrdc.org/bushrecord/wildlife_arctic.asp#474.

Page 151. The National Research Council review of Klamath River issues: Michael Grunwald, "Scientific Report Roils a Salmon War," *Washington Post,* Feb. 4, 2002, p. A01. In late 2003 the National Research Council issued a more complete analysis of the Klamath, concluding that far more drastic steps were needed to save the river's salmon and the endangered suckerfish of Upper Klamath Lake. Dam removal, tighter regulation of logging, and retirement of farmland were among the steps recommended. The panel did conclude that it was not certain whether or not low water flows or high temperatures had caused the massive salmon kill in 2002. The council also indicated that recovery of the suckerfish would be very difficult because agriculture had already damaged Upper Klamath Lake so badly. The Bush administration cited the uncertainty about what had caused the fish kill as justification for its refusal to release adequate water for the fisheries. It conspicuously declined to take a stand on the other recommendations—although the president again went firmly on record as saying that no dams would ever be removed on his watch.

Page 151. Mike Kelley on low morale: Robert F. Kennedy, Jr., "Crimes Against Nature," *Rolling Stone,* Nov. 19, 2003.

Page 152. Studies kept from public release: "Suppressed Government Report Shows Klamath Irrigation Is a Bad Investment," News Release, The Wilderness Society, Nov. 1, 2002.

Page 152. Zeke Grader quoted: "Suppressed Government Report Shows Klamath Irrigation a Bad Investment," Earthjustice press release, Nov. 1, 2002, http://www.earthjustice.org/news/display.html?ID=466.

Page 152. Karl Rove's PowerPoint presentations: Tom Hamburger, "Oregon Water Sage Illuminates Rove's Methods with Agencies," *Wall Street Journal,* July 30, 2003.

Page 152. Inspector general of interior to investigate: Eric Bailey, "Klamath Decisions to Be Probed: The Interior Department Will Investigate Sen. Kerry's Charges That White House Political Interests Determined Water Flows," *Los Angeles Times,* Sept. 5, 2003.

Page 153. Richard Pombo on "radical environmentalists": in David Whitney, "Pombo Lashes Out on Environment," *Sacramento Bee,* June 29, 2003.

Page 153. National Academy of Sciences report on critical habitat: "Science and the Endangered Species Act," Committee on Scientific Issues in the Endangered Species Act, National Research Council, May 1995.

Page 153. Norton suppressed two reports: see Jeffrey Rachinski and Martin Taylor, "Critical Habitat Significantly Increased Endangered Species Recovery,"an analysis of the two unreleased Fish and Wildlife Service reports from June 2003, reported by the Center for Biological Diversity, Oct. 6, 2003, www.biologicaldiversity.org/swcbd/programs/policy/ch/index.html.

Page 154. The National Academy of Sciences warns Abraham: Robert Alvarez, "The Legacy of Hanford," *The Nation,* Aug. 18–25, 2003.

Page 154. The Fish and Wildlife Service report: Michael Grunwald, "Interior's Silence on Corps Plan Questioned," *Washington Post,* Jan. 14, 2002.

Page 154. Jamie Rappaport Clark on the Interior Department stopping comment: in ibid.

Page 155. EPA employees have been "told either not to analyze or not to release information": Jennifer 8. Lee, "Critics Say E.P.A. Won't Analyze Some Clean Air Proposals," *New York Times,* July 14, 2003.

Page 155. Joseph Lieberman on the administration's stifling scientific fact: in ibid.

Page 155. William Ruckelshaus on whether or not analysis is released: in ibid.

Page 156. Pork industry lobbyists persuaded the USDA: Kennedy, "Crimes Against Nature."

Page 156. Bush ordered the EPA not to release perchlorate information: "Rocket Fuel in Drinking Water" and "High Levels of Toxic Rocket Fuel Found in Lettuce," reports by the Environmental Working Group, 2003, http://www.ewg.org/reports/rocketwater/.

Page 156. Schaeffer on "sound science": Eric Schaeffer, "A Natural Selection," Aug. 19, 2003, www.tompaine.com. See http://www.tompaine.com/feature2.cfm/ID/8648.

Chapter 10

Page 158. James Inhofe epigraph: in Elizabeth Kolbert, "Getting Warmer," *The New Yorker,* Nov. 17, 2003.

Page 158. Bill Moyers epigraph: "Now Hear This," interview with Amanda Griscom, *Grist* magazine, Aug. 26, 2003, www.gristmagazine.com/maindish/griscom082603.asp.

Page 159. Nine warmest years of the century: "A Paleo Perspective on Global Warming," National Oceanic and Atmospheric Administration, May 19, 2000.

Page 159. Melting permafrost closes the Matterhorn: Robin McKie, "Decades of Devastation Ahead as Global Warming Melts the Alps," *The Observer,* July 20, 2003.

Page 159. The EPA on arctic temperatures: see U.S. Environmental Protection Agency, Global Warming Impacts–Polar Regions, http://yosemite.epa.gov/oar/globalwarming.nsf/content/ImpactsPolarRegions.html.

Page 160. Baltimore may soon be without orioles: Eric Pianin, "A Baltimore Without Orioles? Study Says Global Warming May Rob Md., Other States of Their Official Birds," *Washington Post,* Mar. 4, 2002.

Page 160 and throughout chapter. All quoted material by Luntz: leaked memo from the Luntz Research Companies entitled "The Environment: A Cleaner, Safer, Healthier America" (original date unknown, but leaked in Feb. 2003), pp. 131–46. See also Jennifer 8. Lee, "A Call for Softer, Greener Language," *New York Times,* Mar. 2, 2003.

Page 161. U.S. power plants' contribution to carbon dioxide emissions: Jeremy Symons, "How Bush and Co. Obscure the Science," *Washington Post,* July 13, 2003.

Page 161. Paul O'Neill's paper calling for a government program on climate change: Robert Novak, "Bush's Global Warming," Mar. 1, 2001, http://www.townhall.com/columnists/robertnovak/rn20010301.shtml.

Page 161. Oil-industry press on Bush's pledge to control carbon dioxide: in ibid.

Page 161. Christie Todd Whitman on carbon dioxide and global warming: see *Crossfire,* Feb. 26, 2001.

Page 162. Symons on the debate that ensued in the administration: Symons, "How Bush and Co. Obscure the Science."

Page 162. O'Neill's second memo: in Amanda Griscom, "The Rollback Machine," *Grist,* Sept. 4, 2003.

Page 162. Novak warned that "the issue is far from settled": Robert Novak, "Bush's Global Warming," Mar. 1, 2001, http://www.townhall.com/columnists/robertnovak/rn20010301.shtml.

Page 162. Whitman at G8 meeting in Italy: Robin Pomeroy, "U.S. Not Backtracking on Global Warming—EPA Chief," Reuters, Mar. 3, 2000.

Page 162. Bush calls global warming science "incomplete": in Ross Gelbspan, "Bush's Global Warmers," *Nation,* Mar. 22, 2001.

Page 162. Germany's Social Democratic spokesperson on the U.S. rejection of the Kyoto Protocol: in Beth Daley and Robert Schlesinger, "Ecologists See Bush Ignoring Data in Greenhouse Gas Step," *Boston Globe,* Mar. 15, 2001.

Page 162. Dick Cheney calls Whitman a "good soldier": in Scott Lindlaw, "Reversing Course: Bush Decides Against Carbon Dioxide Regulations," Associated Press, Mar. 13, 2001.

Page 162. Waiting for sufficient signatures to take effect: for the Kyoto Protocol to take effect, it must be ratified by at least 55 countries that together accounted for at least 55 percent of world carbon dioxide emissions in 1990. As of Sept. 29, 2003, signatories accounted for 44.5 percent of 1990 emissions.

Page 163. Myron Ebell on "a walking corpse": in Joan Lowy, "Bush Faulted on Climate Reversal," Scripps Howard News Service, Mar. 14, 2001.

Page 163. The IPCC's groundbreaking report: "Climate Change 2001: The Scientific Basis," Intergovernmental Panel on Climate Change, 2001, www.grida.no/climate/ipcc_tar/wg1/008.htm.

Page 163. ExxonMobil asks if Robert Watson can be replaced: memo from ExxonMobil to John Howard, White House Council on Environmental Quality, Feb. 6, 2001, cited in "Politics and Science in the Bush Administration," U.S. House of Representatives Committee on Government Reform—Minority Staff Special Investigative Division, prepared for Rep. Henry A. Waxman, Aug. 2003.

Page 163. Effects of global temperature increases: see J. L. Laws, "White House Climate Flap Continues," *Greenwire,* June 6, 2002; see also "Climate Action 2002 Report," Environmental Protection Agency, at http://yosemite.epa.gov/oar/globalwarming.nsf/content/ResourceCenterPublicationsUSClimateActionReport.html.

Page 164. Ebell quotations here and in the following paragraphs: in "Greenpeace Obtains Smoking-Gun Memo: White House/Exxon Link," Sept. 9, 2003, http://dynamic.greenpeace.org/smoking-gun/CEImemo.swf.

Page 164. Bush openly dismissed the EPA report's results: Katharine Q. Seelye, "President Distances Himself from Global Warming Report," *New York Times,* June 5, 2002.

Page 164. Attorneys general of Connecticut and Maine to Ashcroft: letter from Richard Blumenthal and G. Steven Rowe, Aug. 11, 2003; see http://www.cslib.org/attygenl/press/ 2003/enviss/ashcroftlet1.pdf.

Page 164. Bush quoted on rejecting Kyoto: in Laws, "White House Climate Flap Continues."

Page 164. "Major edits" to the global warming section of the EPA report: Andrew C. Revkin with Katharine Q. Seelye, "Report by E.P.A. Leaves Out Data on Climate Change," *New York Times,* June 19, 2003. All subsequent quotes in this paragraph are from the same source.

Page 165. An internal memo from EPA staff: in Symons, "How Bush and Co. Obscure the Science."

Page 165. Lieberman on a new global warming plan: in J. L. Laws, "Lieberman, McCain Lay Out Case for Climate Bill," *Energy & Environment Daily,* Jan. 9, 2003.

Page 165. Lieberman calls EPA refusal "unacceptable": Jennifer 8. Lee, "Critics Say E.P.A. Won't Analyze Some Clean Air Proposals," *New York Times,* July 14, 2003.

Chapter 11

Page 166. John F. Kennedy epigraph: remarks on the 20th anniversary of *Voice of America,* Feb. 26, 1962, archives of the American Presidency Project. Reprinted as "Free Speech Critical During Times of War," University Wire, Feb. 25, 2002.

Page 166. Dick Cheney epigraph: from an interview on the *Larry King Show,* Jan. 29, 2002, cnn.com.

Page 166. Ed Hastey epigraph: personal conversation with Carl Pope, Apr. 2002.

Page 168. Christie Whitman on enhancing anti-terrorism precautions: in an interview at the EPA with Bureau of National Affairs (BNA) reporter Steve Cook, Nov. 21, 2001. See www.StrategicIgnorance.org.

Page 169. Months later it is reported that John Ashcroft had urged agencies to deny Freedom of Information Act requests: Editorial, "The Day Ashcroft Censored Freedom of Information," *San Francisco Chronicle,* Jan. 6, 2002.

Page 169. Ashcroft gave federal agencies reasons to deny FOIA requests: Ashcroft memo to agency heads on Oct. 12, 2001, as reported in Tamara Lytle, "White House Clamps Down on Information; the Administration's Secrecy Has Been Criticized as the Worst in Decades," *Orlando Sentinel,* Mar. 10, 2001.

Page 169. Jon Marvel complained that his organization was cut off from public records: in Launce Rake, "Environmentalists Target Bush Administration," *Las Vegas Sun,* Nov. 29, 2002.

Page 170. Cheney asserted that his task force had not involved bringing in any "outsiders": on *Nightline,* July 25, 2001. See abcnews.go.com/onair/nightline/NightlineIndex.html.

Page 171. The Sierra Club on how the American public was shut out of the process: in "Energy Task Force Pelted with Lawsuits," *Asheville Global Report,* Jan. 25, 2002, http://www.agrnews.org/issues/159/nationalnews.html.

Page 171. The administration once again refused to comply with Sullivan's orders: "Bush administration again refuses to release energy records," Associated Press, Sept. 5, 2002.

Page 171. Laurence Tribe on turning the VP's office "into a giant vacuum cleaner": in personal conversation with Carl Pope, Nov. 2001.

Page 171. On the administration's "unprecedented move": "Bush Administration Ramping Up Secrecy Fight," Sept. 16, 2002, http://www.nrdc.org/media/pressreleases/020916.asp.

Page 172. The Bush team asked the Supreme Court to intervene: Carol Leonnig, "Cheney Seeking Supreme Court Review of Energy Panel Case," *Washington Post*, Sept. 17, 2003.

Page 172. The papers included a detailed map of Iraq's oil fields: AAF [Alison Freeman?], "Cheney Task Force Had Interest in Iraqi Oil Documents," *Greenwire*, July 21, 2003.

Page 173. Oliver Houck on "giving away roughly half of the U.S.": in John McQuaid, "Bush Seeks to Limit NEPA Use Outside U.S. Waters," *Greenwire*, Aug. 12, 2002.

Page 173. Norton complains "it can take six months": in Gale Norton, "Congress Must Cut Red Tape, Help Prevent Forest Fires," *Saint Paul (Minnesota) Pioneer Press*, Sept. 18, 2002.

Page 173. Federal judges ruled that the administration employed "bait-and-switch tactics": see www.defenders.org/publications/forest_report03.pdf.

Page 174. Mary E. Peters complained that "you feel a little bit like that small rodent in a maze": Margaret Kriz, "Bush's Quiet Plan," *National Journal*, Nov. 23, 2002.

Page 174. Tom Voltaggio on "What's past is past": in Stephen Kiehl, "Ehrlich Meets with Officials to Jump-start Plans for ICC; Environmentalists Protest Proposed 18-mile Highway for Washington Suburbs," *Baltimore Sun*, June 12, 2003.

Page 174. The corporate right portrays NEPA as "much abused and outdated": Editorial, "The Greens' Snow Job," *Wall Street Journal*, Nov. 19, 2002.

Page 175. Cards and letters received by the Park Service favored a ban on snowmobiles: "Groups File Suit to Block Yellowstone Snowmobile Decision," *Cyberwest* magazine, Feb. 15, 2003, http://www.cyberwest.com/cw22/yellowstone_snowmobile.shtml.

Page 175. Administration states "It was not a vote" on snowmobiles in Yellowstone: in Katharine Q. Seelye, "Flooded with Comments, Officials Plug Their Ears," *New York Times*, Dec. 4, 2002.

Page 175. The Idaho Cattle Association's recommendation: Kriz, "Bush's Quiet Plan."

Page 175. Administration official on "creating more exclusions": in John Heilprin, "White House Panel Recommends Steps to Exclude Projects from Detailed Environmental Analyses," Associated Press, Sept. 24, 2003.

Page 176. Mark Rey on no longer counting public comments: in "House Subcommittee Reviews Roadless Rule," *The Forestry Source*, Aug. 2002, newspaper of the Society of American Foresters, http://www.safnet.org/archive/802_roadless.cfm.

Page 176. Dale Bosworth defends the new approach: in Dan Berman, "Agency will allow mass e-mails, form letters as public comment," *Greenwire*, Dec. 22, 2003.

Page 176. Teddy Roosevelt quoted: in *The Outlook*, Apr. 20, 1912.

Page 176. Not everyone is going along quietly with the return to secret government: Editorials, "The Fruits of Secrecy," *New York Times*, Nov. 8, 2003; "In the Northwest: Stealth Rule-making Hides Threats to Environment," *Seattle Post-Intelligencer*, Jan. 8, 2003; and "Don't Weaken Environmental Act," *Atlanta Journal-Constitution*, Oct. 14, 2003.

Page 176. John Cornyn on persuading the administration to be less closed: in "Campaign Notebook," *Houston Chronicle*, Sept. 26, 2002.

Page 177. The White House was "irritated by pesky questions": Dana Milbank, "White House Puts Limits on Queries from Democrats," *Washington Post,* Nov. 7, 2003.

Chapter 12

Page 178. William Golding epigraph: Remarks during a reading of his novel *Lord of the Flies.*

Page 178. Theodore Roosevelt epigraph: Third Annual Message to Congress, Dec. 7, 1903.

Page 179. Blair was arrested: John Blair, "Criticize Cheney, Go to Jail," *Counterpunch,* Feb. 8, 2002, http://www.counterpunch.org/blair1.html.

Page 180. Halliburton's illegal oil deals with Hussein: Martin A. Lee, "Cheney Made Millions off Oil Deals with Hussein," *San Francisco Bay Guardian,* Nov. 13, 2000.

Page 180. The EPA's lack of enforcement for clean water violators: Guy Gugliotta and Eric Pianin, "EPA: Few Fined for Polluting Water," *Washington Post,* June 6, 2003.

Page 181. Bush justification of EPA budget cuts: Jennifer A. Dlouhy, "Endangered Species: Bush Wants Control," *Seattle Post-Intelligencer,* Apr. 11, 2001.

Page 181. Federalist Society alumni in the administration: report by People for the American Way, "The Federalist Society: From Obscurity to Power," Aug. 2001, http://www.pfaw.org/pfaw/general/default.aspx?oid=652.

Page 181. John Ashcroft had voted to allow real-estate developers: S. 2271—Property Rights Implementation Act of 1998, July 13, 1998. See http://www.lcv.org/images/client/pdfs/scorecard98.pdf.

Page 183. Bush cabinet's ties to corporations: "13 of 16 Cabinet Members Have Ties to 'Class Action' Targeted Companies," Foundation for Taxpayer and Consumer Rights press release, Oct. 20, 2003.

Page 183. Al Gore's speech: speech delivered to MoveOn.org at New York University, Aug. 7, 2003.

Page 184. Atmosphere of intimidation in Elko County: Jim Carlton, "Bitter Battle over Rural West," *Wall Street Journal,* Feb. 16, 2001.

Page 184. Mike Leavitt refused to make public his plans: "Three Cases Speak Volumes About New EPA Choice," *Earthjustice,* Aug. 13, 2003.

Page 185. Some of the RS-2477 claims are narrow slot canyons with waterfalls: see photos at www.suwa.org/page.php?page_id=95.

Page 185. Tenth Circuit Court of Appeals decision: Donna Kemp Spangler, "Utah Trails Aren't Roads," *Deseret Morning News,* July 2, 2003.

Page 185. Heidi McIntosh on the law of the land in Utah: ibid.

Page 185. Many of these places had rights-of-way across them that only the state could define: see http://www.earthjustice.org/news/display.html?ID=667.

Page 186. Ashcroft swears to defend the Roadless Rule: text of Ashcroft Confirmation Hearing, Day Two, Jan. 17, 2001.

Page 186. Ann Veneman on protecting roadless values: USDA News Release No. 0075.01, "USDA Upholds Roadless Protections Rule," May 4, 2001.

Page 186. Edward Lodge used the administration's own arguments in his injunction: see http://www.allears.org/litigation/.

Page 186. Ashcroft has "done almost nothing" to defend the Roadless Rule: Editorial, "Poor Marks on the Environment," *New York Times,* Jan. 28, 2002.

Page 187. Brimmer's investments in energy development: Clarence A. Brimmer's Financial Disclosure Form for Calendar Year 2002, Committee on Financial Disclosure, Administrative Office of the United States Courts, April 7, 2003.

Page 187. Justice Department argued against environmentalists' right of appeal: Jack Sullivan, "Bush Administration Argues Against Appeal of Roadless Decision," Associated Press, Nov. 13, 2003.

Page 188. A billion fish died in North Carolina's Neuse River in 1991: from Neuse riverkeeper Rick Dove's testimonial before the Senate Committee on Government Affairs, Mar. 13, 2002. See http://www.newfarm.org/depts/pig_page/rick_dove/index.shtm.

Page 188. The toxic microbe *Pfiesteria piscidia:* Joby Warrick, "The Feeding Frenzy of a Morphing 'Cell From Hell,'" *Washington Post,* June 9, 1997.

Page 188. Well-connected campaign contributors appeared to have a direct pipeline to the legal exemption table. As soon as Christie Whitman left the EPA, the administration exempted from pollution industrial laundries that clean towels contaminated with industrial solvents. New EPA Administrator Mike Leavitt took up the plight of this rather specialized industrial segment when it turned out that the owners of Cintas Corporation, the major beneficiary of the exemption, were enormous Bush campaign contributors. Cintas founder Richard Farmer is a Pioneer—that is, he has donated $100,000 or more to Bush. Together with his wife, his son (the current Cintas CEO), and the Cintas vice chairman, Farmer has contributed more than $2 million to Bush and the GOP since 1997. (Federal Election Commission Data Base.)

Page 188. The lobbying firm, in secret, proposed to the EPA an amnesty agreement: letter to EPA Administrator Christie Whitman from Lloyd Eagan, president, State and Territorial Air Pollution Program Administrators, and Ellen Garvey, president, Association of Local Air Pollution Control Officials, Apr. 7, 2003, in which STAPPA and ALAPCO "object to EPA entering into a safe harbor agreement with the CAFO industry."

Page 189. Other observers put the figure (of wetlands now unprotected) at 60 percent: At the time the proposed rule was originally announced, an EPA spokesperson said that the guidance could withdraw federal protection from up to 20 million acres of wetlands outside Alaska, which equals 20 percent of the wetlands in the lower 48. The rule deals with isolated waters, not just wetlands, so intermittent and ephemeral streams could lose protection as well. The EPA's 1998 Water Quality Inventory (Appendix A-1) estimated that about 50 percent of streams were either non-perennial or canals (which also lose protection). Scientists say the percentage is actually much higher because the smallest streams rarely show up on topographical maps. The 60 percent figure is a conservative estimate based on these data; it was first cited by Julian Borger in the *(London) Guardian,* Jan. 17, 2003.

Page 189. Bill Henck audited: John D. McKinnon, "IRS Lawyer Claims Politics Influenced Halt of Synfuel Tax Credit Crackdown," *Wall Street Journal,* Nov. 28, 2003.

Page 190. J. Steven Griles swears to prevent the appearance of any improprieties: in Eric Pianin, "Official's Lobbying Ties Decried," *Washington Post,* Sept. 25, 2002.

Page 190. Ashcroft has yet to appoint a special prosecutor for Griles: Pete Yost, "Environmental Groups Seek Special Counsel to Investigate No. 2 Official at Interior," Associated Press, June 3, 2003.

Page 190. Whitman dissolved Martin's position: "Senate Passes Bill to Reinstate EPA Ombudsman," *Greenwire,* May 22, 2003.

Page 191. Competitive Enterprise Institute crowed: "Experts Ponder Whitman's Future," *Greenwire,* May 22, 2003.

Page 191. Leavitt fired a Division of Wildlife Resources official: Hartt Wixom and John Holt, "Kill the Fish to Save the Fishery," *Outdoor Life* 197, no. 4 (Apr. 1996).

Page 191. Utah joined Texas as one of the country's worst water polluters: Jerry Spangler, "Utah Coalition Slams Leavitt," *Deseret Morning News,* Sept. 17, 2003.

Page 191. Leavitt says mining industry toxic release "is not pollution": Jerry Spangler, "Utah Decries EPA's Report on 'Pollution,'" *Deseret Morning News,* June 16, 1999.

Page 192. Phil Hardberger on cases getting "anti-consumer": in Michael Scherer, "The Making of the Corporate Judiciary," *Mother Jones,* Nov./Dec. 2003.

Page 192. David Sentelle ridicules the Endangered Species Act: Dissenting Opinion, United States Court of Appeals, District of Columbia Circuit, Case No. 96-5354, Dec. 5, 1997. See http://pacer.cadc.uscourts.gov/common/opinions/199712/96-5354a.txt.

Page 192. Federal judge forbade students to celebrate Earth Day: "Hostile Environment," Community Rights Counsel, NRDC, and Alliance for Justice, July 18, 2001. For a full text of the report, see www.communityrights.org/PDFs/HE.pdf.

Page 192. William Pryor on environmental policy: Jen Koons, "Senate Advances Controversial Circuit Nominee," *Greenwire,* July 24, 2003.

Page 192. Janice Rogers Brown quoted: "Janice Rogers Brown and the Environment: A Dangerous Choice for a Critical Court," report by the Community Rights Counsel and Earthjustice, Oct. 21, 2003.

Page 193. Estrada refused to express any opinions on the issues of the day: "Floor Statement Delivered by U.S. Senator Dianne Feinstein on the Nomination of Miguel Estrada," Feb. 10, 2003. See http://feinstein.senate.gov/03Speeches/estradafinal.htm.

Page 193. Victor Wolski argues against Clean Water Act protection for migratory birds: Brief Amicus Curiae of Pacific Legal Foundation at 5, *Cargill, Inc. v. United States,* cert. denied, 516 U.S. 955 (1995) (no. 95-73).

Page 193. Wolski bragged to the *National Journal:* statement of Senator Patrick Leahy on the Senate Floor, press release, office of Senator Leahy, July 9, 2003.

Page 193. U.S. Court of Federal Claims ruled in favor: *Tulare Lake Basin Water Storage District v. United States,* No. 98-101 L (Fed. Cl. April 30, 2001) at 19 (slip op.), cited in "Hostile Environment," a report by Community Rights Counsel, July 18, 2001, www.communityrights.org.

Page 194. J. Michael Luttig rejected the idea: ibid.

Chapter 13

Page 196. DeLong epigraph: James V. DeLong, "Privatizing Superfund: How to Clean Up Hazardous Waste," Cato Policy Analysis No. 247, Dec. 18, 1995. DeLong is a lawyer and an adjunct scholar of the Competitive Enterprise Institute.

Page 196. Byrd epigraph: Remarks by U.S. Senator Robert C. Byrd to Senate Conference Committee on Energy, Nov. 7, 2003.

Page 196. Roosevelt epigraph: speech, Chicago, Ill., June 17, 1912.

Page 198. Luntz warned GOP politicians: Frank Luntz, "The Environment: A Cleaner, Safer, Healthier America," a memo leaked to the Environmental Working Group. See http://www.ewg.org/briefings/luntzmemo/pdf/LuntzResearch_environment.pdf.

Page 198. Origins of Superfund as a response to Love Canal: "Love Canal: The Beginning," On-line Ethics Center for Engineering and Science, Case Western University, May 13, 2002, http://onlineethics.org/environment/lcanal/history.html.

Page 199. Eight hundred and forty of some 2,000 Superfund sites have been cleaned up: see http://www.pirg.org/enviro/superfund/superfund.asp?id2=6096&id3=superfund&.

Page 200. PERC complains about Superfund standards: Dana Joel Gattuso, "EPA Hinders Urban Cleanups," Political Economy Research Center, Dec. 2000, http://www.perc.org/publications/percreports/dec2000/war.php?s=2.

Page 201. Superfund statistics: Office of Inspector General, EPA, "Annual Superfund Report to Congress, Fiscal 2002," Report EPA-350-R-03-001, Mar. 2003.

Page 201. Mark Plamondon on being afraid the toxic site "will be brushed under the carpet": "New Hampshire Communities at Risk: How Bush Administration Policies Harm Four New Hampshire Communities," Sierra Club Report, July 2003, www.nhsierraclub.org/jahia/Jahia/pid/1231.

Page 202. The Bush administration proposes that the government stop seeking repayment from tank owners: Editorial, "Panel Should Pull Plug on Outdated Energy Plan," *Atlanta Journal-Constitution,* Oct. 8, 2003.

Page 203. In 1972, two-thirds of America's lakes, rivers, and beaches were too polluted for swimming or fishing: Marguerite Young, "California State Water Status Summary," Clean Water Action Project, San Francisco, 1997. See http://www.wcei.org/california/303dsummary.html.

Page 203. Only 40 percent of nation's waterways remained polluted when Bush took office: the EPA's most recent report, "Quality of the Nation's Rivers and Streams" (2000), estimates that 61 percent of rivers, 55 percent of lakes, and 49 percent of estuaries are safe for fishing and swimming. See http://www.epa.gov/owow/monitoring/nationswaters/quality.htm.

Page 204. Report on Hamilton County homeowners' "dirty little secret": Hagit Limor, "Hamilton County Sewage," WCPO-9 I-Team News Report, Sept. 5, 2003. For a transcript, see http://www.wcpo.com/wcpo/localshows.iteam/090503.html.

Page 204. A near-record 12,000 beach closings due to sewage spills in 2002: "Beach Closures and Advisories Second Highest in a Decade," Press Release, NRDC, Aug. 13, 2003.

Page 204. Christie Whitman on the funding gap for new water-pollution-control facilities: in "Whitman Says Water Treatment Needs Outstrip Funding," *Washington Post,* Oct. 1, 2002.

Page 205. Fernald radioactive waste dumped untreated into the Great Miami River: "Water Treatment Bypass Process," News Update, Fernald Closure Project, U.S. Department of Energy, 2003. See http://www.fernald.gov/Cleanup/WaterBypass.htm.

Page 205. Luntz on the number one hot button to most voters: in his memo, "The Environment: A Cleaner, Safer, Healthier America."

Page 206. Michael Case on inherently compatible activities: Jingle Davis, "Victory at Fort Stewart: Army Makes Peace with Woodpecker," *Atlanta Journal-Constitution,* Jan. 30, 2003.

Page 206. The Pentagon "fact sheet": titled "Encroachment Impacts on Army Installations," provided to the Sierra Club on Mar. 13, 2003. It can be found on www .StrategicIgnorance.org.

Page 206. Army documents on "training realism": Mike Cast, "Training Lands Management," Winter 2000, U.S. Army Environmental Center, http://aec.army.mil/usaec/publicaffairs/ update/win00/win0002.htm.

Page 206. Gordon England on not making local accommodations: Margaret Kriz, "Pre-emptive Exemptions," *National Journal* 35, no. 17 (Apr. 26, 2003).

Page 207. David Horowitz on "this siege against science and good sense": in Harold Johnson, "Environmentalist Overkill Threatens Military Lives," *FrontPage* magazine, Mar. 20, 2003, http://www.frontpagemag.com/Articles/Printable.asp?ID=6748.

Page 207. Anniston's Army depot chemical weapons disposal: Tina Susman, "Afraid to Keep It, Afraid to Burn It: Alabama Town Wary as Army Begins Destroying Weapons Stockpile," *Newsday,* Aug. 5, 2003.

Page 208. Mike Abrams on the Pentagon's investment of $500 million: ibid.

Page 208. Craig Williams on a poor, black community in Alabama being targeted for incineration: ibid.

Page 208. Fred Shuttlesworth on fighting for "freedom from this toxic oppression": Elizabeth Crowe, "In Alabama 'Burning Chemical Weapons Is Dead Wrong,'" Chemical Weapons Working Group, Aug. 16, 2003. See http://www.cwwg.org/pr_08.16.03alrally.html.

Page 209. EPA officials on the magnitude of the Kentucky coal sludge spill: Roger Alford, "Coal Sludge Taking Its Toll on Fish, Wildlife," Associated Press, Oct. 19, 2000.

Page 209. Martin County Coal on restoring the community: in Roger Alford, "Coal Company President Apologizes for Sludge Spill," Associated Press, Nov. 28, 2000.

Page 209. Martin County Coal calls sludge spill "an act of God": "Coal Sludge Spill an Act of God, Company Claims," Associated Press, Nov. 30, 2000.

Page 209. Jack Spadaro's firing: James Dao, "Mine Safety Official Critical of Policies Faces Firing," *New York Times,* Nov. 9, 2003.

Page 210. A license to pollute: the administration was well aware of how serious the problem was. An interagency administration panel added up the toll from two decades of mountain-top removal mining, reporting that 724 miles of streams had been destroyed and 7 percent of the region's forests exterminated. Astonishingly, the administration used these results to weaken further the restraints on coal companies—ensuring that the numbers of streams and forests destroyed would continue to grow and leaving behind even more reclamation problems to be addressed by future generations. (Elizabeth Shogren, "Mining Damage in Appalachia Extensive, U.S. Finds," *Los Angeles Times,* May 30, 2003.)

Page 210. Luntz on "becoming a champion of national parks and forests": in his memo, "The Environment: A Cleaner, Safer, Healthier America."

Page 211. Popularity of Land and Water Conservation Fund in the U.S. House of Representatives: "Reps Young and Miller Announce Overwhelming House Support for Historic Conservation Bill," Press Release, Committee on Resources, U.S. House of Representatives, Feb. 16, 2000.

Page 211. Phil Gramm on a "dangerous concept": Audrey Hudson and Amy Fagan, "Conservatives Upset by Environment Part of Faith-based Bill," *Washington Times,* June 18, 2002.

Page 211. Carol LaGrasse on "a land grab program": in ibid.

Page 211. Norton's plan to privatize the Park Service: Kerry Tremain, "Pink Slips in the Parks: The Bush Administration Privatizes Our Public Treasures," *Sierra* 88, no. 5 (Sept./Oct. 2003).

Page 212. Bob Barbee on the need for "a strong cadre of professionals": in ibid.

Page 212. Fran Mainella on "serious consequences": in ibid.

Page 212. A report card on Bush's park stewardship: "Administration Earns D– on National Parks; Report Card Highlights Administration's Failure to Protect Parks," *U.S. Newswire,* June 11, 2003.

Page 212. Grover Norquist on abolishing government: in an interview with Mara Liasson, Morning Edition, National Public Radio, Mar. 25, 2001.

Chapter 14

Page 214. Powell epigraph: Secretary of State Colin Powell, "Remarks on the Launch of President Bush's Initiative Against Illegal Logging," Press Release, State Department, July 28, 2003.

Page 214. Krauthammer epigraph: Charles Krauthammer, "The Bush Doctrine: ABM, Kyoto, and the New American Unilateralism," *Weekly Standard,* June 4, 2001.

Page 214. Caligula quotation used by Kiesling: in Paul Krugman, "Let Them Hate as Long as They Fear," *New York Times,* Mar. 7, 2003.

Page 215. Wall Street Journal editor's assessment: personal communication with Carl Pope, Feb. 2003.

Page 215. International pledges to rebuild Iraq: Steven R. Weisman, "U.S. Wins Commitments for At Least $13 Billion in Aid for Iraq," *New York Times,* Oct. 24, 2003.

Page 215. British poll results: "U.K. Poll: Bush a Threat to World Peace," CBSNews.com, Feb. 28, 2003.

Page 215. Krauthammer on Bush's withdrawal from Kyoto: in Krauthammer, "The Bush Doctrine."

Page 216. U.S. emissions figures: Kevin A. Baumert and Nancy Kete, "The U.S., Developing Countries, and Climate Protection: Leadership or Stalemate?" World Resources Institute, June 2001.

Page 216. Whitman on her meeting with environmental ministers: in a letter from Whitman to Bush, Mar. 6, 2001. For a full transcript of the letter, see www.washingtonpost.com/wpsrv/onpolitics/transcripts/whitmanmemo032601.htm.

Page 217. Carbon dioxide emissions in relation to Kyoto: "Analysis of President Bush's Climate Change Plan," Pew Center on Global Climate Change, Feb. 2002, http://www.pewclimate.org/policy_center/analyses/response_bushpolicy.cfm.

Page 217. UNEP figures on mercury: "Global Mercury Assessment Report," United Nations Environment Program, Dec. 2002.

Page 218. Bush administration position on mercury: Eryn Gable, "Internal Document Outlines U.S. Resistance to Future U.N. Treaty," *Greenwire,* Jan. 28, 2003.

Page 218. Michael Bender on the U.S. proposition being "barely more than doing nothing": in ibid.

Page 218. Henry Waxman and Patrick Leahy letter: in J. R. Pegg, "Bush Aims to Slow Mercury Reduction Efforts," *Environmental News Service,* Feb. 25, 2003.

Page 219. Statistics on yanked UNFPA funds: David S. Broder, "Deadly Politics," *Washington Post,* July 28, 2002.

Page 219. State Department fact-finding mission on voluntary UNFPA programs in China: ibid.

Page 219. The decision to withdraw funding "underscored long-running tensions": Todd S. Purdum, "U.S. Blocks Money for Family Clinics Promoted by U.N.," *New York Times,* July 23, 2002.

Page 219. Barbara Boxer on the gag rule: in "Senate Repeals Global Gag Rule," Reuters, July 10, 2003.

Page 219. Wendy Wright in support of the gag rule: in "US exports anti-abortion policy," *BBC News,* June 28, 2003, http://news.bbc.co.uk/1/hi/world/americas/3028820.stm.

Page 220. Klaus Toepfer begged the meeting for "a concrete action plan": in Sylvia Thompson, "Horizons," *Irish Times,* June 1, 2002.

Page 220. Emil Salim of Indonesia: quoted in Kelly Jones, "U.S. Mask Slips in Bali; World Sustainability Hearings," *Earth Island Journal,* Sept. 22, 2002.

Page 220. Georgina Mace on the failure of the Bali meeting: in Jeremy Lovell, "World Earth Summit All Set for Major Flop," Reuters, June 17, 2002.

Page 221. Kofi Annan summing up the conference: in James Dao, "Protesters Interrupt Powell Speech as U.N. Talks End," *New York Times,* Sept. 5, 2002.

Page 221. Food and Agriculture Organization of the United Nations estimates on overharvested fisheries: see Food and Agriculture Organization, Fisheries, Databases and Statistics, http://www.fao.org/fi/statist.asp.

Page 222. Skin cancer risks soaring in Australia: Sharon Beder, *The Hole Story: Ozone Depletion Research in the Areas of Medical, Biological and Veterinary Science, Physics, Pharmacy and Physiology* (Environmental Education Project, University of Sydney, 1992).

Page 222. David Doniger and Joe Farman on the U.S. demand that the phaseout of ozone-destroying methyl bromide be halted: in Geoffrey Lean, "Bush Ready to Wreck Ozone Layer Treaty," *(London) Independent,* July 20, 2003.

Page 223. Administration feeds market for endangered species: Shankar Vedantam, "U.S. May Expand Access to Endangered Species," *Washington Post,* Oct. 11, 2003.

Page 223. Jane Goodall on the Bush policy on international wildlife trade: in Frank Sweeney, "Primate Expert Blasts Bush," *San Jose Mercury News,* Oct. 12, 2003.

Page 223. JFK quoted: John F. Kennedy, Inaugural Address, Jan. 20, 1961.

Chapter 15

Page 224. Warren Rudman epigraph: in Jonathan Weisman, "Alarms Sounded on Cost of GOP Bills; Lawmakers Increase Spending to Win Votes," *Washington Post,* Nov. 24, 2003.

Page 224. Thoreau epigraph: Henry David Thoreau, letter dated May 20, 1860, to Harrison Blake, in *The Writings of Henry David Thoreau,* vol. 6 (Boston: Houghton Mifflin, 1906), p. 360.

Page 224. Muir epigraph: John Muir, "Save the Redwoods," *Sierra Club Bulletin* 11, no. 1 (Jan. 1920).

Page 225. 234 million acres stripped of protections: see note for sixth bullet item, chapter 1.

Page 229. Statistics on fuel efficiency of projected vehicle fleet: "Building a Better SUV," Union of Concerned Scientists, Sept. 2003, http://www.ucsusa.org/publications.

Page 229. Statistics on falling GM production: John Porretto, "Toyota Is Poised to Outsell Ford and Chevrolet This Year," *Corpus Christi Caller-Times,* Sept. 2, 2003.

Page 230. The United States burns 25 percent of the world's oil but has only 5 percent of the world's population: *World Factbook 2003,* at www.bartleby.com/151/fields/82.html and www.bartleby.com/151/fields/20.html.

Page 230. Apollo Project could create three million new jobs: see www.apolloalliance.org.

Page 231. Statistics on lives saved from cleaning up power plants sued by the Clinton administration: "Power to Kill," Clean Air Task Force report, July 2001.

Page 231. Mercury levels in fish from the Everglades: Eric Pianin, "Mercury Rules Work," *Washington Post,* Nov. 6, 2003.

Page 231. Leopold quote: Aldo Leopold, *A Sand County Almanac* (1948; reissue, New York: Ballantine Books, 1986).

Page 232. Prevent wildfire destruction with Community Protection Zones: see American Lands Alliance's "Community Protection Plan," http://www.americanlands.org/community_protection_plan.htm.

Page 233. National Forests provide only 4 percent of our need for timber: "Scientists to Bush: Stop Logging National Forests," Native Forest Network, Apr. 16, 2002, http://www.nativeforest.org/campaigns/public_lands/stb_5_30_02.htm.

Page 233. Restoration potential: see, for example, http://arcata.fws.gov/jitw/reports/accomplishments/pdf on the Jobs in the Woods program, which has provided 1,309 jobs in Oregon alone since 1994. This program restores and revitalizes forest lands.

Page 234. Statistics on preventing abortion and deaths from pregnancy-related problems: Shanti R. Conly and Shyami de Silva, "Paying Their Fair Share?" Population Action International, 1999.

Page 235. Reducing emissions not by the 22 percent envisaged in Kyoto but by 60 percent or more: Dr. Margo Thorning, "Kyoto Protocol and Beyond: 'Whither the Targets?'" International Council Capital Formation, Nov. 2002.

Further Reading

This annotated, selective list of works emphasizes the political background of Bush's environmental recklessness more than specific environmental policy issues.

Banerjee, Subhankar. *Arctic National Wildlife Refuge: Seasons of Life and Land.* Seattle: Mountaineers Press, 2003. The book behind the exhibit the Smithsonian Institution tried to bury. Gorgeous photographs with a first-person account of the contested Arctic Refuge.

Barnes, Peter. *Who Owns the Sky? Our Common Assets and the Future of Capitalism.* Washington, D.C.: Island Press, 2001. The best linkage of the issues of commons management and global warming.

Behan, Richard W. *Plundered Promise: Capitalism, Politics, and the Fate of the Federal Lands.* Washington, D.C.: Island Press, 2001. A good description of the evolution of federal lands management policy.

Bliese, John R. E., John Ross, and Edward Bliese. *The Greening of Conservative America.* New York: Westview Press, 2001. The best description from a conservative viewpoint of the hijacking of the fusionist tradition by corporatist perspectives.

Bollier, David. "Reclaiming the Commons." *Boston Review,* Aug. 19, 2002. Based on material included in Bollier's *Silent Theft: The Private Plunder of Our Common Wealth.* New York: Routledge, 2002. A good discussion of the current dialogue on management of common resources.

Brown, Lester R. *Eco-Economy: Building an Economy for the Earth.* New York: W. W. Norton, 2002. Lays out a vision of how we might take the next steps toward a sustainable future.

Carson, Rachel. *Silent Spring.* Boston: Houghton Mifflin, 1962. A classic on the emergence of the ecological and environmental perspectives.

Dombeck, Michael P., et al. *From Conquest to Conservation: Our Public Lands Legacy.* Washington, D.C.: Island Press, 2003. One of the two best books on Clinton-era environmental perspectives, from one of the major protagonists.

Gelbspan, Ross. *The Heat Is On: The Climate Crisis, the Cover-Up, the Prescription.* New York: Perseus Books, 1998. No longer up to date, but the classic work on global warming.

Gore, Al. *Earth in the Balance: Forging a New Common Purpose.* Boston: Houghton Mifflin, 1992. The other best book on Clinton-era environmental perspectives, from another of the major protagonists.

Hawken, Paul, Amory Lovins, and Hunter Lovins. *Natural Capitalism: Creating the Next Industrial Revolution.* New York: Back Bay Books, 2000. An alternative to exploitation; argues that capitalism can provide answers to environmental dilemmas.

Heinzerling, Lisa, and Frank Ackerman. "Pricing the Priceless: Inside the Strange World of Cost-Benefit Analysis." Washington, D.C.: Georgetown Environmental Law and Policy Institute, 2002. A good analysis of the problems with cost-benefit analysis. The full report is available online at www.ase.tufts.edu/gdae/publications/ C-B%20pamphlet%20final.pdf. Another book by Ackerman and Heinzerling, *Priceless: Human Health, the Environment, and the Limits of the Market,* was published by the New Press in early 2004.

Ivins, Molly, and Lou Dubose. *Shrub: The Short but Happy Political Life of George W. Bush.* New York: Vintage Books, 2000. For background on Bush in Texas and Texas political traditions; see also Lind, below.

Lash, Jonathan, et al. *A Season of Spoils: The Reagan Administration's Attack on the Environment.* New York: Pantheon Books, 1984. A look at the Reagan assault on environmental protection.

Leal, Donald R., and Roger E. Meiners. *Government vs. Environment.* Lanham, Md.: Rowman & Littlefield, 2002. Packages the hard-right perspective that government is intrinsically the enemy of environmental protection.

Leopold, Aldo. *A Sand County Almanac.* New York: Oxford University Press, 1948 (reissued, New York: Ballantine Books, 1986). Another classic book on the emergence of ecological and environmental perspectives.

Lind, Michael. *Made in Texas: George W. Bush and the Southern Takeover of American Politics.* New York: Basic Books, 2003. For background on Bush in Texas and Texas political traditions; see also Ivins and Dubose, above.

Miller, Char. *Gifford Pinchot and the Making of Modern Environmentalism.* Washington, D.C.: Island Press, 2001. Tells the story of progressive conservationism from Pinchot's perspective rather than that of his contemporaries Theodore Roosevelt or John Muir.

Pyne, Stephen J. *Fire: A Brief History.* Seattle: University of Washington Press, 2001. Pyne is the classic source for a scientific and historical overview of wildfire.

Reisner, Marc. *Cadillac Desert: The American West and Its Disappearing Water.* Rev. ed. New York: Penguin USA, 1993. You can't understand the West without understanding water, and you can't understand water without reading Reisner.

Scarlett, Lynn. "Evolutionary Ecology." *Reason Magazine,* May 1996. A sophisticated effort to reconcile the libertarian hostility to government with the realities of pollution by the present assistant secretary of the Interior. Scarlett would have been a much more interesting choice at EPA than at Interior, because she is not, based on this article, a quietist about pollution. But just as Christie Whitman might have been too green for the corporatists if put in charge of Interior, Scarlett was slotted for that department, where her hostility to public lands fitted the boomer perspective much more neatly.

Stegner, Wallace. *Where the Bluebird Sings to the Lemonade Springs: Living and Writing in the West.* New York: Random House, 1992. A good collection of essays on the history of attitudes toward environmental protection in the rural West.

Index